IMAGES
of America

BEECH GROVE

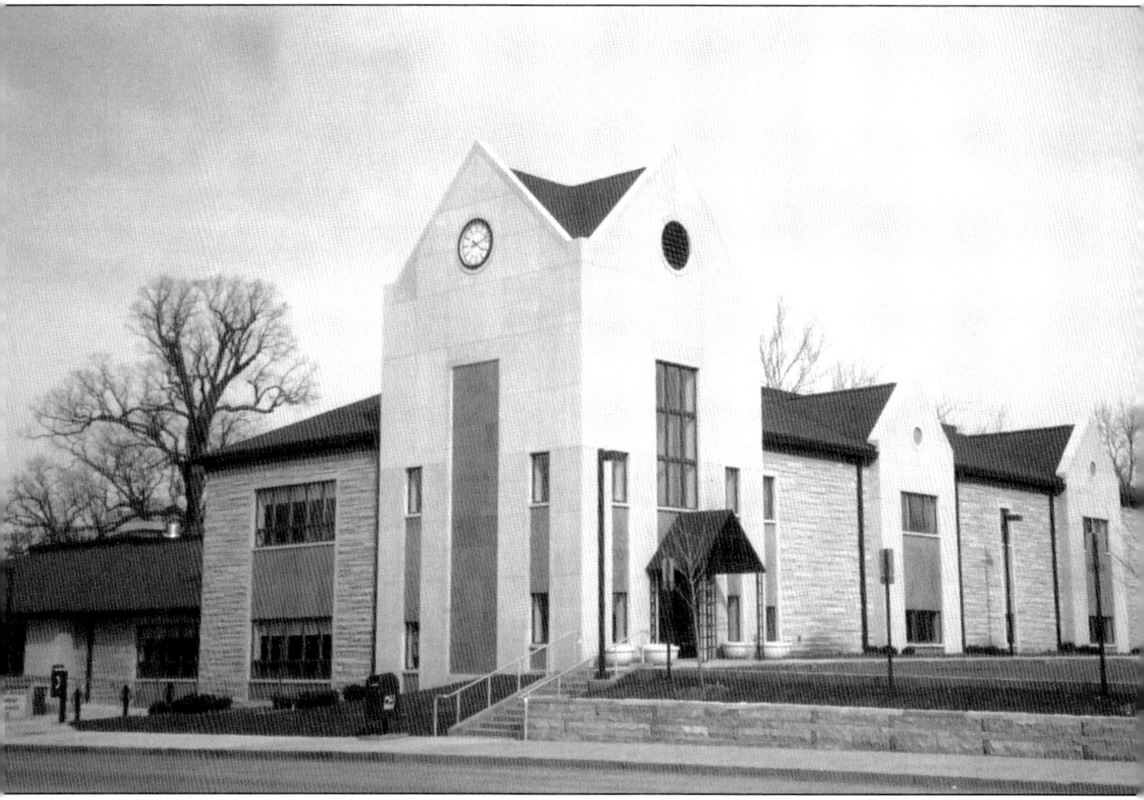

The first location of the Beech Grove Public Library was converted store frontage at 504 Main Street. The facility quickly outgrew this temporary space, and just a year later, in October 1952, ground-breaking occurred for the new and current home. The library's history room houses the collection of the local historical society, as well as the library's own historical archives, both comprising the primary source of photographs in this book. (Beech Grove Public Library.)

On the Cover: Bands played, flags waved, crowds came, and speeches were made as the Big Four Locomotive Erection Shop was formally dedicated in 1908. Construction of the massive facility began in 1904 and was the magnet that drew thousands of workers and their families, leading to the incorporation of the town of Beech Grove in 1906. The facility remains a significant employer in the city more than a century later. (Beech Grove Public Library.)

IMAGES
of America

BEECH GROVE

Jim Hillman and John Murphy with
the Beech Grove Public Library

ARCADIA
PUBLISHING

Copyright © 2011 by Jim Hillman and John Murphy with the Beech Grove Public Library
ISBN 978-0-7385-8357-0

Published by Arcadia Publishing
Charleston, South Carolina

Printed in the United States of America

Library of Congress Control Number: 2010928676

For all general information, please contact Arcadia Publishing:
Telephone 843-853-2070
Fax 843-853-0044
E-mail sales@arcadiapublishing.com
For customer service and orders:
Toll-Free 1-888-313-2665

Visit us on the Internet at www.arcadiapublishing.com

This book is dedicated to the memory of the many entrepreneurs whose vision changed a small area of Indiana wilderness into a center of the railroad industry in the Midwest, inspiring the spirit that keeps the city vibrant today.

Contents

FOREWORD

Incorporated as a town a little more than a century ago and as a city three decades later, modern-day Beech Grove is primarily a residential community of approximately 15,000 citizens.

An early dairy cattle farm that had several groves of native beech trees first adopted the name Beech Grove Farm. The farming and cattle business gave rise to a small station on the railroad, which also adopted the name. Then, beginning in 1904, the loosely knit agricultural community experienced explosive growth with the establishment of a major railroad yard and locomotive erection shop. It was that growth that led to the incorporation of the town in 1906.

The early prominent families in the town were the Churchmans, McGregors, Boltons, and Cottmans. One of the best-known early Grovers was poet Sarah T. Bolton, famous as the creator of *Paddle Your Own Canoe* and numerous other works. The former Bolton family farm is today the principal city park, named in her honor, located at Thirteenth and Churchman Avenues.

Only a year after incorporation, the first Beech Grove school opened on the second floor of William Wheat's store on Main Street. From that humble beginning, the city has developed an award-winning school system, capped by Beech Grove High School that sits on the land of the former McGregor family farm. Our schools and public library are among the best in Indiana.

Established as a town in 1906, Beech Grove became a fifth-class city in 1935. The city's status was elevated to a fourth-class city in 1961. In 1969, the City of Indianapolis and Marion County merged their governing structures to create a unified city-county system that in theory would incorporate the entire county. During that process, Beech Grove acted to be excluded and remained as an independent city, albeit entirely surrounded by Indianapolis.

A mayor, clerk-treasurer, and seven council members govern the city. All municipal services, including police, fire, streets, parks, and the senior citizen center, are provided by the city administration. The school and library systems likewise remain independent and serve only the city itself.

Today the residents of Beech Grove enjoy a safe small-town atmosphere while benefiting from the proximity of the business and amenities of the Indianapolis metropolitan area and easy access to major interstate highways and air travel—the best of all worlds.

Looking forward, our downtown business corridor is scheduled for a major revitalization in 2011, construction will soon begin on our new greenway trail, and the city will be among the leaders in establishing a broadband wireless network. Each of these projects is designed to improve our citizens' quality of life, improve personal wealth, and promote community pride and ownership.

Reflecting on our past and having celebrated our centennial in 2006, we look toward the next century, continuing to work together to make our city a better, brighter Beech Grove—a place our children and grandchildren will be proud to call home.

We hope you enjoy your visit to Beech Grove through this pictorial history and will be moved to visit our city in person to experience our small town in the midst of the metropolis.

—Mayor Donald Joe Wright
Beech Grove, Indiana

ACKNOWLEDGMENTS

We could have not even begun this work without the cooperation of the Beech Grove Public Library. The library staff and volunteers not only provided us with access to their archives, they became partners in our efforts to search through information and images. We also extend our heartfelt thanks to all who contributed their time, shared memories, stories, and legends, and to those who provided a photograph or two or just a lead about where to look for information. That list includes many individuals, businesses, religious organizations, the Beech Grove Public Library, City of Beech Grove employees, Mayor Wright and his staff, and many others.

Among those offering assistance, there are a few that must be thanked individually. Michele Patterson, Beech Grove Public Library's Reference/Technical Services Librarian, had assisted us during previous research projects; she once again opened the library's archives, contributing her personal reflections and local knowledge. In the library history room, we were joined for untold hours by volunteer Richard Carman, who assisted in the mundane tasks of searching files and albums, while relating stories and adding facts to the photographs based on his years of living in Beech Grove and his long time association with the historical society. Michele and Richard also provided invaluable introductions and contacts with local government offices and business promoters, who each added to the story of the city. We offer a special word of thanks to Joe Seiter, who shared his wonderful postcard collection and encouraged our efforts. In addition to all the above assistance, the people we met all conveyed a remarkable sense of local pride and ownership in their city, an attitude that explains how this community, now surrounded by Indianapolis, retains the small-town atmosphere that makes it such a desirable home for her citizens.

Unless otherwise noted, all the images presented in this book are from the archives of the Beech Grove Public Library.

Of course, none of this would be possible without the support of Kathy and Rita, who allow us the time and encourage us throughout each project and in life every day.

INTRODUCTION

From a scattering of farmhouses, open fields, and groves of beech trees, the town of Beech Grove was incorporated on November 12, 1906. The organization of the town was a direct result of the construction of a massive railroad facility, known as the Big Four Shops, which commenced in 1904; the town grew in unison with the locomotive, passenger, and freight-car maintenance operations. But in mid-1907, the town of Beech Grove consisted of little more than four homes and two businesses.

By 1908, as the Shops arose out of the clearing across from the developed areas of town, employment opportunities brought an explosion of interest in the planned community, and as population swelled the sounds of industry were heard in the humming of machinery, cacophony of steam hammers, pounding of blacksmiths, clanking of coins in Main Street business cash boxes, and whistling of trains. Noting the importance of the Shops, and auxiliary support businesses, to the origination and development of Beech Grove, it is likewise important to note that the town managed to blossom as an independent and unique community outside the redbrick walls of the area's largest industry.

Even though the Shops fueled growth and demand for big-city amenities—and Indianapolis was just six or so miles northwest of town—travel from Beech Grove to the capital city was rare in the early years. The city of Indianapolis's development went as far as what is now known as Fountain Square, with the transportation route of Virginia Avenue being unreliable and often a muddy mess. Churchman Pike, the main roadway to the southeast of Indianapolis, was relatively new, and with many sections under construction the stretch was prone to flooding. The only reliable way to Indianapolis was by horse and buggy, or by the Cleveland, Cincinnati, Chicago and St. Louis Railway, which was considered costly at the time for such a short ride. The transportation situation improved with the arrival of the trolley network, enhanced and affordable trains, buses, paved roads, and increased ownership of automobiles.

Because of the relative isolation of the community, a true small-town consciousness permeated the emerging population. Residents gathered for rabbit hunts, barn dances, poker and gambling nights, backyard picnics, "chopping bees" to clear the heavily forested land to the south, and swimming in Lick Creek. The community invented its entertainment, socialized among themselves, and remained close-knit well into the 1940s. Residents worked hard on their farms, at the Shops, or in their Main Street businesses, and then the town came alive in the evenings and on the weekends.

Early town residents included the Clapp brothers with their grocery, dry goods, and shoe sales operation. William R. Wheat, a competitor of the brothers, also sold groceries but added hardware items to his retail mix. Fourth Avenue's Jane McGregor was known for her big heart and even bigger fresh-baked apple pies. Catholic pastor Fr. Peter Killian was a friendly and kind gentleman, remembered for his community improvement efforts. Among other early familiar faces seen around town were members of the Achgill, Baker, Clawson, Curry, Geshwiler, Gilliland, Hunter, Kuntz, Logan, Mendenhall, Skaggs, Terhune, Timmermon, and Vandiver families.

The affluent Churchman family, whose stately Victorian mansion once stood on land now occupied by the Churchman Hill Plaza at the corner of Churchman and Emerson Avenues, was active in community financing and development. Included in the Churchman family's legacy is a book written and self-published by Frank Lindley Churchman, grandson of Francis M. Churchman, founder of Hillside, the Churchman's Beech Grove farm. The book, entitled *So This Was Hillside*, is an excellent resource that details early Indiana farm and Beech Grove town life.

The Churchman cattle farm, along with the 55-acre farm known as Beechbank, reflected the abundance of beech trees in the area, groves that provided the impetus for the naming of the community. Several beech trees can still be found on the southern boundary of the remaining 35 acres of Beechbank—home of famed women's rights activist and poet Sarah Tittle (Barret) Bolton—which are now the major Beech Grove city park. The first railroad stop in the area was named Ingallstown; that name was considered for the community, however, the railroad stop adopted the Beech Grove name, and that name was then assumed when the town was incorporated.

Aside from financier Francis Churchman and poet Sarah Bolton, Beech Grove was the birthplace of Broadway and film actor Clifton Webb, as well as legendary contemporary actor—and the "King of Cool"—Steve McQueen, though neither Webb nor McQueen spent their childhoods in Beech Grove. Another brush with the famous arrived in Beech Grove on October 15, 1948, when Pres. Harry S. Truman visited the community during his whistle-stop reelection campaign and attended ceremonies at the town's Masonic Lodge.

There were a few Beech Grove residents within the circles of high society, but most citizens were farmers or blue-collar laborers, although as the town grew it did attract a fair share of entrepreneurs and railroad executives. As the local St. Francis Hospital evolved to become the flagship of the large St. Francis Hospital and Health Centers, a wave of medical professionals relocated to the city. Through the services of the hospital, the wealth of the Churchmans, the words of Bolton, the acting of Webb and McQueen, and the trains and industry of the town, the citizenry of Beech Grove has impacted Indiana, the nation, and international locales.

The first town board met on November 12, 1906. The town of Beech Grove became a fifth-class city in 1935, and it was upgraded to a fourth-class city in 1961. Prior to 1935, three ward-elected board members and a clerk-treasurer governed the town. Unique to Beech Grove was the fact that officials were elected from locally grown political parties that ran on the People's, Progressive's, Citizen's, and other tickets. The city's first mayor, Progressive-turned-Republican Charles Adams, held office from 1935 until 1942. It is interesting to note that in Beech Grove, home of feminist poet Sarah Bolton, Democrat Alice Stratton became one of the first female candidates in the state of Indiana to run for the office of mayor in 1951. Although a woman has yet to hold that position in Beech Grove, Mary Bates became the first woman to serve on the Beech Grove City Council in 1961.

With the transition mandated by Unigov legislation in Marion County, the City of Indianapolis's and Marion County's governance and municipal services were blended, making all of Marion County the new Indianapolis. Beech Grove chose to exempt itself from the new county-city government structure and remained a separate city, albeit totally surrounded by the now enlarged Indianapolis. In a unique arrangement resulting from the city-within-a-city circumstance, the residents of Beech Grove are allowed to vote for the office of mayor in both Indianapolis and their own city.

Widespread crime has never been significant in Beech Grove; the streets are relatively safe, clean, and graffiti free. As Indianapolis has become one of the country's largest urban areas, Beech Grove has been able to keep serious crime from crossing its borders. Since J. C. Johnson was appointed the first town marshal in 1906, and Charles E. Lough became the first police chief in 1936, Beech Grove's police department has been recognized for excellence across Indiana. The first functioning fire department originated in 1906, and the exploits of the town's sole firefighter, Billy Trusdale, along with Nip and Tuck—the two equine members of the firefighting team—are the stuff of local legends. Billy, Nip, and Tuck continued fighting fires with rudimentary equipment until a Little Giant fire engine was purchased to improve their abilities. In 1922, a 350-gallon Stutz fire engine replaced the horse-drawn apparatus.

While area schooling began around 1868 in the old Poplar Grove one-room schoolhouse—known as "No. 9"—in 1907, open space above the Wheat Grocery Store at 423 Main Street became the town's first public school, a location that remains today the oldest standing building in the city. Multiple relocations and building projects, including the construction of several modern structures, have occurred throughout Beech Grove's school history. The first high school graduates were presented with diplomas in 1922.

Blessed Sacrament Roman Catholic Parish, now known as Holy Name of Jesus, is the oldest established congregation in Beech Grove. Fr. Peter Killian conducted services in the upstairs area of his home, beginning in 1908. Shortly thereafter, the Clapp family residence provided the meeting space for Methodist Episcopal services, evolving into the Beech Grove United Methodist Church congregation. A lunchtime prayer meeting at the Shops resulted in the 1910 organization of the Beech Grove Christian Church, followed by the First Baptist Church in 1912. Other denominations established locations in Beech Grove, including the Pilgrim's Holiness Church, which became the Wesleyan Church (1920s), the Independent Nazarene Church (1950s), Faith Assembly of God (1958), South Emerson Church of God (1961), Ascension Lutheran Church (1972), and other larger, contemporary, nondenominational worship centers.

The Catholic Church has had a profound impact on the quality of Beech Grove life. While Killian was busy establishing a vibrant parish, the Sisters of St. Francis of Perpetual Adoration founded St. Francis Hospital, which developed into one of the leading hospital networks in Indiana. In the 1950s, a group of Sisters of the Order of St. Benedict came from Immaculate Conception Monastery in Ferdinand, Indiana, and established Our Lady of Grace Monastery. Since their arrival in Beech Grove, the sisters have achieved separate status as an independent monastery. They founded Our Lady of Grace Academy, an all-female high school, as well as St. Paul Hermitage, a senior residential living center. After the high school closed, the amenities transitioned into the Benedict Inn and Conference Center, a multi-use facility that has retreat facilities and sleeping rooms, a gymnasium, and an indoor swimming pool.

Beech Grove life has been enriched by a variety of civic organizations. The Beech Grove Masonic Lodge was chartered in 1913. Mary Rutledge is credited with introducing the Girl Scouts to the city in 1929. The Lions Club (1937), American Legion Post 276 (1939), Beech Grove Business and Professional Women's Club (1945), Veterans of Foreign Wars Post 5626 (1946), Little League (1955), and Beech Grove Senior Services (1973) are just a few of the civic organizations operating to improve the quality of Beech Grove living. An active Promoters Club (1953) is responsible for annual Fourth of July fireworks, an annual fall festival, and community awards. The city of 15,000 residents continues to enjoy success beyond the rail yards.

It is not the authors' intent to provide an in-depth, up-to-date, and definitive history of Beech Grove, which is an ambitious project yet to be tackled. Through months of research, the authors uncovered many conflicting dates and varied spelling of names, referenced buildings found to be unknown or their locations disputed, and interviewed residents who had memories that challenged information in formal resources. While the authors do not wish to perpetuate inaccuracies, textual decisions sometimes needed to be made in line with the best, most consistent information available. In cases where assumed facts may be conflicted, or vivid memories contradicted, please allow the images to tell the story.

One

Trains to Town

By 1900, Indianapolis had become a hub of both passenger and freight railroad traffic, and several railroad companies had established business offices and maintenance facilities in the city. In 1904, the Cleveland, Cincinnati, Chicago and St. Louis Railway, commonly called "The Big Four Line," acted to make a far larger investment in the Indianapolis area. The company purchased approximately 2,400 acres for the establishment of a major rail yard and mechanical shop to be located about five miles southeast of the city.

The selected location was just north of an existing stop along the Big Four tracks called "Beech Grove." The yard would expand the company's ability to serve the area's ever-growing agricultural and industrial freight traffic, which increased to include two major grain storage and shipping operations. The Big Four Shop was envisioned as a major steam locomotive erection and maintenance complex that would serve the entire New York Central system.

With the development of the locomotive facility came a migration of tradesmen, eager for steady work during the anticipated three years of construction, followed by a wave of laborers seeking employment in the locomotive shop itself. Almost overnight, the loosely organized agricultural area acquired an industrial complex that would require housing and services for a much more urban community. While the construction workers were viewed as somewhat transient, it was clear that long-term employment opportunities at the railroad complex mandated the establishment of permanent and affordable housing, government services, and social opportunities.

In 1906, the community incorporated as the town of Beech Grove. Of the original 2,400 acres the railroad had acquired, 640 acres were reserved for the Shops and rail operations, and the balance formed the original land for the town itself. The Beech Grove Improvement Company was formed and engaged in the buying, holding, and selling of real estate. This firm established the first formal plats and began the development of residential and commercial areas of the town.

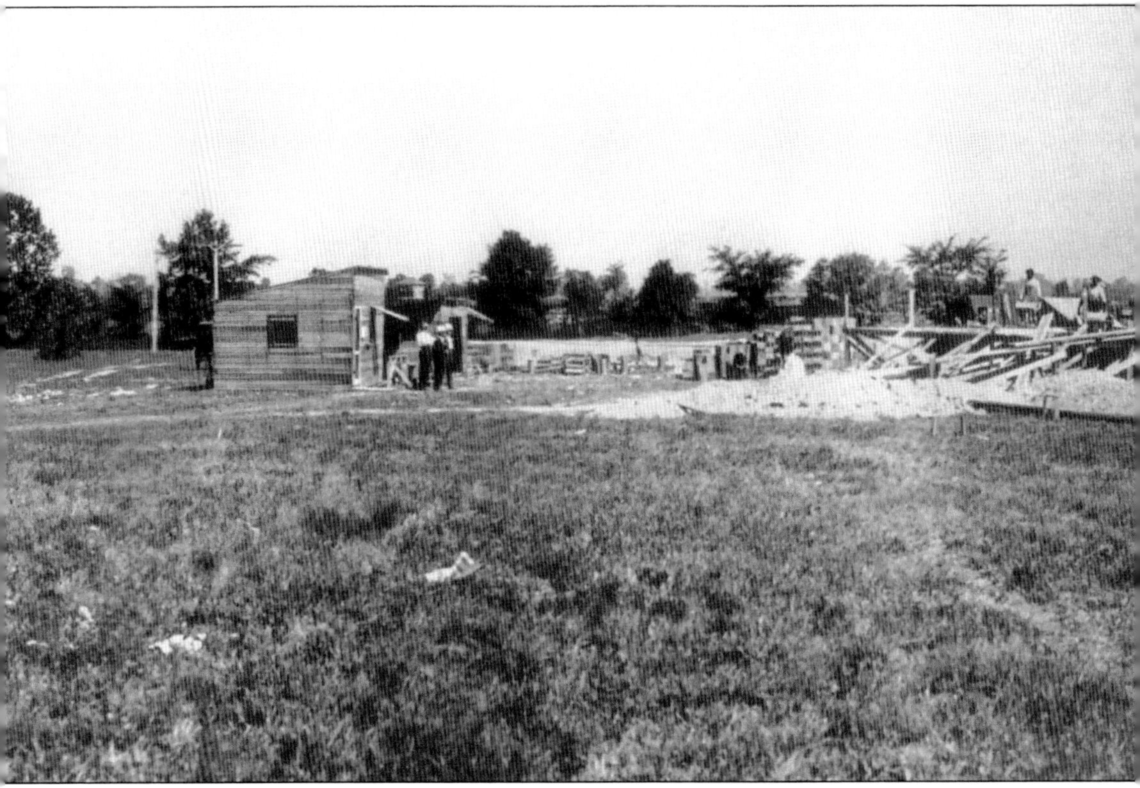

By late summer 1904, construction crews were laying the foundations for the locomotive erection shop. Typical for construction of the time, there was precious little large machinery on the site, and the vast majority of the work was done by manual labor. A project of this scope required a large labor force of varying skill levels, including laborers, forming carpenters, and concrete finishers. As quickly as the foundations for one building were completed, the concrete crew would move to the next, quickly being replaced by ironworkers to erect the framework. Once the frame was completed, crews of roofers, brick masons, plumbers, and electricians occupied the site to complete the structure. With the project estimated to consume three years of construction, literally hundreds of tradesmen found full-time employment at the rural site. In a time before the private automobile, travel to and from the work site was difficult, time-consuming, and expensive.

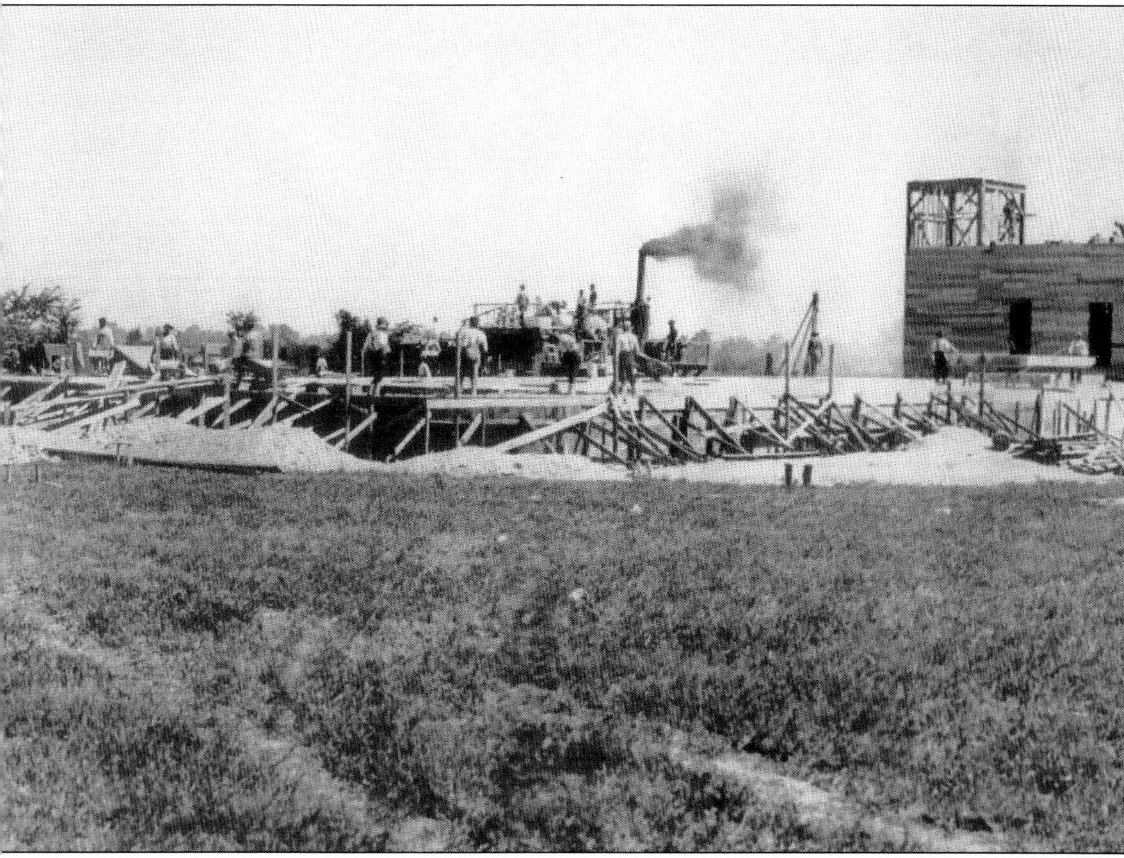

The concrete finishers are smoothing the floor on the first erection bay. The smokestack seen in this photograph is the coal-fired, steam-driven concrete plant that was erected on the site. Just as commuting to the site was a chore for workers, transportation of materials to the site presented its own set of obstacles. The solution to this issue was to bring the raw materials, sand, gravel, and cement by rail and mix the concrete on site. Virtually all of the bulky or heavy construction materials—such as brick, steel-frame sections, steel-roofing panels, crane beams, and large electrical apparatus—were delivered to the site on Big Four railcars. Even though the site was eventually covered with rails to service the operations, several temporary rail sections were built during construction to accommodate the movement of materials from the adjacent rail line onto the construction site.

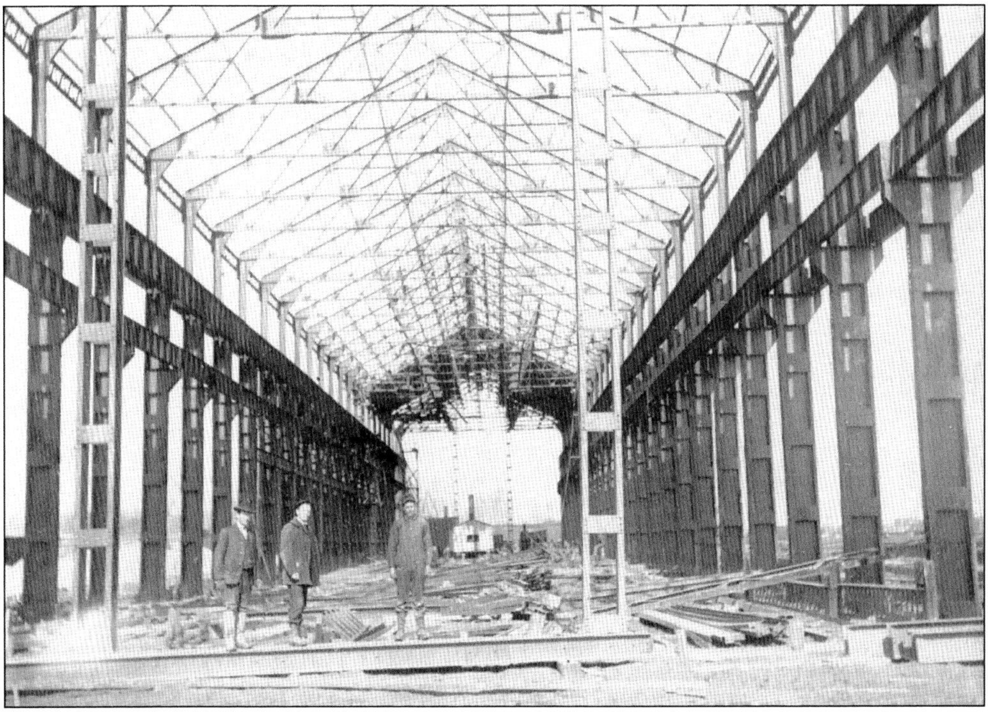

The three ironworkers standing in the photograph above give some idea of the size of the shop buildings. The central building is 309 feet wide and 578 feet long, contains two locomotive bays, as seen in these photographs, and is connected by a central shop area for the staging and preparation of parts. The very large steel columns that support the roof also carry rails for the installation of overhead cranes, with a capacity of 120 tons, which traverse the length of the bay. Once the steel structure was fully erected, the frame was enclosed by a steel roof and brick exterior. In the photograph below, the roof is being installed on the completed frame of one locomotive bay.

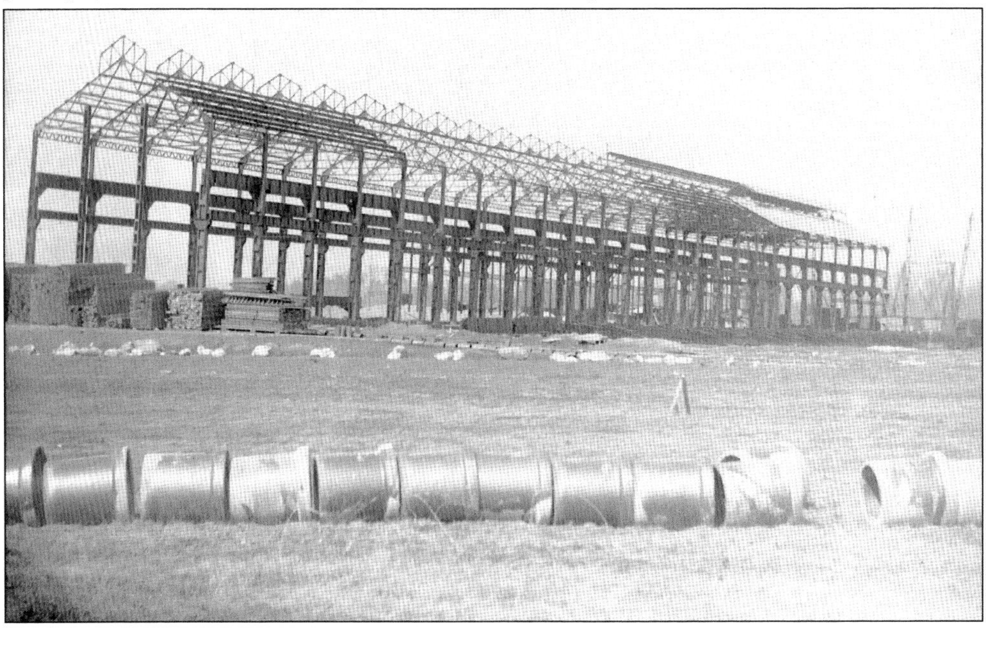

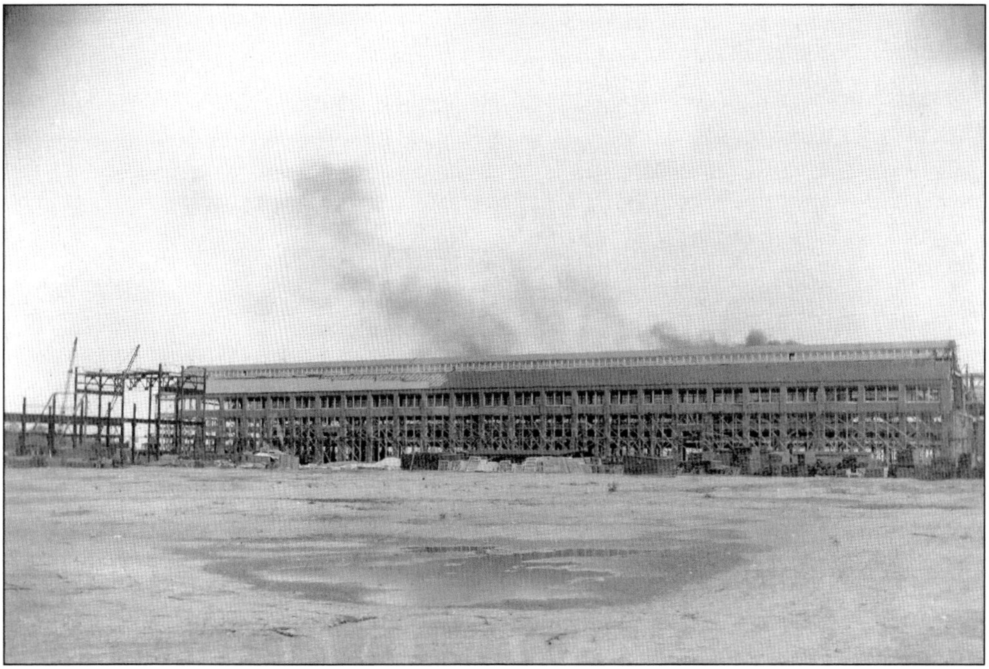

As the roof was installed, and the brick exterior was completed, the massive locomotive bay began to take its final shape. Typical of industrial buildings of the time, the walls were largely steel-framed windows and rows of upper skylights ran the full length of the roof peak. The large expanse of glass was necessary to provide adequate light and ventilation in the building.

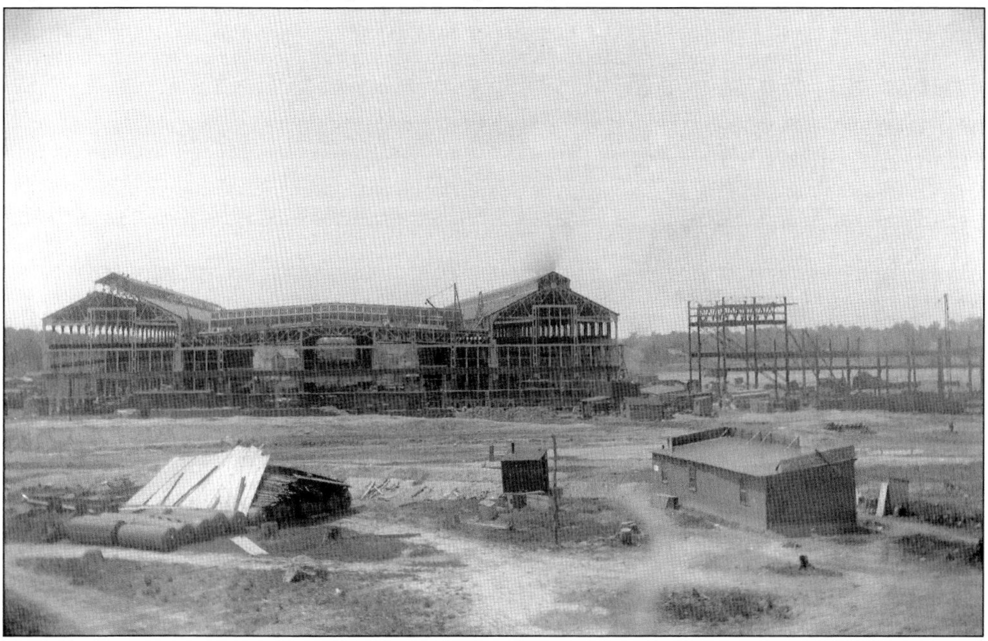

This 1907 photograph shows the central locomotive shop building with the locomotive bays and central shop area clearly visible. This view is the rear of the building, and to this day this image reflects the familiar view of the facility from Emerson Avenue, the sight that most local residents are accustomed to seeing.

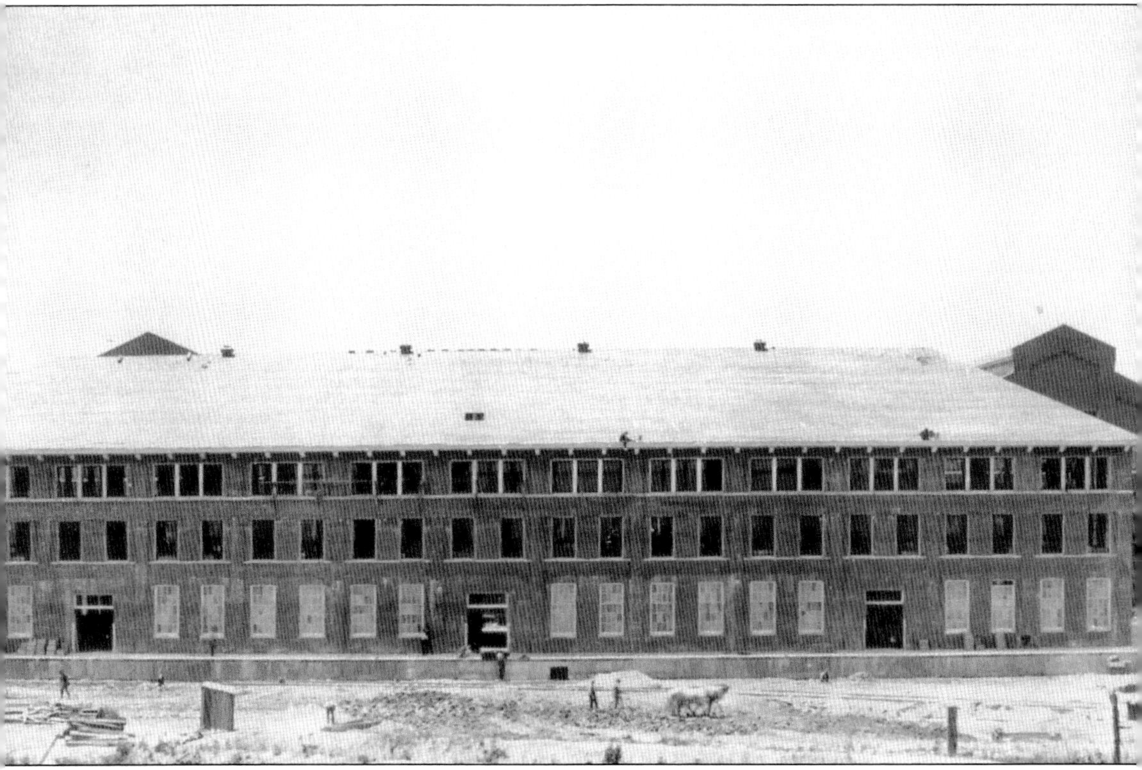

As massive as the structure of the locomotive shop is, it only formed the core of the complex. In this photograph, the twin peaks of the locomotive bays are seen behind another shop building under construction. In addition to the locomotive shop itself, the facility initially included the powerhouse, administrative building, blacksmith shop, forge, warehouse, and a few additional shops dedicated to freight and passenger car repair and refurbishment operations. In later years, a freight car paint shop, as well as a passenger car trim and paint shop, were added. Once completed, the entire complex consisted of more than 100 acres of land, nearly 18 of which were under roof, all serviced by more than 10 miles of yard track within the fences. Immediately adjacent to the maintenance facility itself, another area of more than 500 acres was occupied by a general rail yard that served two local grain shipping facilities, switching of cars to assemble trains, and provided storage and staging for inbound and outbound cars and locomotives for the shop.

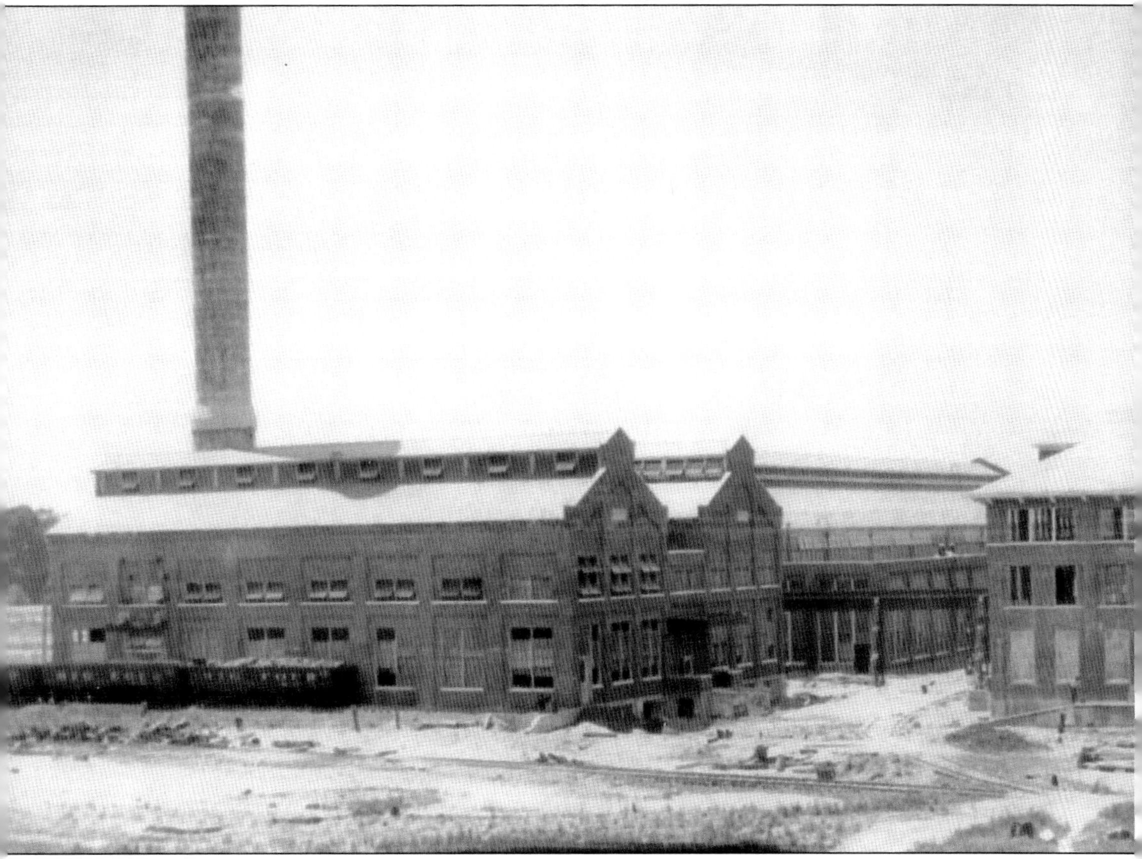

While virtually all major industrial complexes built in the early 1900s included a powerhouse, most were located in, or near, the central city services. In Indianapolis, electricity and steam were both produced by a local utility company power plant near downtown, and the powerhouses at industrial locations dealt mostly with internal distribution of steam and electricity supplied by the utility company. This complex, with its rural location, faced the challenge of providing the massive steam and electrical supplies required to operate without having the benefit of a local utility company with the capacity to meet their needs. In order for this industrial complex to function in the rural setting, the power required had to be produced on-site. Like the locomotives the complex would build and service, the powerhouse was a coal-fired, steam-generating plant that fed high-pressure steam into a spiderweb of piping to distribute heat and power throughout the complex.

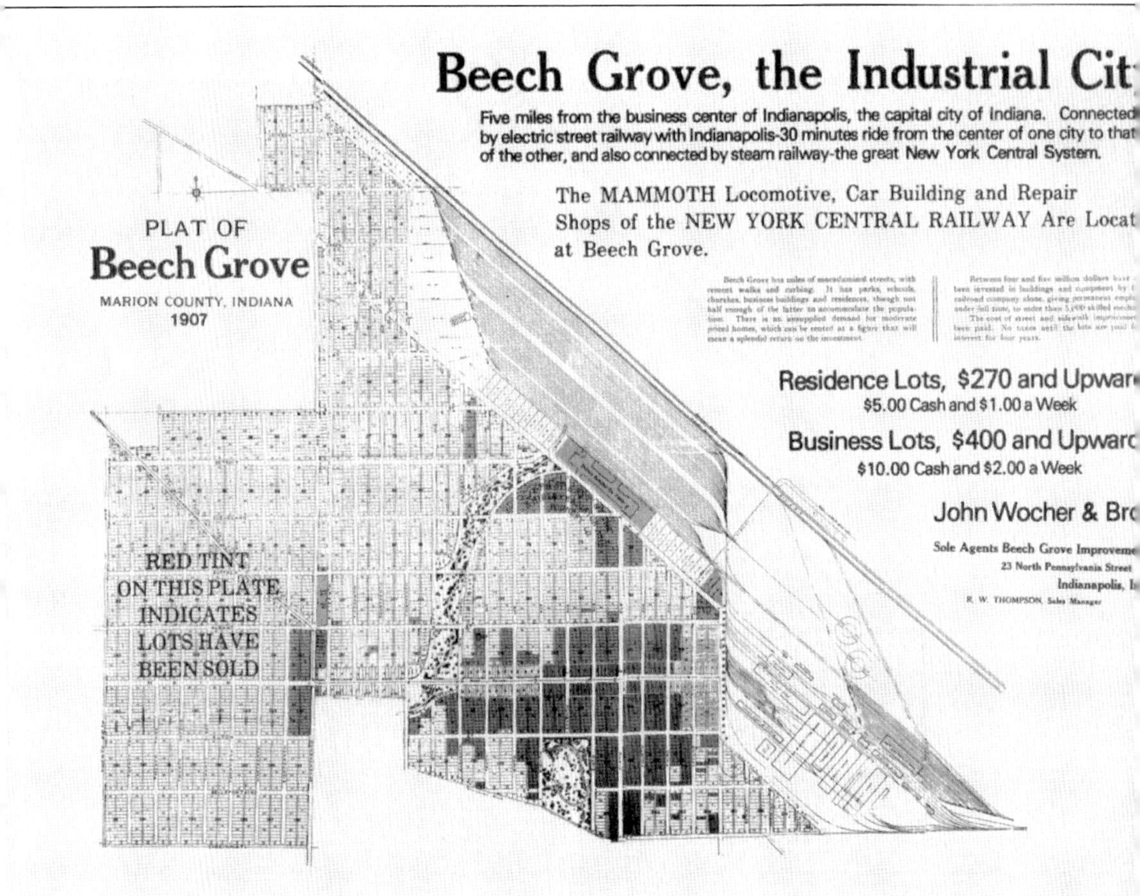

When the New York Central Lines—owner of the Cleveland, Cincinnati, Chicago and St. Louis Railway—laid the plans for the Beech Grove complex, it allocated one quarter of the land acquired to railroad operations. The balance of the land was developed as residential and commercial property, primarily to house the employees of the railroad shop complex. While this plan did accommodate employees, it was also a significant business venture for the railroad, because it already owned the land that it planned to develop. The railroad created the Beech Grove Improvement Company for development purposes and platted the town of Beech Grove during 1906 and 1907. In the plat map and sales brochure seen here, the town is directly adjacent to the Shops, with the idea that employees could easily walk to work. When the town was platted, many streets were named for major points along the New York Central routes. Today residents still live and travel on Albany Street, Detroit Street, Cleveland Street, and others recalling the major cities the railroad served.

Two

Locomotives Drive the Future

For more than a century, the complex known nationwide as "The Beech Grove Shops" has served the railroad industry and been a mainstay of the Beech Grove community, but the trip has not always been a smooth ride. Between 1904 and 1908, the Shops were built by the Big Four Line—the Cleveland, Cincinnati, Chicago and St. Louis Railway—resulting in the maintenance and repair complex becoming the Big Four Shops in common parlance. The Shops erected and maintained steam locomotives, freight, and passenger cars for the next 15 years.

In 1922, the Big Four Line was absorbed into its parent company, the New York Central Lines. Little changed in the operations, but the name changed to the New York Central Shops in 1923. Under the new leadership, freight and passenger car paint and trim shops were added in 1923 and 1930.

During World War II, the Shops reached their peak activity, employing more than 5,000 men and women to keep the trains operating for the war effort. The Shops set several records for their speed in servicing locomotives and returning them to service.

After the war, rail passenger service declined, and the Shops gradually became primarily focused on freight car repair. The workforce declined as the New York Central Lines experienced financial difficulties and eventually merged with the Pennsylvania Railroad to become the Penn Central Railroad in 1968.

The (now) Penn Central Shops continued to operate at a fraction of capacity and the facility fell into gradual decline until the federal government created the Amtrak passenger rail system. Amtrak needed a central facility for repair and upgrade of rolling stock, and much of that work came to the Penn Central Shops. In 1975, Amtrak took control of part of the facility, sharing space and workforce with Penn Central.

In 1986, Amtrak assumed total ownership of the Shops, renaming the facility once again as the Amtrak Shops. Today the facility is known as a premier locomotive and car shop, maintaining, repairing, and upgrading Amtrak's fleet for the entire nationwide system.

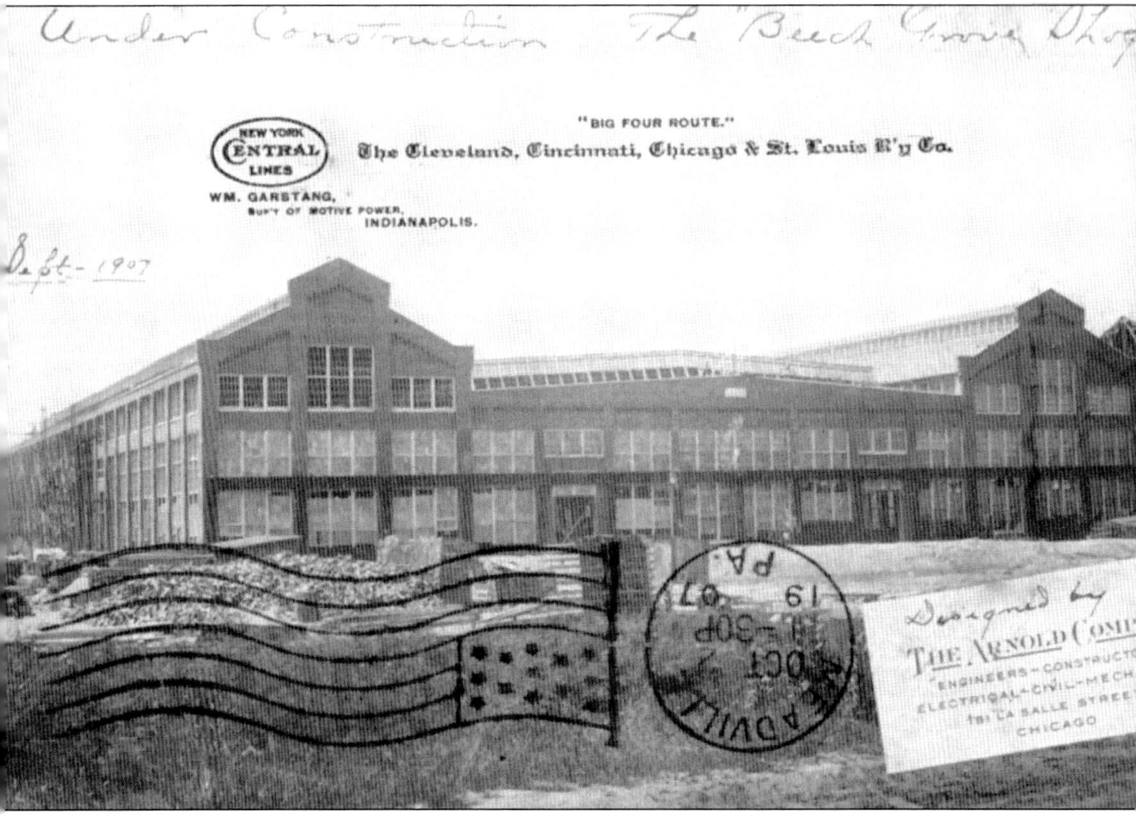

This unique postcard image from 1907 shows the Shops under construction. Note that the names of the New York Central Lines; the Cleveland, Cincinnati, Chicago and St. Louis Railway Company; and the Big Four Route are all printed on the card. The New York Central Lines was the majority owner, and effectively the parent company, of the Cleveland, Cincinnati, Chicago and St. Louis Railway Company that was generally referred to as the Big Four. The sender of the card has added in the note across the top that the picture is of the "Beech Grove Shops," however the Shops actually adopted the "Big Four Shops" name in common parlance. In addition to the railway company names, the card identifies the Arnold Company of Chicago as the design and engineering firm for the project. William Garstang is identified as the superintendent of motive power, located at the Indianapolis headquarters. The present-day administration building is located on Garstang Street, named in memory of the first superintendent. (Joe Seiter collection.)

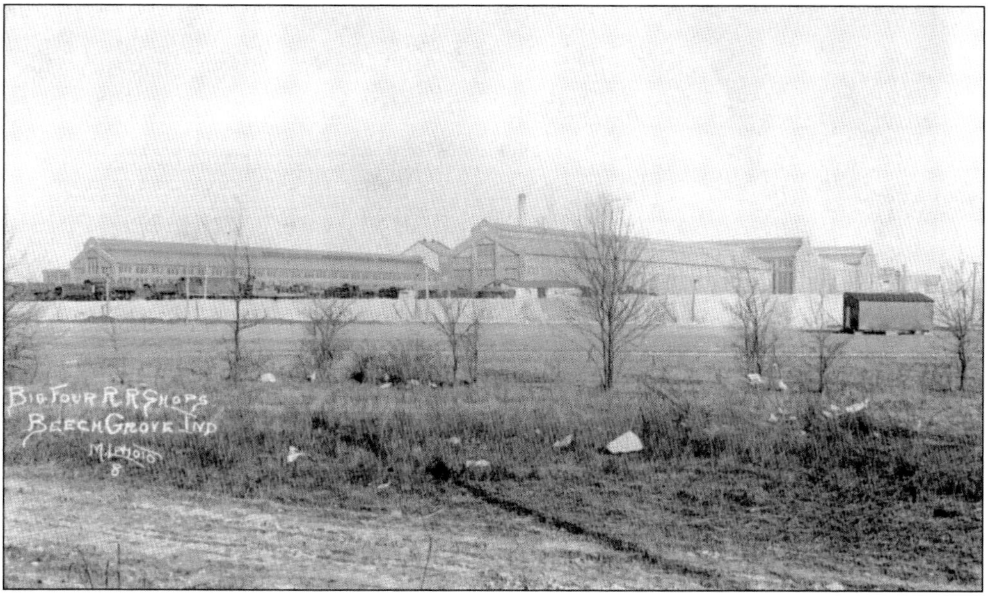

This postcard image from 1910 shows the now completed and operational Big Four Shops as viewed from the southwest. Several steam locomotives can be seen on the staging tracks in front of the locomotive erection bays of the main building. The Shops had the capacity to service and maintain up to 1,000 locomotives, far more than the Big Four Line owned at the time. (Joe Seiter collection.)

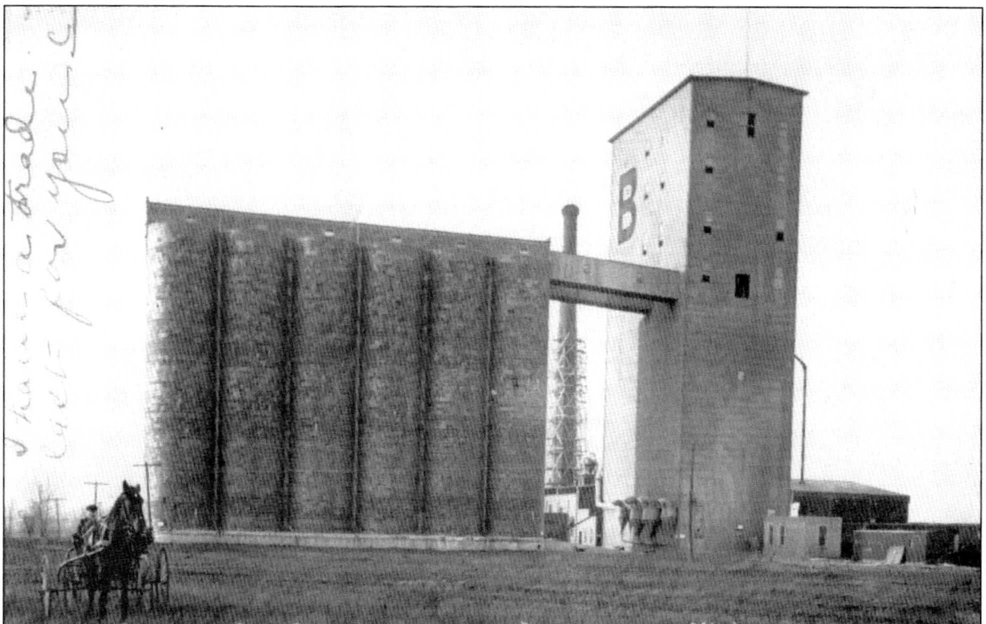

By the time of this 1910 postcard, the economic impact of the rail yard and Shops was evident in the ancillary business that developed to either supply the Shops with parts and supplies or were located where they could access the railroad service. The Cleveland Grain Company located a major elevator and shipping depot adjacent to the yard. Today two major grain elevators are serviced by the Beech Grove rail yard. (Joe Seiter collection.)

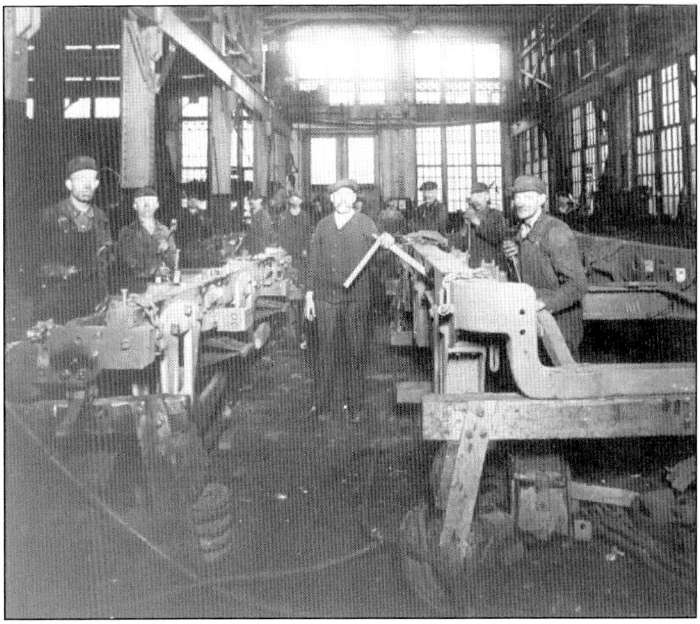

This 1910 picture of a frame crew illustrates the working conditions in the Shops during the early years. The Shops were typical of any heavy industrial plant of the time with few power tools and lighting provided primarily by the large glass areas of the walls. Even the most skilled tradesmen labored in less than ideal conditions to create the mechanically complex locomotives. There was nothing easy or comfortable about shop work in heavy industry in the early 1900s.

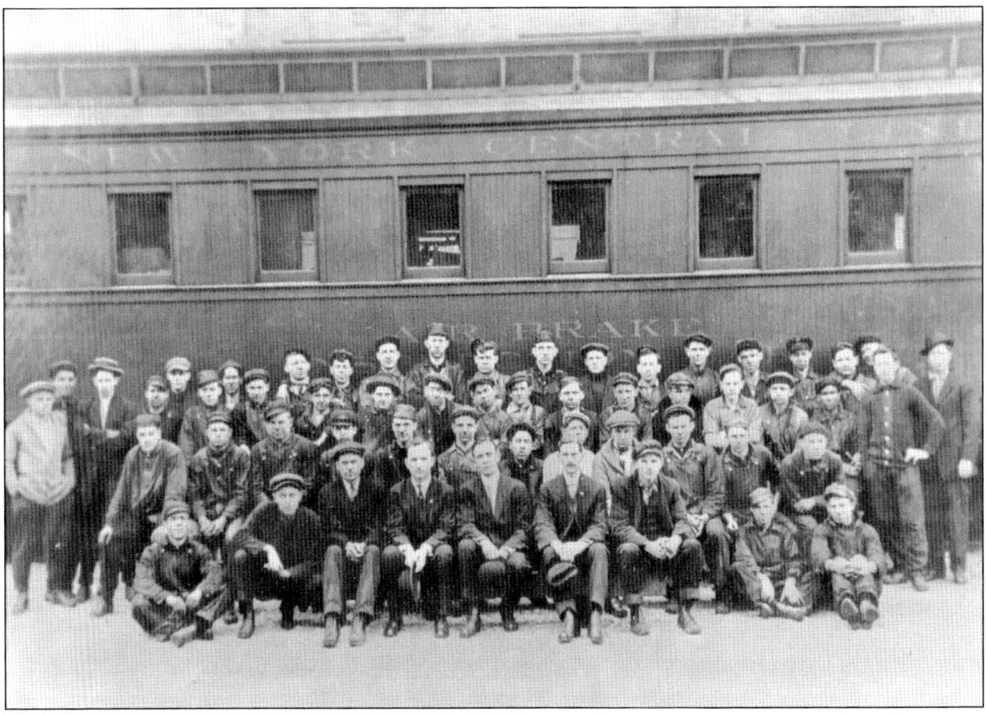

The apprentice class of 1913 poses for a photograph with their supervisors, pictured in the center front row in ties and coats, standing in front of a typical New York Central Lines passenger car. Over the next few years, the apprentices were trained to build and maintain locomotives and cars such as this that provided popular passenger service all across the eastern United States.

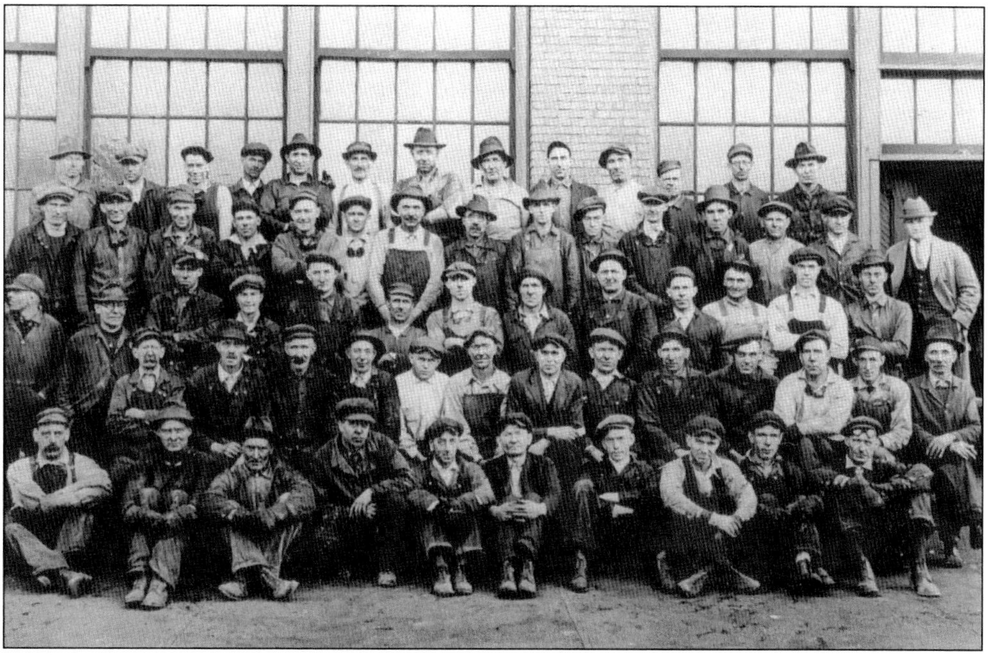

It is likely that some of the 1913 apprentice class is also seen in this 1920 photograph of a locomotive shop crew. Even though the work was hard and conditions less than pleasant, most employees remained with the Shops for their entire careers, since the railroad offered higher than average wages and long-term job security.

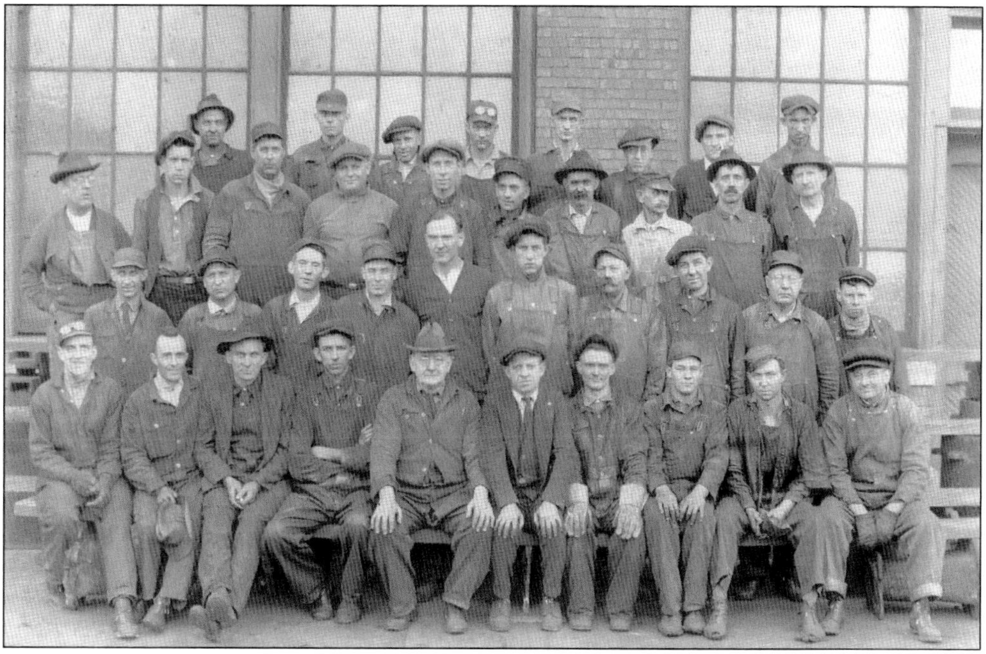

While the erecting crews generally received the credit for the end products, they were supported by a number of smaller departments that provided the various subassemblies required to actually erect the locomotive. This 1924 photograph shows the driving box wheel gang. This work crew provided some of the critical units for the final assembly operations.

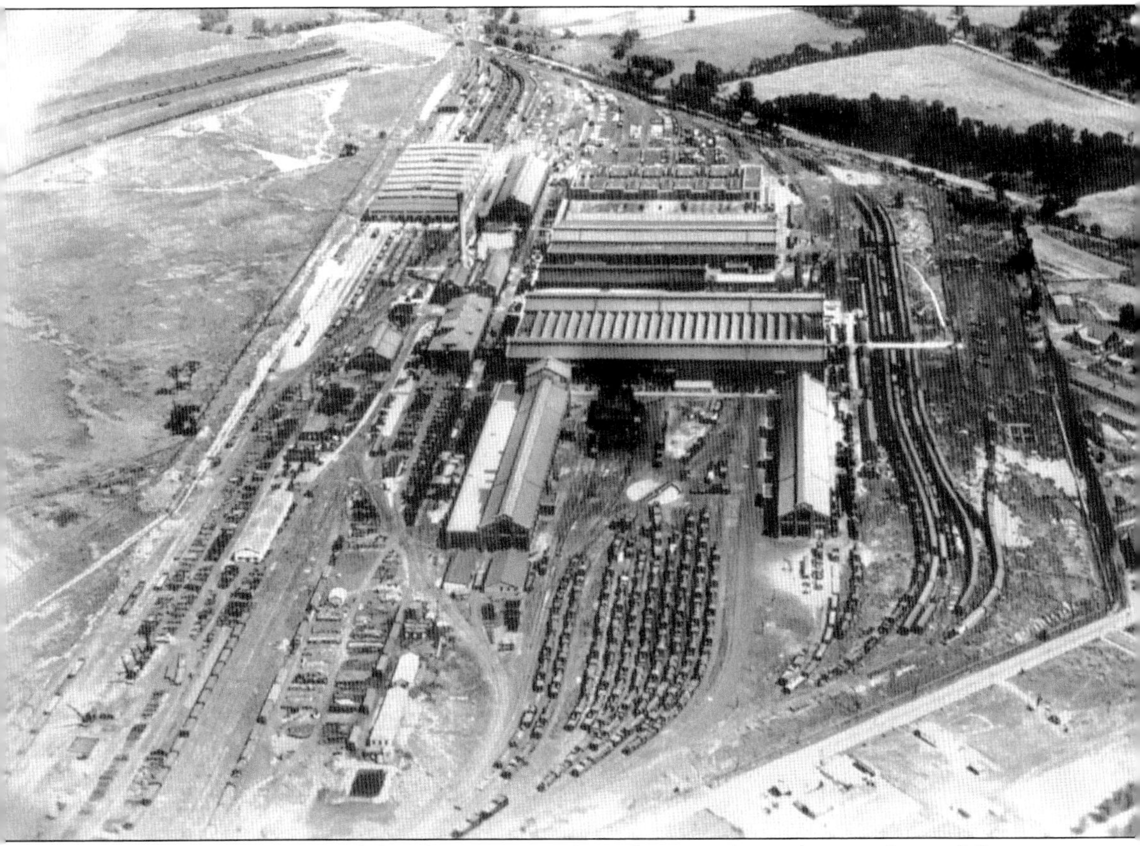

This 1930 aerial view of the Shops, as seen from the west, shows the complex in full operation following the recent addition of a new passenger car trim and paint shop. By the time of this photograph, the facility had been transferred to the control of the New York Central Lines, which operated more than 2,000 miles of track in the eastern half of the country, providing both freight and passenger service from the East Coast to the Mississippi River. At this time, the railroads were the travel method of choice for any long trip. The various railroad companies competed for passenger business by introducing express routes between major cities and offering more comfortable travel with dining and club cars and sleeping accommodations. All of the staging tracks at the Shops are seen here filled with cars awaiting either maintenance or upgrading. The Beech Grove Shops developed a reputation for first-class workmanship and innovation, providing passengers on the New York Central Lines the most modern amenities.

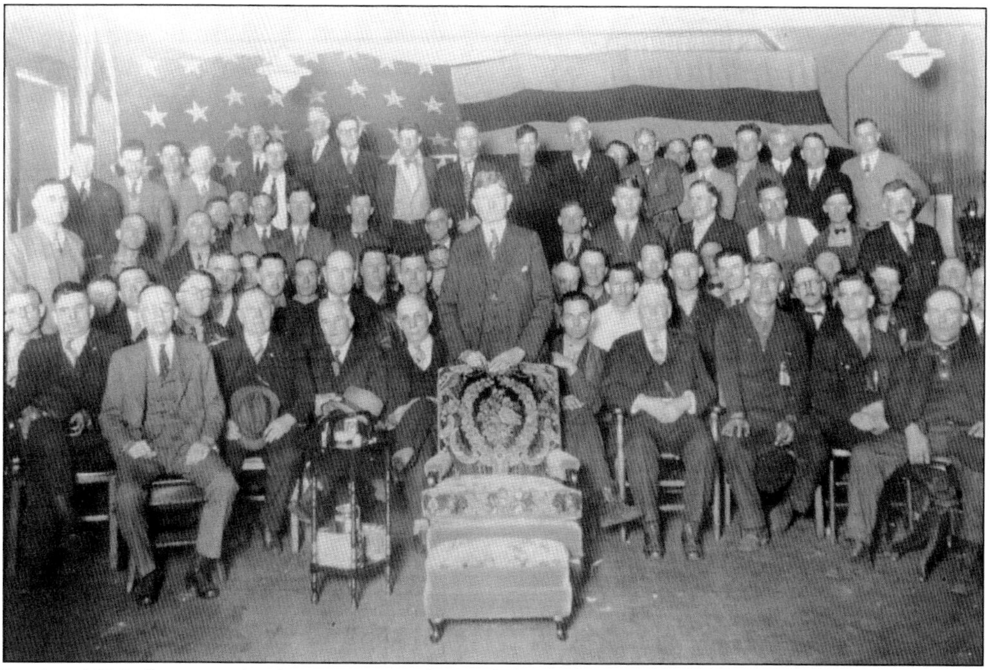

In this 1930 photograph, the superintendent of the Beech Grove Shops (standing) poses with his all-male clerical staff. Although by 1930 women were becoming common in office and clerical departments in many businesses, the railroad Shops were a primarily male workplace, and promotion to an office position was generally seen as a benefit of having spent many years on the shop floor.

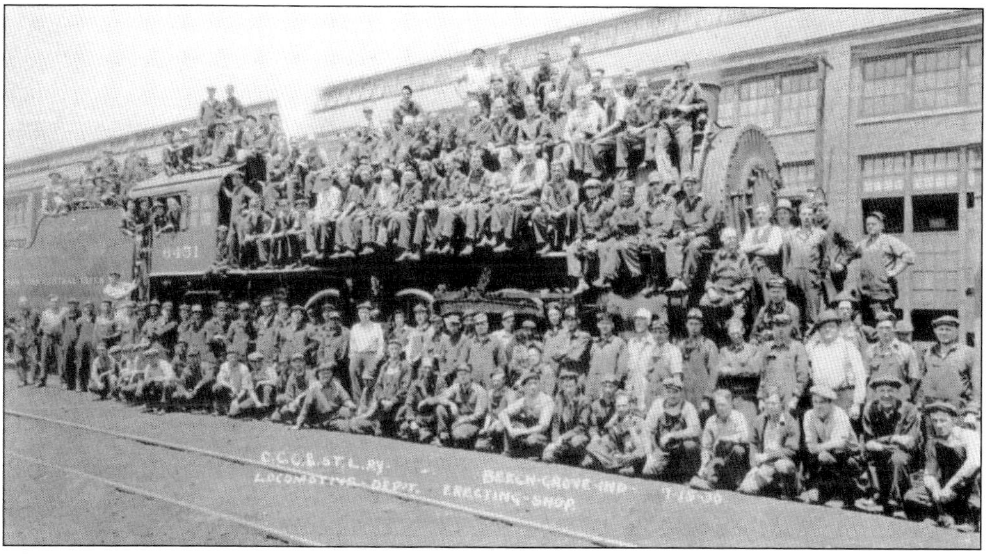

The Locomotive Erecting Shop crew poses with New York Central No. 6451 as it prepares to leave the Shops to enter service in 1930. The photograph not only illustrates the immense size of the locomotive itself, it demonstrates the size of the crew required to produce and maintain the powerful, mechanically complicated steam engines. The crew includes metal fabricators, welders, pipe fitters, mechanics, and several other skilled men needed to complete the erection of a locomotive.

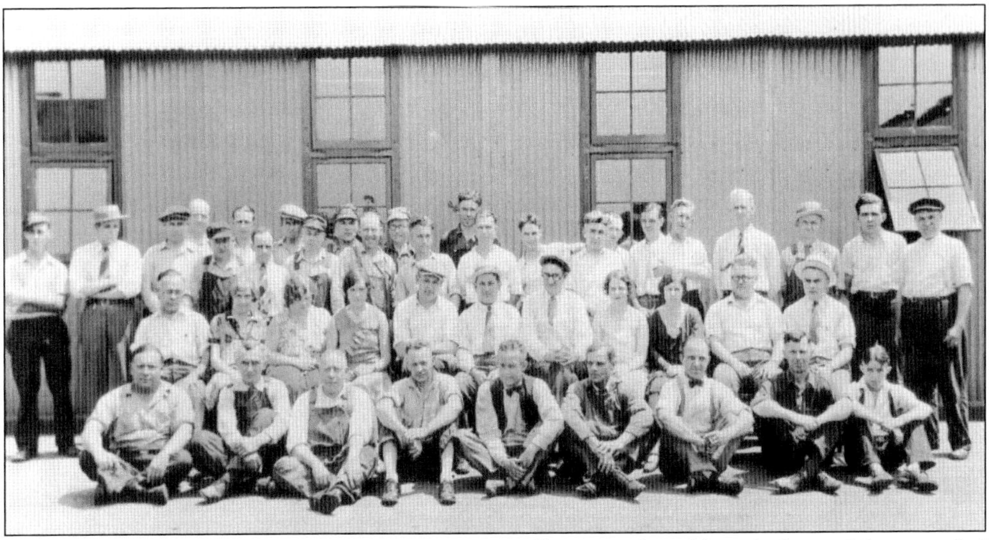

This 1930 photograph of the piecework department illustrates that although the workforce tended to be male dominated, a number of women were employed in certain departments. Many of the females were employed as seamstresses in the car trim and upholstery departments and similar operations. The outbreak of World War II brought many more female employees into all aspects of shop operations.

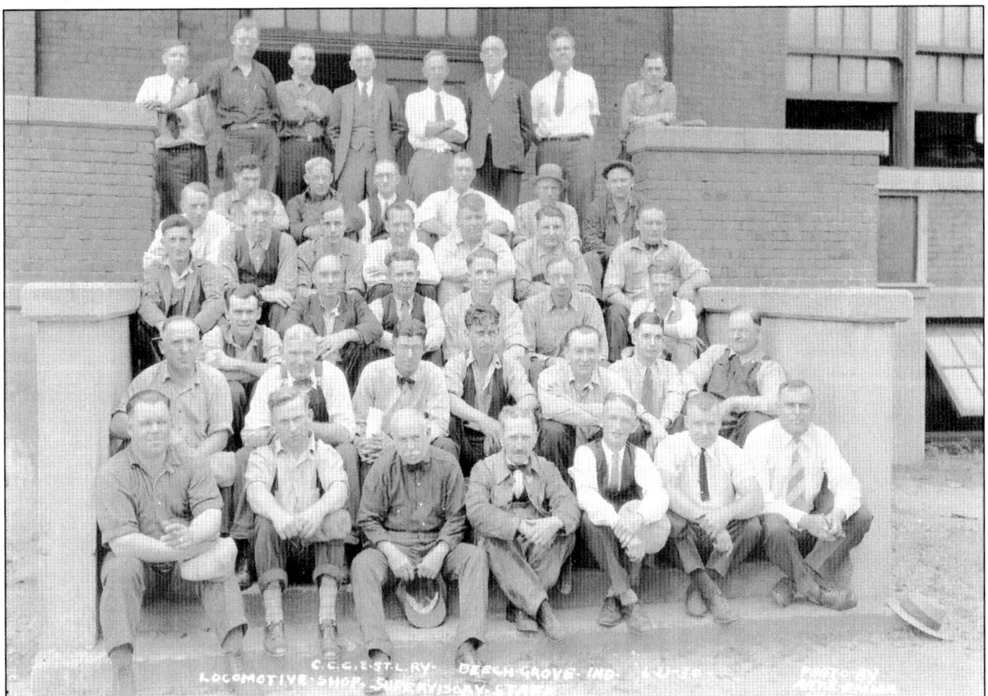

By 1930, the Shops had achieved an industry-wide reputation for high-quality work and efficient, cost-effective operations. Pictured on the steps to the entrance of the main building in June 1930 is the supervisory staff of the locomotive department; these are the managers and floor supervisors responsible for the daily operations of erection and maintenance of the New York Central Lines' motive power.

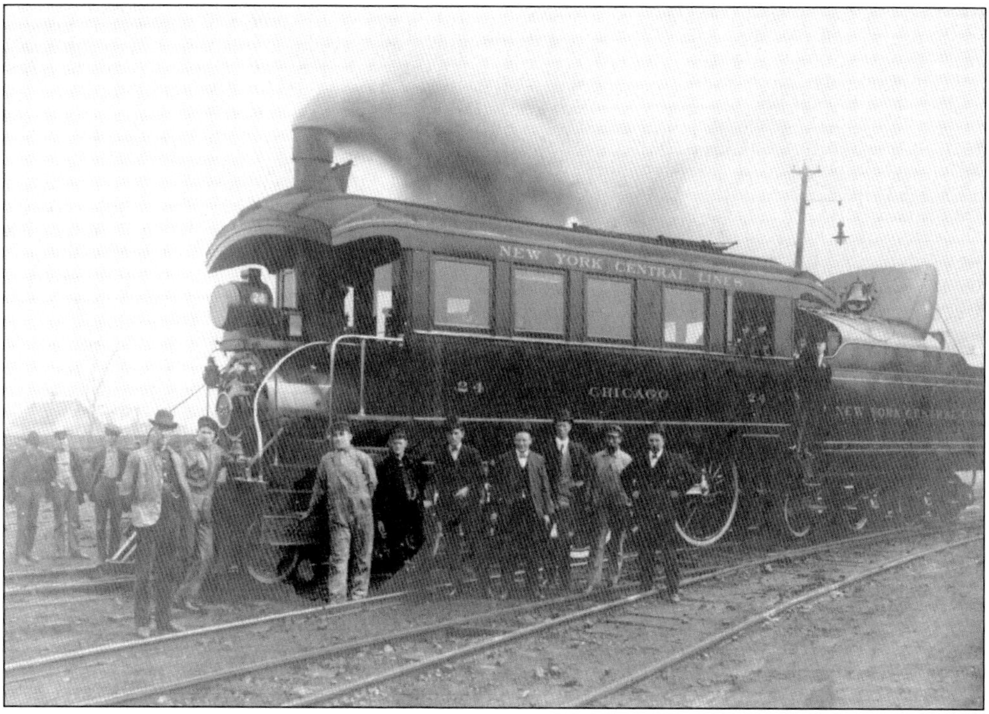

The Shops developed a reputation for the ability to construct different and innovative locomotives. In this 1930s photograph, the crew is ready to do a road test with a uniquely designed locomotive and tender. The cab encloses most of the boiler, and the smokestack goes through the roof. This unit was specifically designed for use by rail inspection and testing crews.

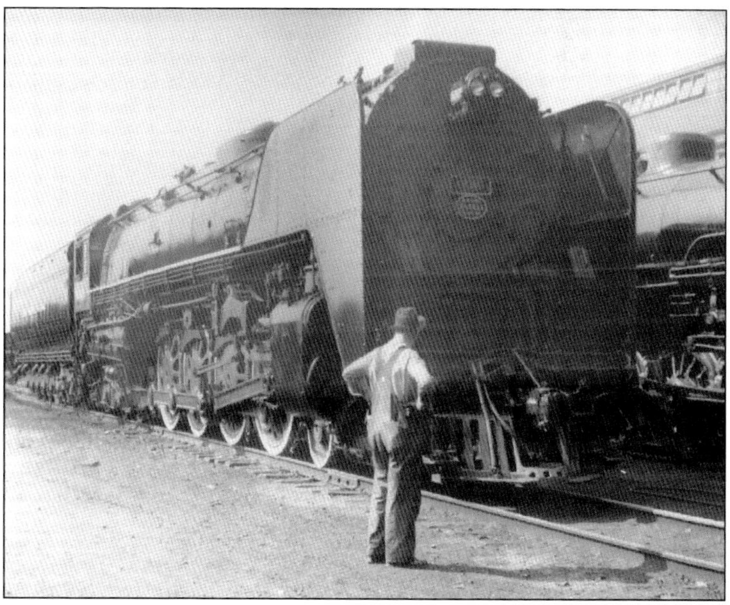

Pipe-fitter foreman Charlie Brunsma looks over two New York Central locomotives ready to return to service in 1945. Locomotives such as these were the workhorses that moved troops, equipment, and materials throughout World War II. The Beech Grove Shops were widely acclaimed as the best facility in the nation for the maintenance of these critical wartime assets.

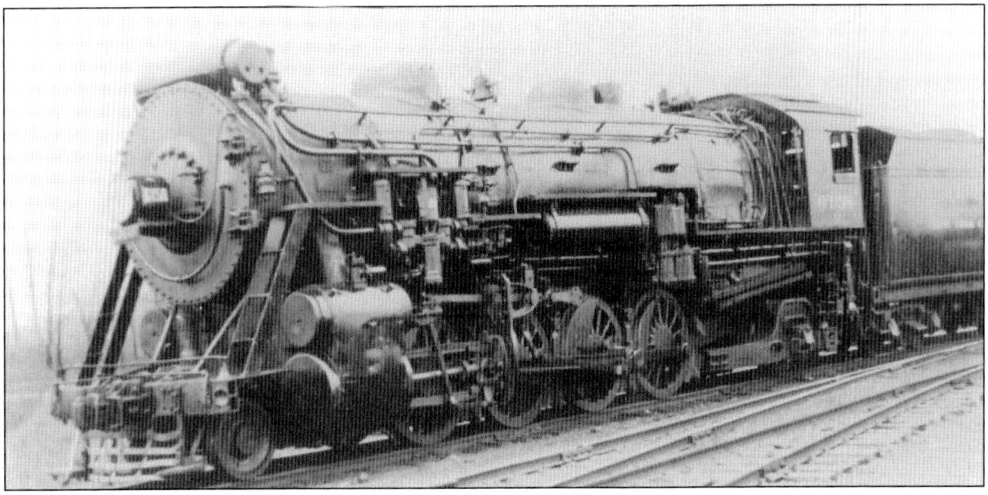

As New York Central No. 6158 prepares to depart the Shops in this 1950 image, the passenger business was in decline—a victim of both the new airline industry and the post-war emergence of the family automobile. Employment at the Shops had peaked during the war years at near 5,000, but employee numbers declined as the passenger cars that had been their main business were retired.

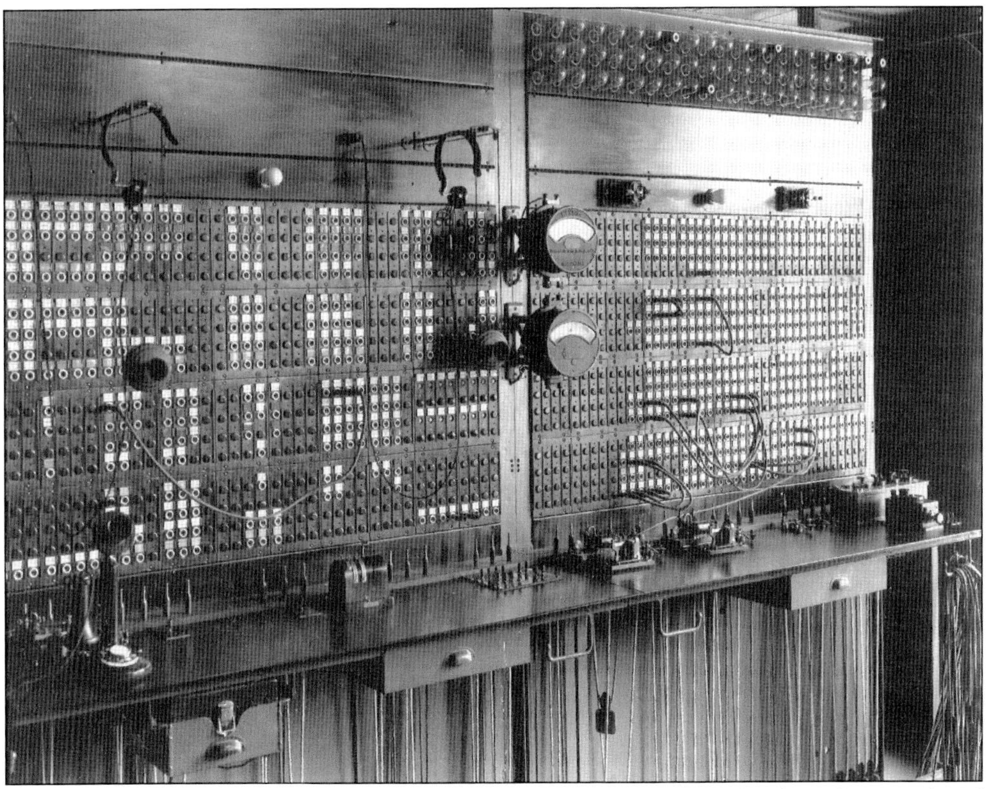

The telephone switchboard, seen here in 1950, illustrates the aging technology that was found throughout the Shops. The steam locomotives and passenger cars that had been the principal products for 50 years were about to be retired, and the financial difficulties of the major railroad companies had slowed any investments or upgrading of the facility. The future was uncertain.

The late 1950s and early 1960s saw little of the traditional work that had earned the Shops its enviable reputation, such as this refurbished dining car. As the major railroads struggled to retain what they could of passenger traffic, the reality was that the work arriving at the Shops was becoming more centered around freight cars and their new diesel-electric prime movers. The winds of change were howling through the staid old industrial buildings.

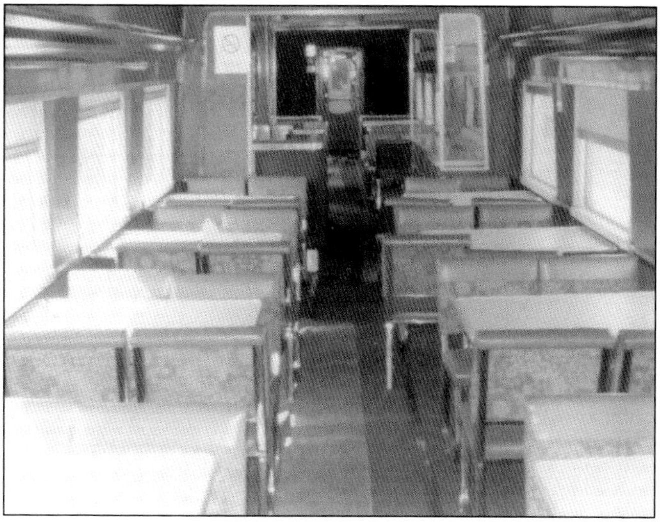

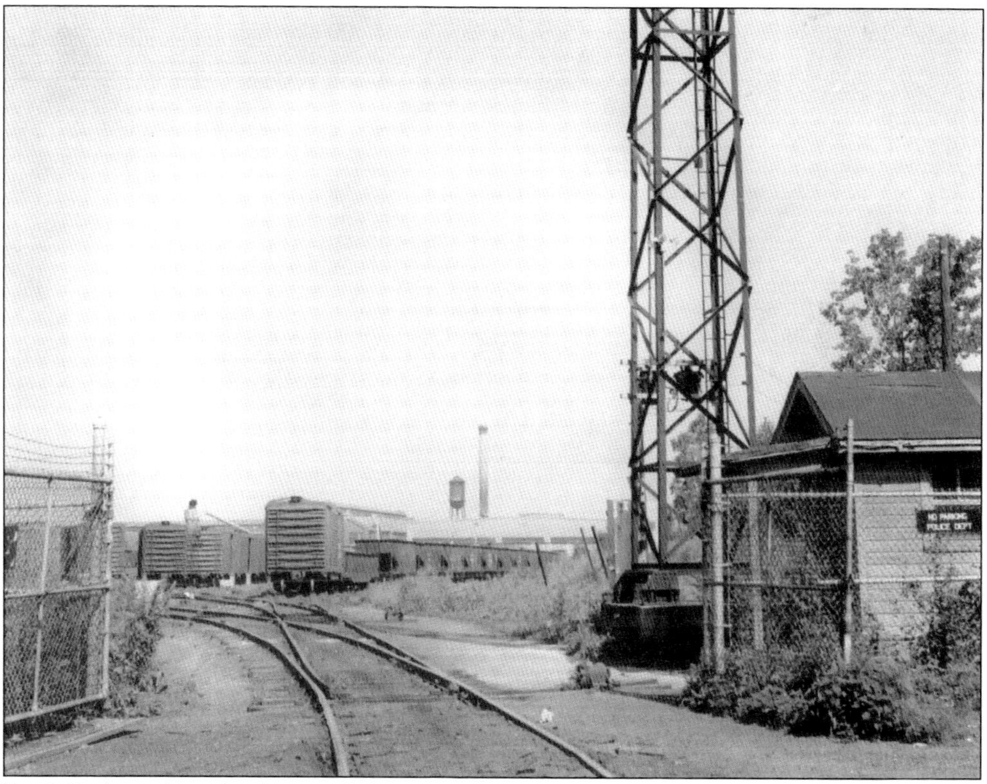

By 1960, the rails in the shop yard that once showcased gleaming and plush passenger cars were filled with freight cars of all descriptions. No fine wood trim and upholstery work was required to keep these heavy haulers on the road. Mechanical service, some sheet metal work, and an occasional paint job were all that was required for the freight service.

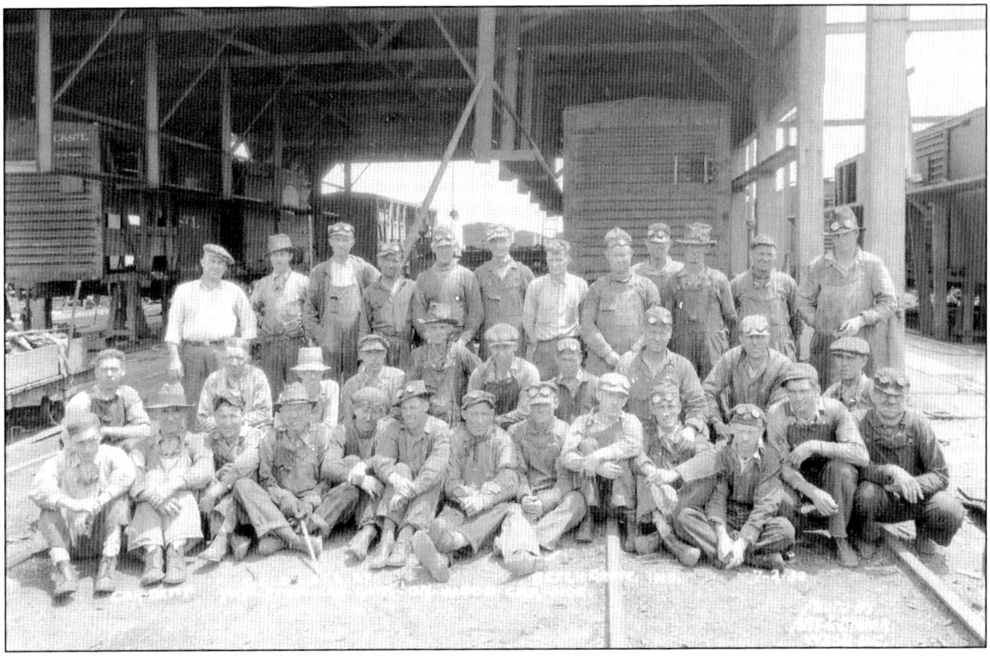

When these photographs of the freight car shop crews were taken in 1930, the work they were doing was a minor part of the business, as it was overshadowed by the locomotives and passenger car work that accounted for virtually all of the significant production. The photograph above shows the wood-sided cars being converted to steel cladding, with the work primarily done in an outdoor shed-type structure. In the photograph below, another part of the freight car crew is seen in front of the cavernous shop building in which the freight cars were finished and painted. By 1960, the steam locomotive and passenger car work was gone for all practical purposes, and crews such as these had become the mainstay of the shop operations.

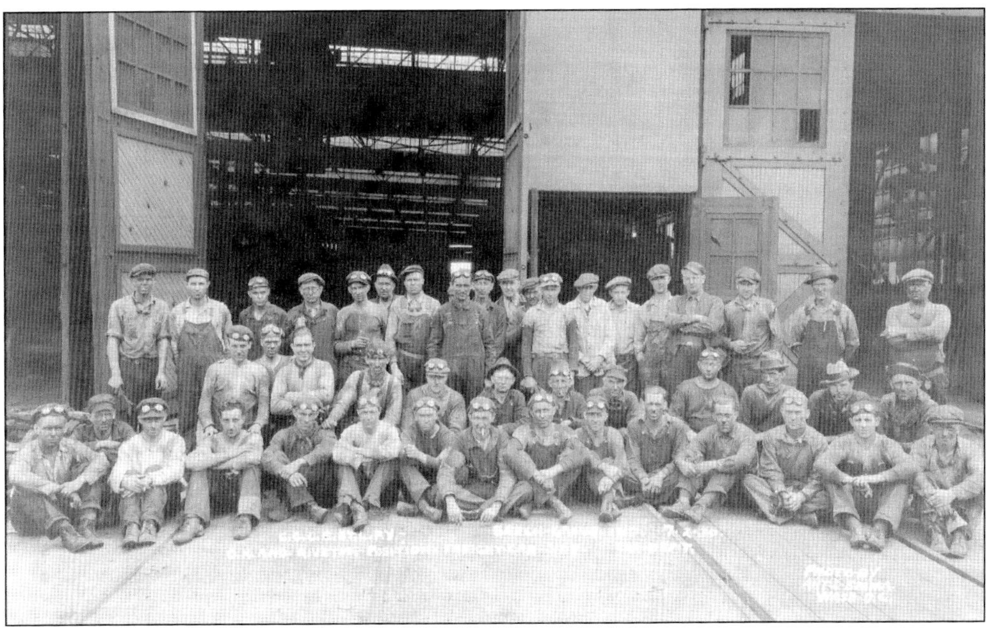

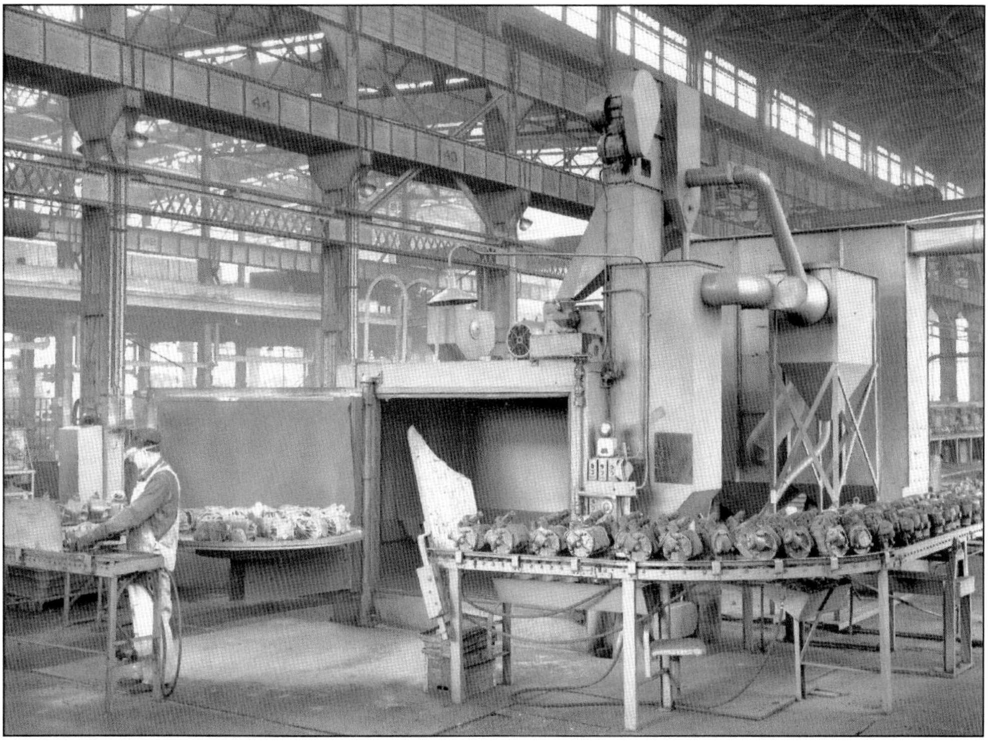

Rebuilding air brake valves became a high-volume operation by 1960. The transition to freight cars meant an increased number of cars to be serviced and likewise resulted in some capital investments in shop machinery. Here Floyd Lewis is seen loading valve assemblies into the Wheelabrator table blast machine for removal of rust and corrosion prior to the rebuilding of the internal components.

Air brake foreman R. B. Bailey (left) and assistant foreman Harold Inler are inspecting the results of the blast cleaning process on valve assemblies prior to rework. The valve assembly on the left is typical of the incoming condition of parts: covered with rust and corrosion from long service in the field. The valve assembly on the right shows the condition after the blast cleaning operation is complete.

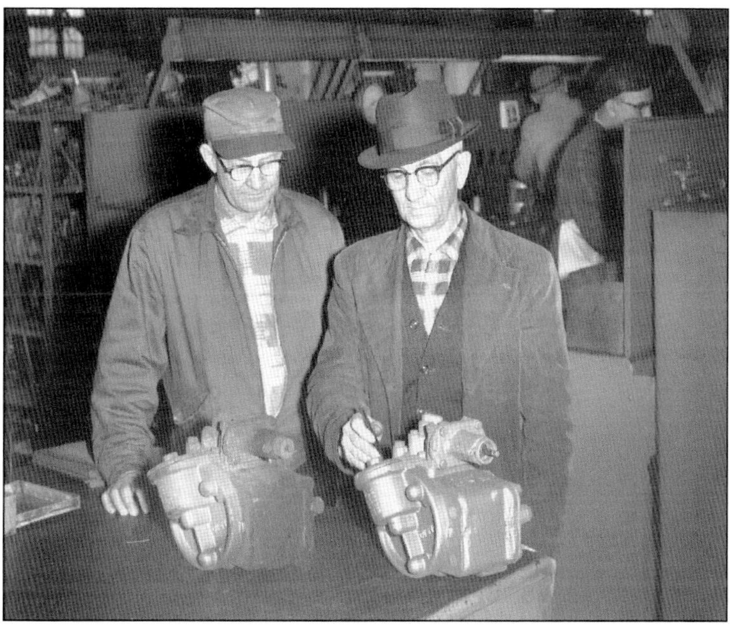

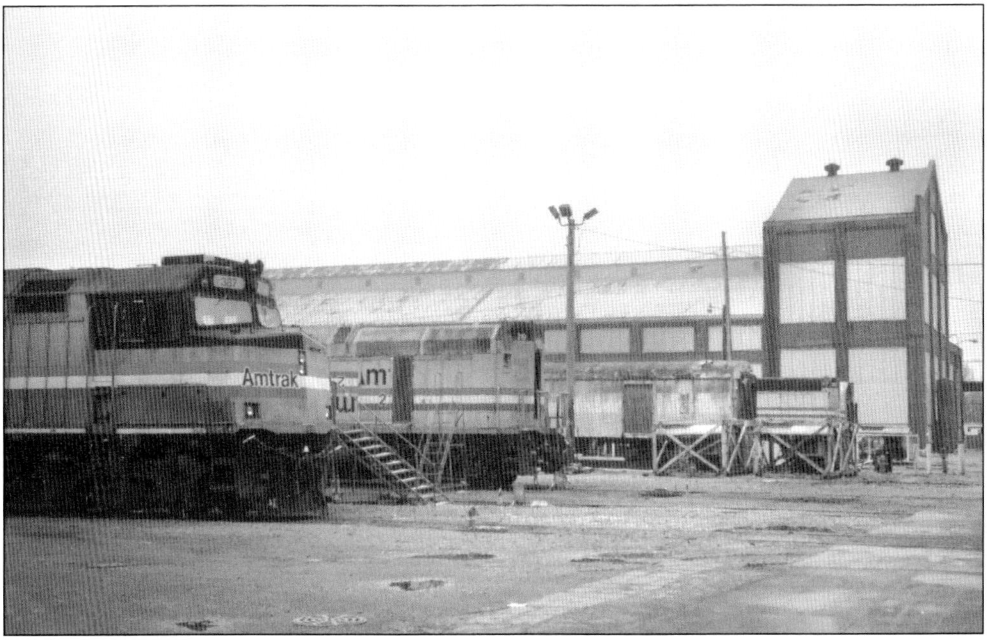

New life was breathed into the Shops when the federal government created the Amtrak passenger system, choosing Beech Grove as the location of the principal nationwide service and rebuilding facility. Once again, the rebuilding of passenger equipment became the cornerstone of operations. Seen on the staging rails, a locomotive and a few Amtrak cars await major renovation work.

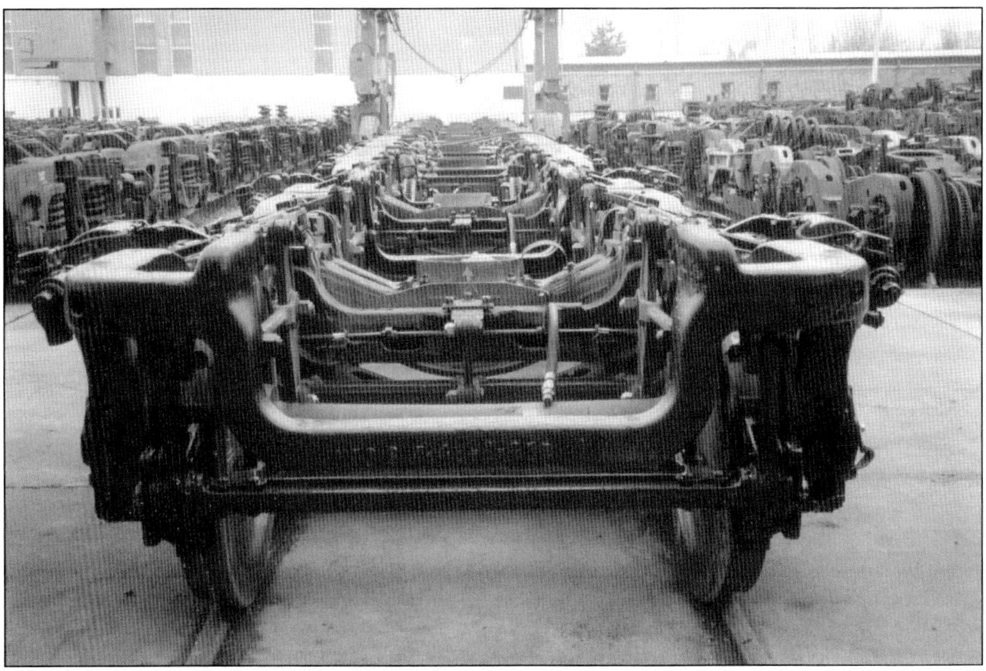

When Amtrak acquired the equipment of the financially struggling older lines to establish the new passenger service, most of the rolling stock had deteriorated from heavy use and deferred maintenance; Amtrak's entire fleet was in need of major upgrading. Pictured on the storage rails rest newly restored rolling frames in rows being staged to move to the erection bays.

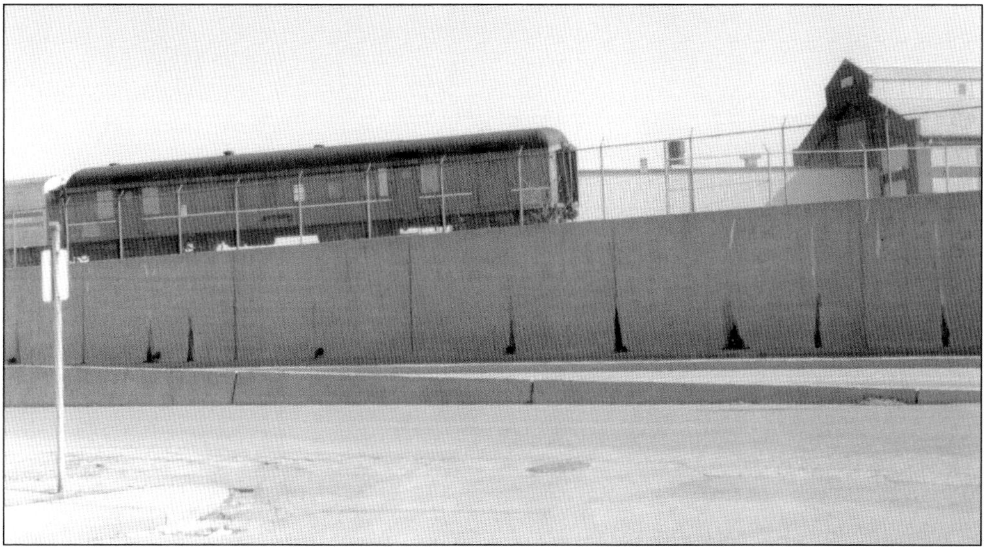

A long-retired Penn Central passenger car is seen arriving at the Shops to be renovated for Amtrak service. The Shop employees are skilled in the mechanical, sheet metal, paint, and detailed trim work required for repairs and upgrades to the retired cars, as well as those damaged by wrecks and heavy use. This car will leave the Shops fully refurbished and clad in the familiar Amtrak stainless steel ready to provide years of service in its second life.

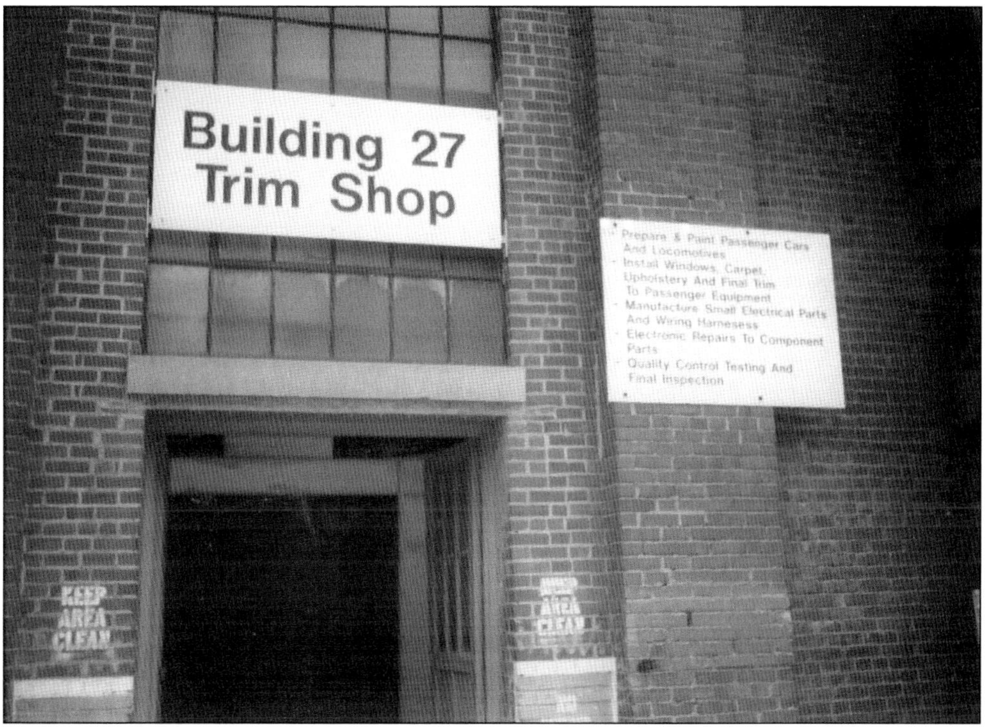

While the locomotives, cars, and their components have changed dramatically over the past century, the brick and stone exteriors of the buildings, with their large expanses of steel-framed windows, remain essentially as they were built between 1904 and 1908. New signage was added in 1997 to inform visitors about the operations in each building.

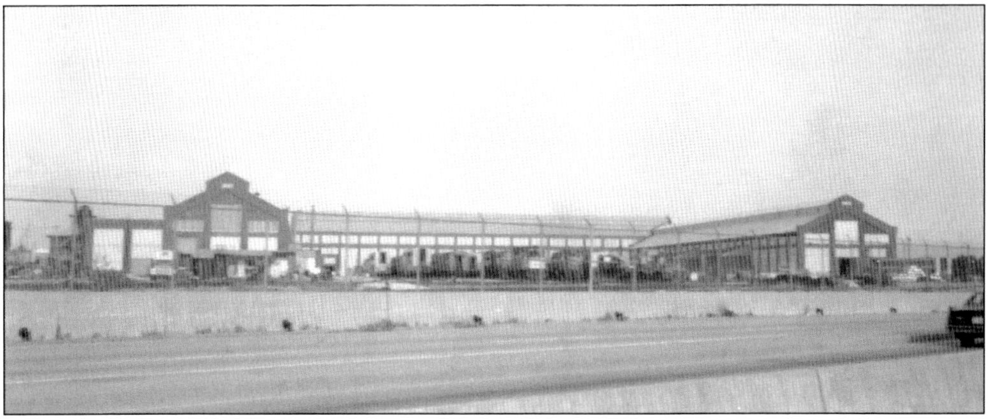

The photograph above is the view of the Beech Grove Shops that greeted visitors entering the city along Emerson Avenue, the principal north-south thoroughfare along the east side of the city. Although this image shows the yard filled with Amtrak locomotives, the view was essentially the same when the yard was lined with steam locomotives. The old, rust-stained concrete wall and high security fencing did little to offer an attractive entrance to Beech Grove. Over the past decade, the city engaged in a major reconstruction of Emerson Avenue, seeking to enhance the atmosphere all along the street. Amtrak joined with the city to upgrade the appearance of the Shops and to create the unique architectural features seen in the photograph below. Today the rehabilitated street and upgraded Shops present a unique and welcoming entryway into the city. (Below, authors' collection.)

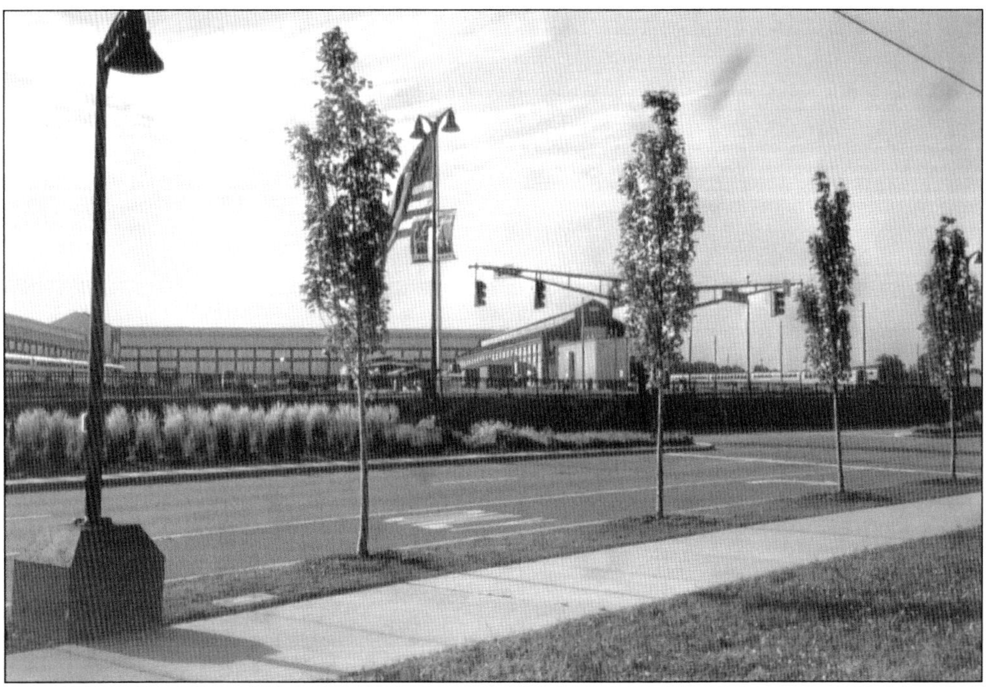

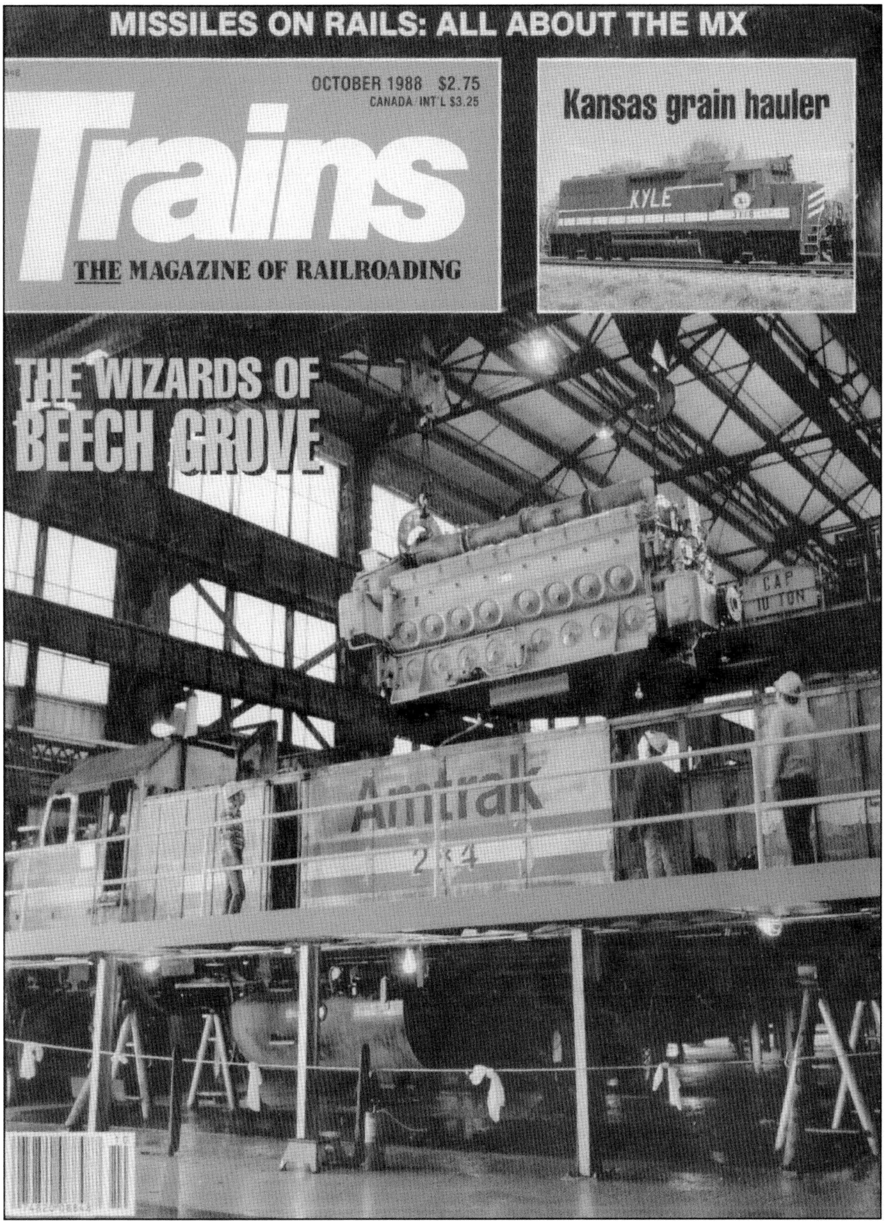

With the transition from steam to modern diesel locomotives, almost every aspect of the Shops has undergone dramatic change. The introduction of contemporary equipment and tools, and the entirely different technology required, make it unlikely that the Shops will ever again reach the employment levels of 50 years ago. The one constant factor has been the reputation of the Beech Grove facility to produce high-quality and innovative results on a daily basis. In this October 1988 edition of *Trains* magazine, the cover image and feature article expound on the virtues of the "Wizards of Beech Grove." The *Railroad Gazette*, in the November 29, 1907, issue referred to the facility in its earliest days as "one of the notable Shops in the country," and it remains so more than a century later. Whether officially named the Big Four Shops, The New York Central Shops, the Penn Central Shops, or the Amtrak Shops, this will always be the Beech Grove Shops, or most commonly just "the Grove." (Authors' collection.)

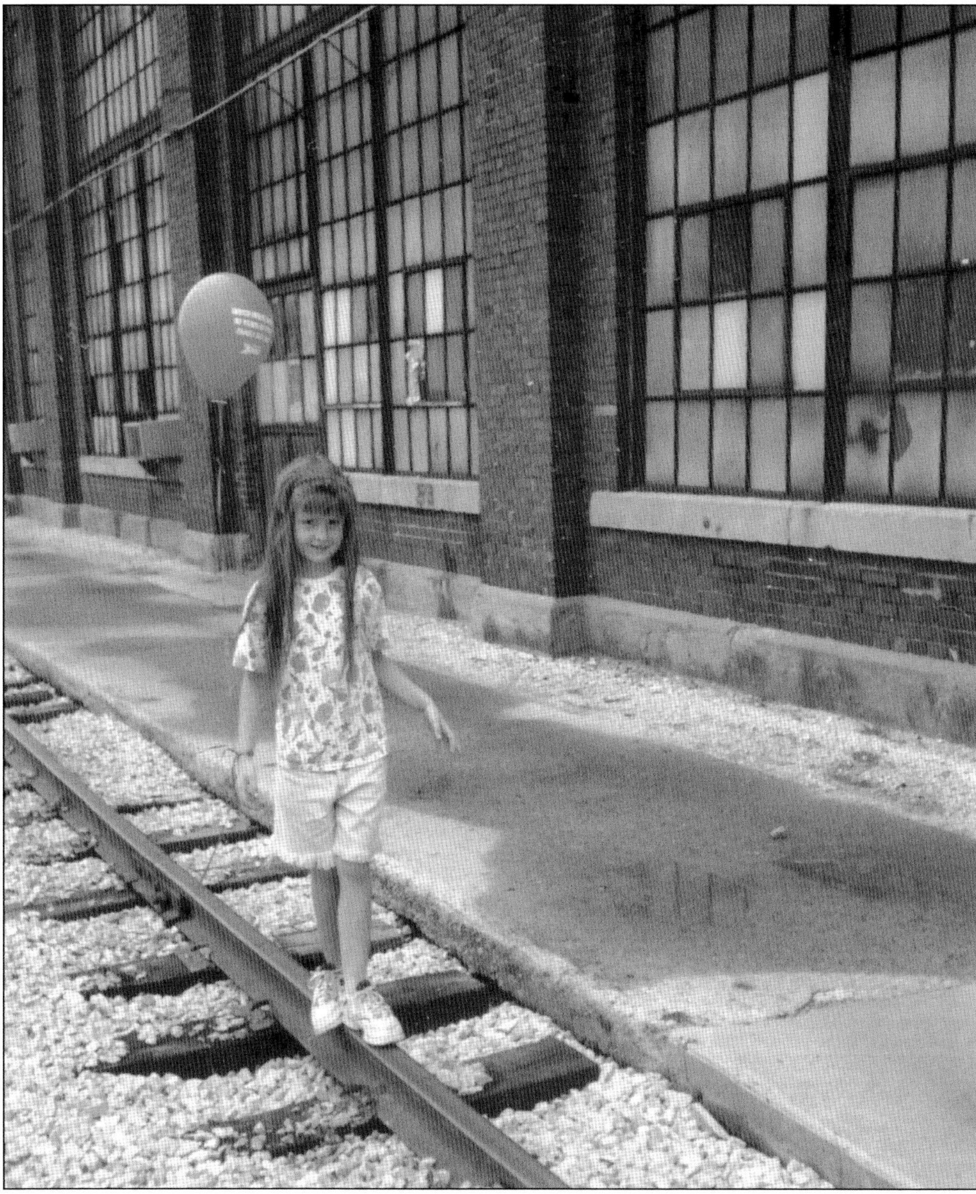

Proving that some things never change, a young girl attending the Amtrak Family Day in the summer of 1997 repeats the generations-old ritual of walking a rail against the backdrop of a century-old locomotive erection building, the birthplace of many of the massive machines the rails were designed to carry. The Shops continue to be part and parcel of the Beech Grove community, a major economic and employment engine that produced and nurtured the eggs from which the city hatched. For the railroad industry, and rail enthusiasts everywhere, the Shops are revered as the birthplace of the powerhouses of the steam age, the early streamliners, and the contemporary stainless steel coaches that carry Amtrak's passengers across the country. For those who grew up nearby during the steam age, the Shops are the birthplace of youthful fascination with the sounds of escaping steam, wailing whistle, and clanging bell as a locomotive strained to pull its load from the yards on a summer evening—the sounds that engendered childhood dreams of riding the rails to faraway places.

Three

More Than Just a Train Stop

While little formal history has been written about the central Indiana countryside prior to the 1800s, passing historical references document the struggles of transient Native American and pioneer wanderers. Once the relatively flat and fertile land was tamed, it became a loosely connected network of homesteads and farms, with an occasional stream or wooded patch separating the fields. There was the one-room Poplar Grove schoolhouse, a meeting hall built in 1837, a small cemetery, and a tollgate and road connecting area farms, but not much else.

Francis McClintock Churchman, a financier representing the Indianapolis firm of Fletcher and Churchman, bought 80 acres of land, known as the Snyder Farm in the mid-1860s, and established a permanent residence among the beech trees. Churchman immediately grew fond of his "beech tree grove on the hillside" and set forth to acquire 160 additional acres from John Pogue of Virginia for $3,000, paid in gold.

The new acreage became locally known as "Beech Grove Farm." The land lay along the Big Four Line running from Indianapolis to Cincinnati and was near the Ingall Station railroad stop, often called Ingallstown, which was named for the Big Four railroad's Cincinnati division president at the time. Churchman's business partner, George Patton, began importing Jersey cattle, pedigreed from the Isle of Jersey, to the farm. Activity was steady and growing, and eventually a railroad siding was constructed, facilitating the movement of cattle. The Ingall station gradually assumed the Beech Grove name as the entire area became generally known as Beech Grove.

In 1904, the Big Four Line announced intentions to build a large facility in the Beech Grove area. Along with some acreage owned by Churchman, several community farms totaling more than 2,600 acres were purchased by the railroad. The railroad dedicated approximately 640 acres to the shop and associated yard facilities before creating the Beech Grove Development Company to develop the balance of the land into a planned community for the housing of shop employees. New families and businesses were drawn to Beech Grove, which was incorporated as a town in 1906.

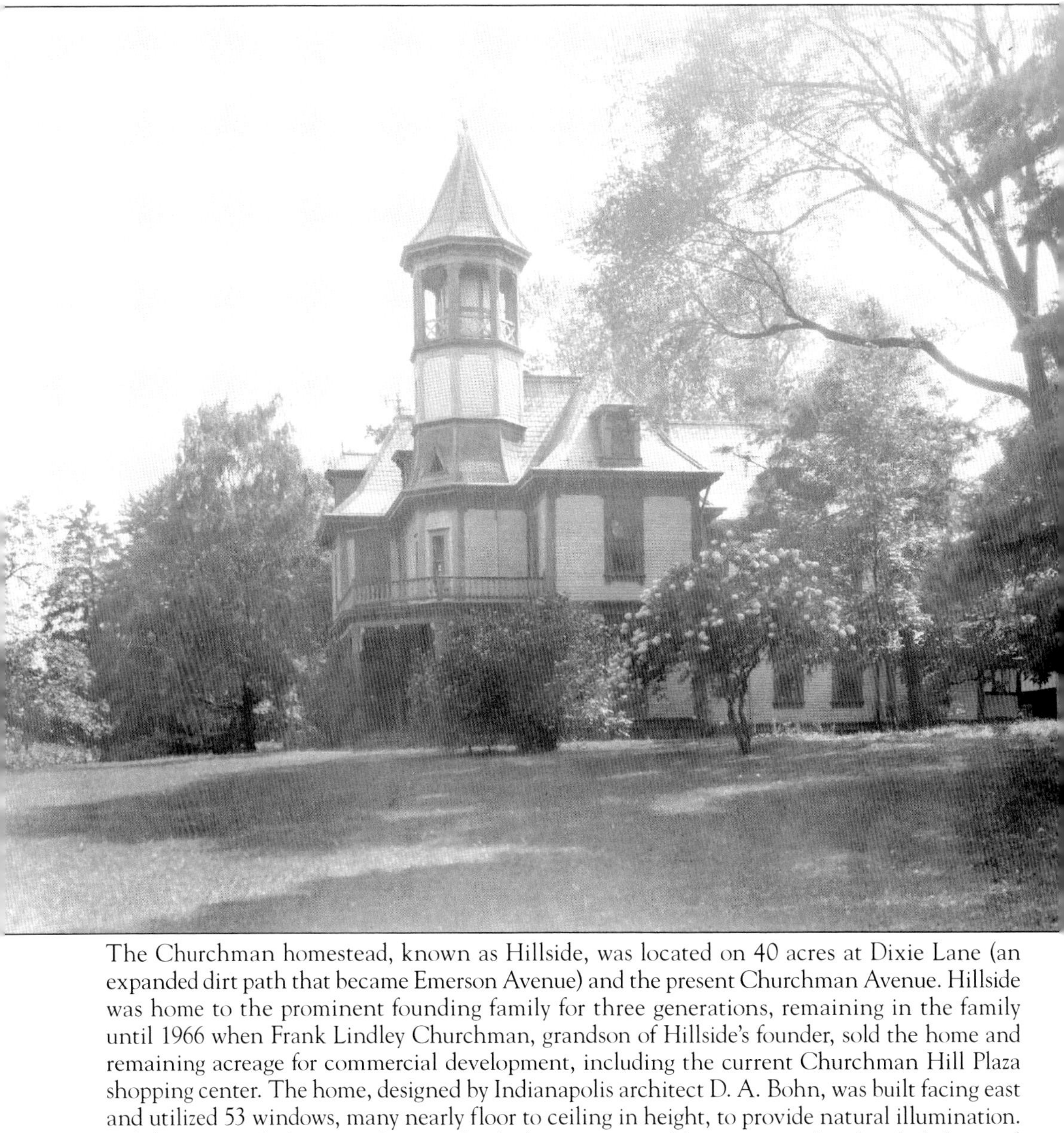

The Churchman homestead, known as Hillside, was located on 40 acres at Dixie Lane (an expanded dirt path that became Emerson Avenue) and the present Churchman Avenue. Hillside was home to the prominent founding family for three generations, remaining in the family until 1966 when Frank Lindley Churchman, grandson of Hillside's founder, sold the home and remaining acreage for commercial development, including the current Churchman Hill Plaza shopping center. The home, designed by Indianapolis architect D. A. Bohn, was built facing east and utilized 53 windows, many nearly floor to ceiling in height, to provide natural illumination. While not overtly fancy on the outside, the house was sturdily constructed and included several upscale interior features, including natural gas chandelier lighting, one-inch thick wall plaster, two-inch thick doors, ornate moldings, and ceiling rosettes. Compared to other large estates of the late 1800s, Hillside's imposing facade and Victorian-style construction was relatively plain and simple, focusing on practicality and convenience instead of show.

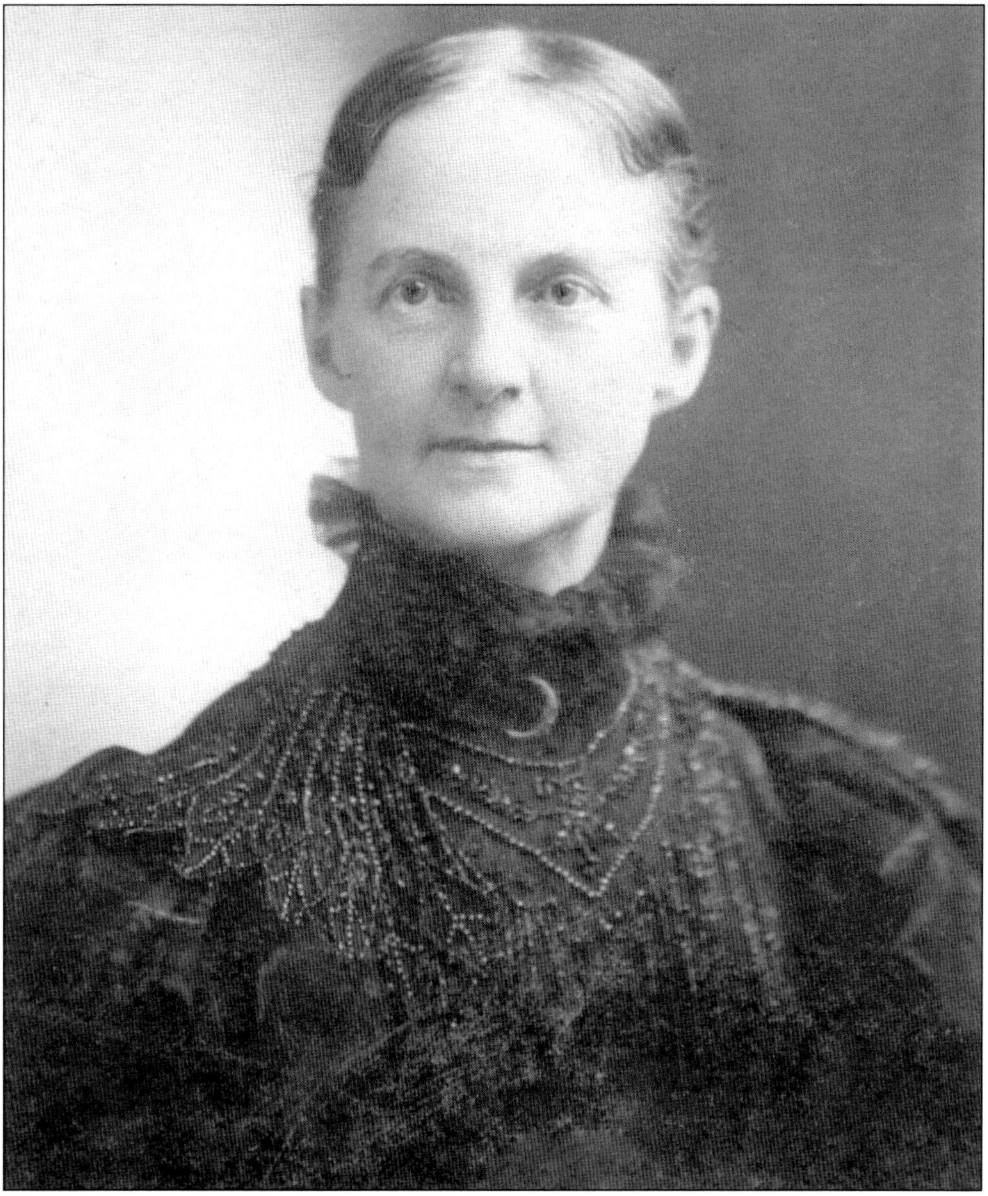

Anna Churchman, in a rare picture from 1897, was the matriarch of Hillside. She married Francis McClintock Churchman on October 12, 1859, in Janesville, Wisconsin. The couple eventually had seven children. Her husband, being of English and Quaker heritage, was a reputable, hard-working man noted for his integrity. He began his career at age 19 as a clerk at S. A. Fletcher Bank on Washington Street, the predecessor of the American Fletcher National Bank of Indianapolis, Indiana, and within five years made managing partner, a position he held until his death. Within the then-relatively small, but close-knit, Indianapolis business community, Churchman was highly regarded for his ability to make loans based solely on the character of the applicant and a firm handshake. While not much for going out on the town, rather preferring to keep private and tending to his family, Francis was well known and likewise knew many people. He is one of only a few Hoosiers to have had their likenesses immortalized in a portrait by Indiana artist T. C. Steele.

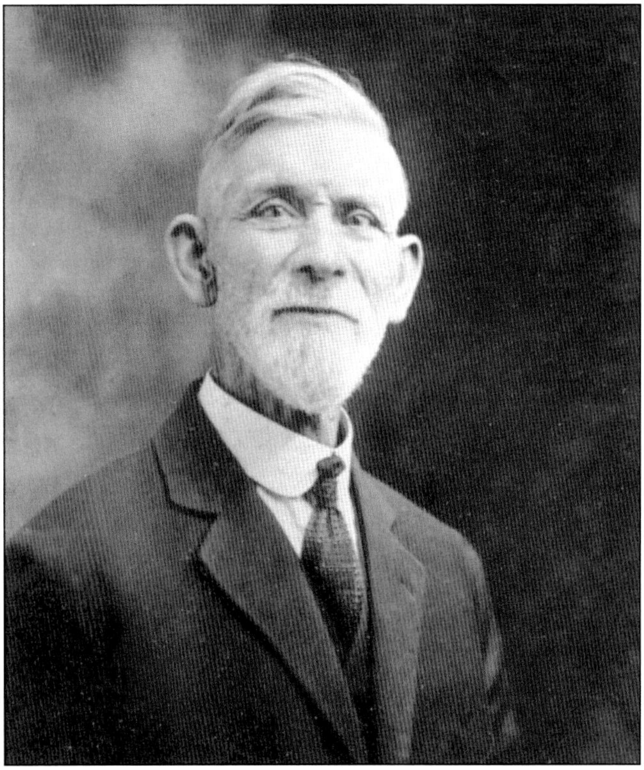

Physicians began arriving in the Beech Grove area in the late 1800s. Dr. Clark Farabee, one of the first Beech Grove doctors, had an office at Seventh Avenue and Main Street. It was 1913 before the Order of the Sisters of St. Francis of Perpetual Adoration, a Catholic religious community, constructed the first hospital in the community, opening with 75 patient beds.

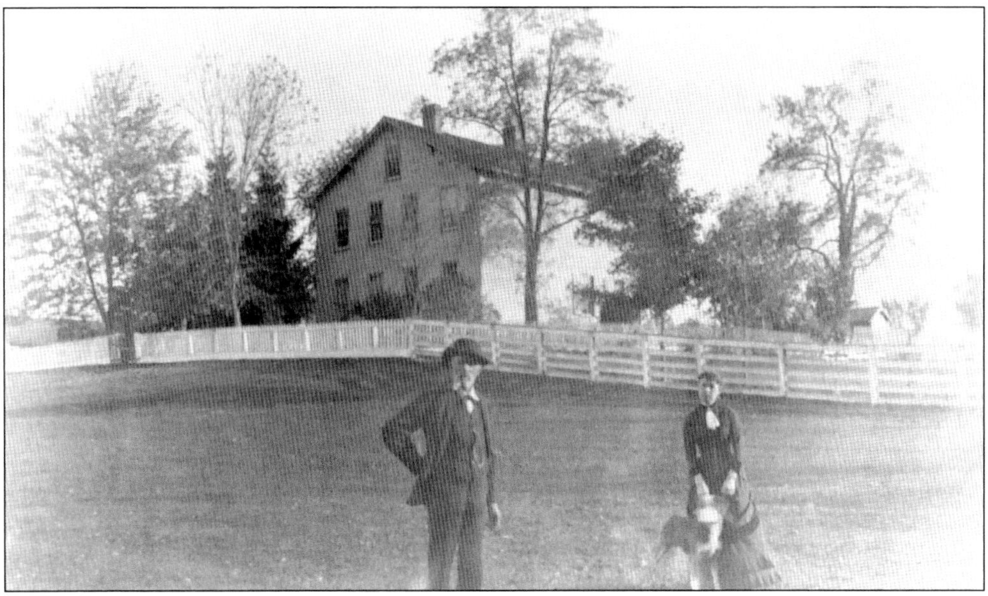

Among the early inhabitants of the Beech Grove area was the Fletcher family. This photograph of their home shows that like most families during the settlement years, the Fletchers had several acres for farming, hunting, and hosting gatherings, a large house to accommodate a growing family, and obligatory barn and white picket fence. While the Beech Grove area consisted primarily of similar farms dotting the countryside, often several miles apart, there remained a strong sense of community.

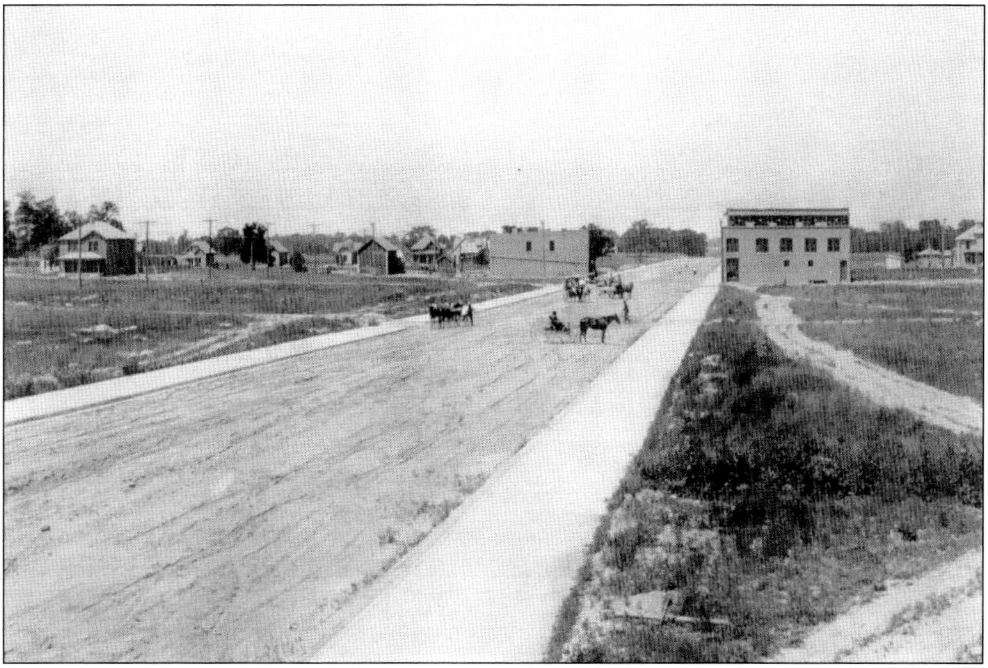

This page showcases the first known photographs of the town of Beech Grove. Evident in these 1906 pictures is the very rural character of the community, still in its infancy, complete with horse-drawn buggies. The land had been cleared to make way for the housing and businesses to service the employment needs of the Big Four Shops. It was not long before a dramatic change occurred and the town was transformed, as the streets filled with motorized modes of transportation, including the interurban. Beech Grove, a planned community, was developed primarily by the Beech Grove Improvement Company on land acquired by the railroad for this purpose.

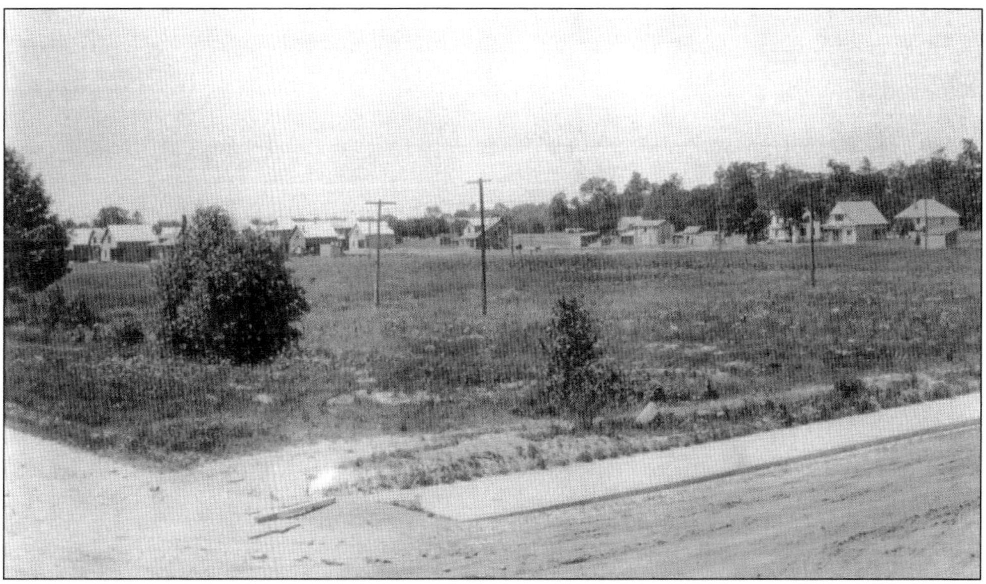

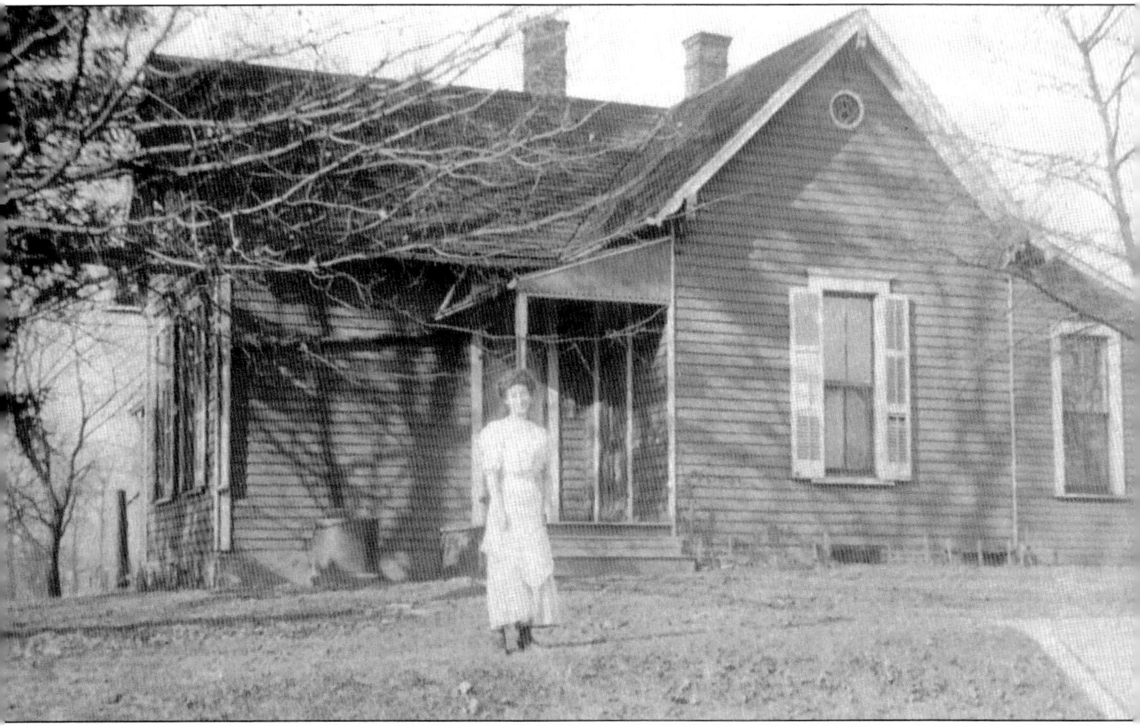

Ruth McGregor was Beech Grove's first telephone operator. She is seen in this 1908 photograph at the Beech Grove Telephone Exchange at 222 South Fourth Avenue. Ruth's quiet job of servicing calls for a few hundred residents quickly expanded with the increase in population. Within 25 years, the town of Beech Grove grew to sport more paved streets per capita than any other Indiana community of like size. By the early 1930s, Beech Grove had numerous transportation options, gas and electric utilities, modern and affordable housing, a state-of-the-art sanitary and storm sewer system, and a well-educated citizenry. Even with Indianapolis as accessible as a 10¢ bus or streetcar fare, Beech Grove has been able to maintain a unique and independent quality, rare in a modern city that now is home to 15,000 people.

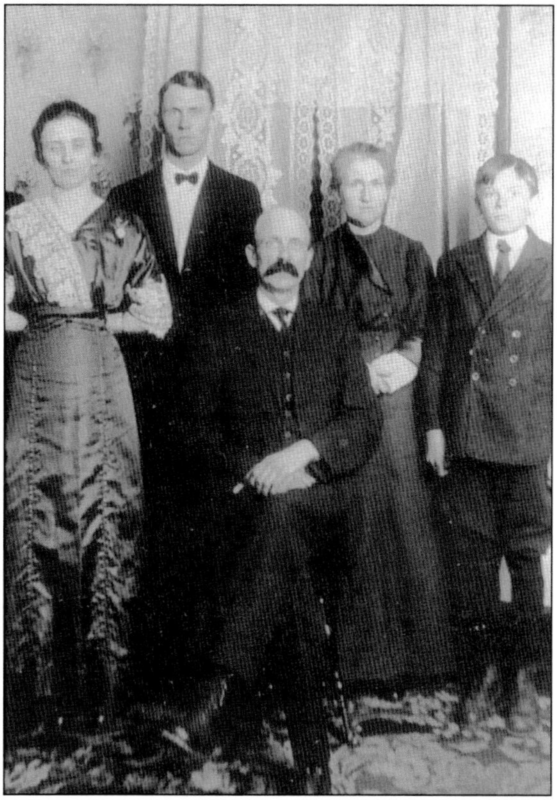

The Wheat family patriarch is pictured front and center with his family. The Wheat family was well known within the community for its retail operation. Wheat's Grocery was the first grocery and general merchandise store in town. For years, it remained the main source of quality, affordable food and other products for Beech Grove residents, eliminating the need to travel to Indianapolis or produce all necessities locally.

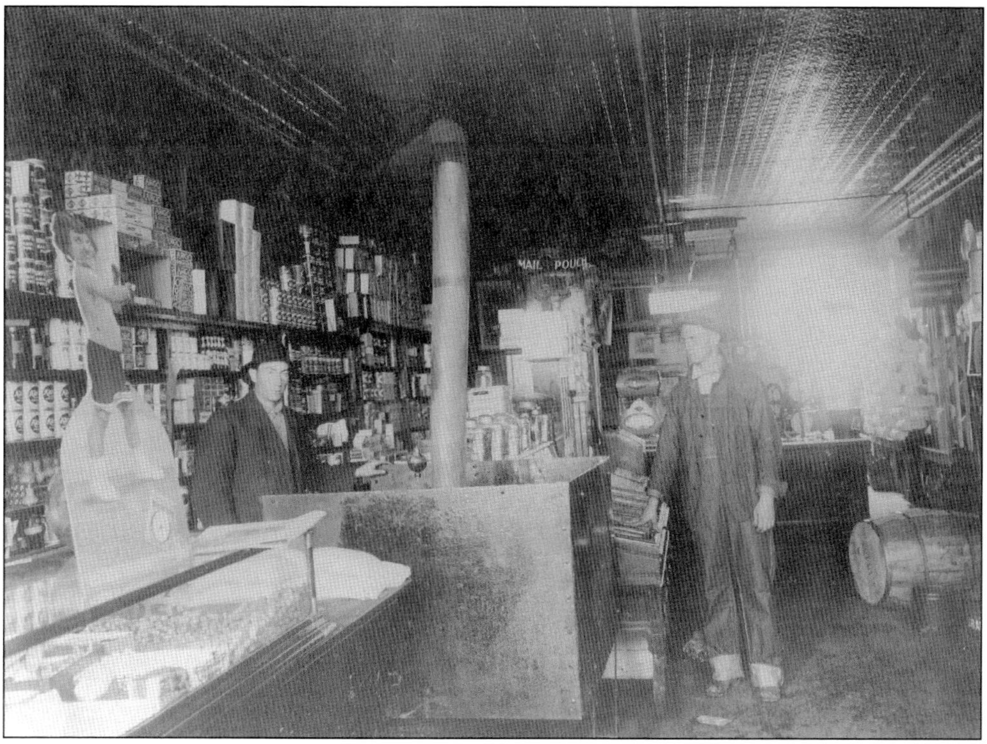

This interior photograph of Wheat's Grocery was taken in 1908. Wheat's Grocery was more than just a place to buy needed supplies, it was a community gathering spot, a place to "warm up" in the winter, and the spot to visit and catch wind of local gossip. Clifford Wheat is smiling behind the counter with Herman Wheat at center right.

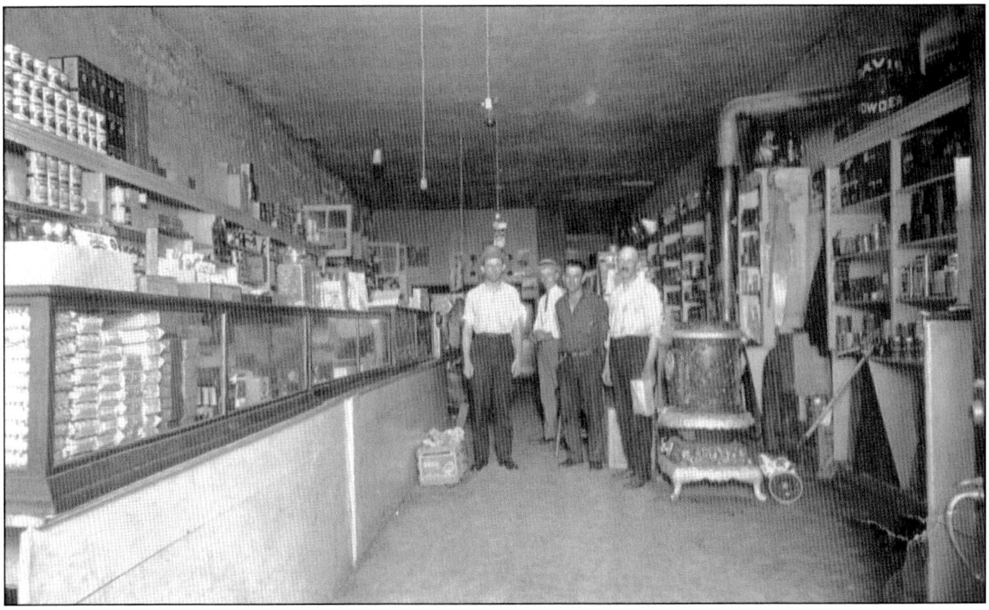

The photograph above depicts a well-stocked and well-organized Wheat's Grocery and shows, from left to right, Clifford Wheat, Herman Wheat (Bill's son), Tip Russell, and Bill Wheat in the early 1920s. Clearly visible is the warming furnace that drew in the locals for cold weather chatting. Most early businesses were family operations with several generations of the family working in multiple capacities. To this day, the majority of Main Street businesses are independent or family operations. In the photograph below, George Clifford Wheat is seen behind the counter and surrounded by stacks of merchandise. It was common that the Wheat family knew everybody in town by name and often, like F. M. Churchman at Fletcher's Bank, extended credit with a handshake (and receipt ledger). (Above, Woodhull family collection.)

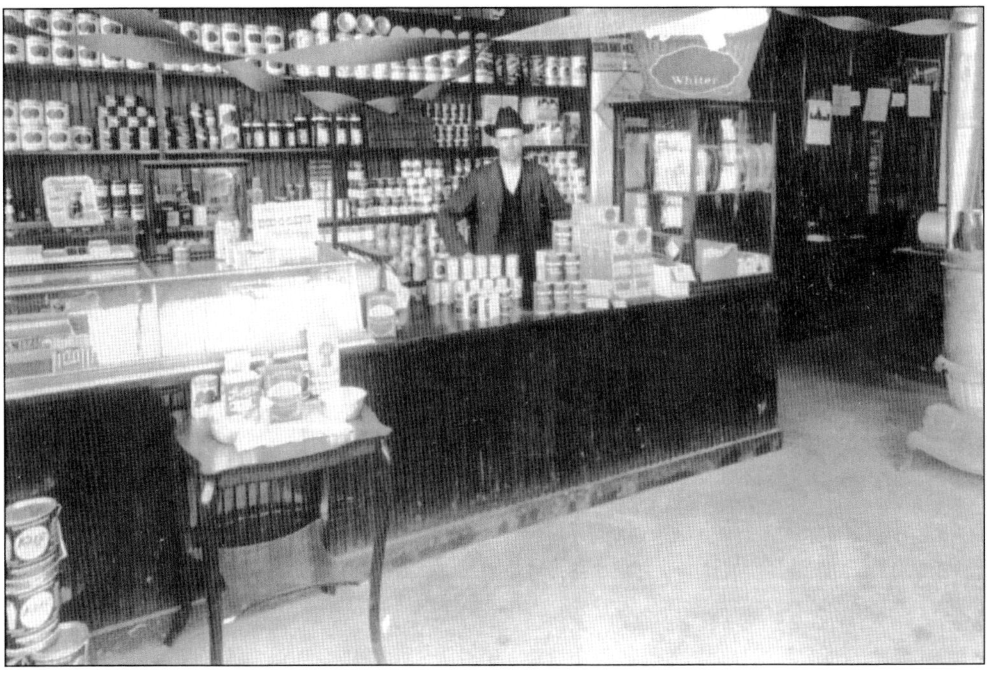

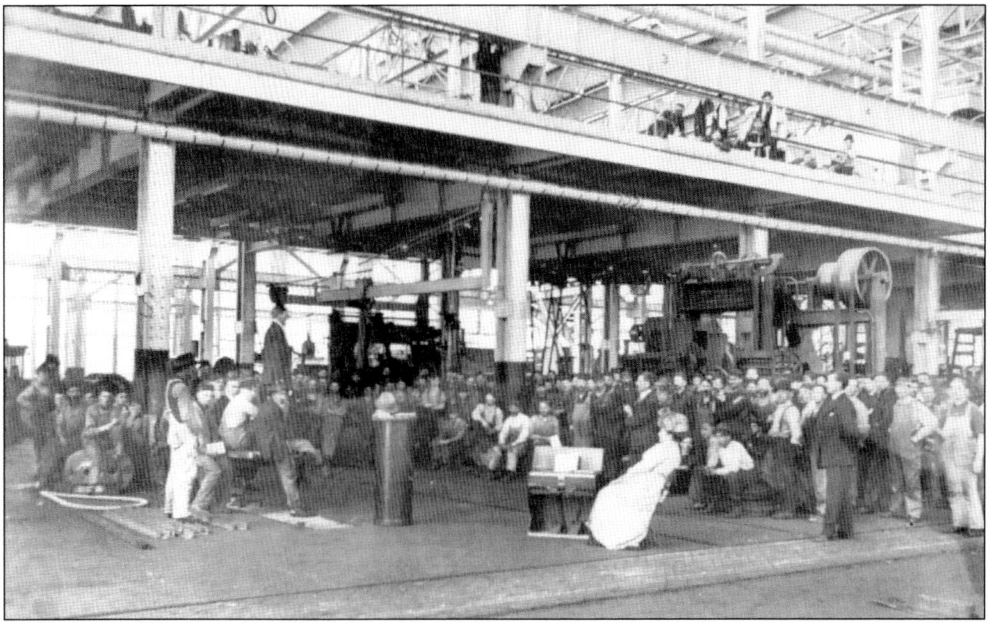

This lunchtime scene at the Big Four Stores Department platform in 1911 shows workers and community members at a church service meeting, complete with organist. These meetings, initiated in 1910 by Newton Griggs, C. M. Hamilton, Bert and Fred Long, Fred Parker, and R. F. Turner, developed into a large congregation, culminating in a move to a tent revival and eventually the founding of the Beech Grove Christian Church.

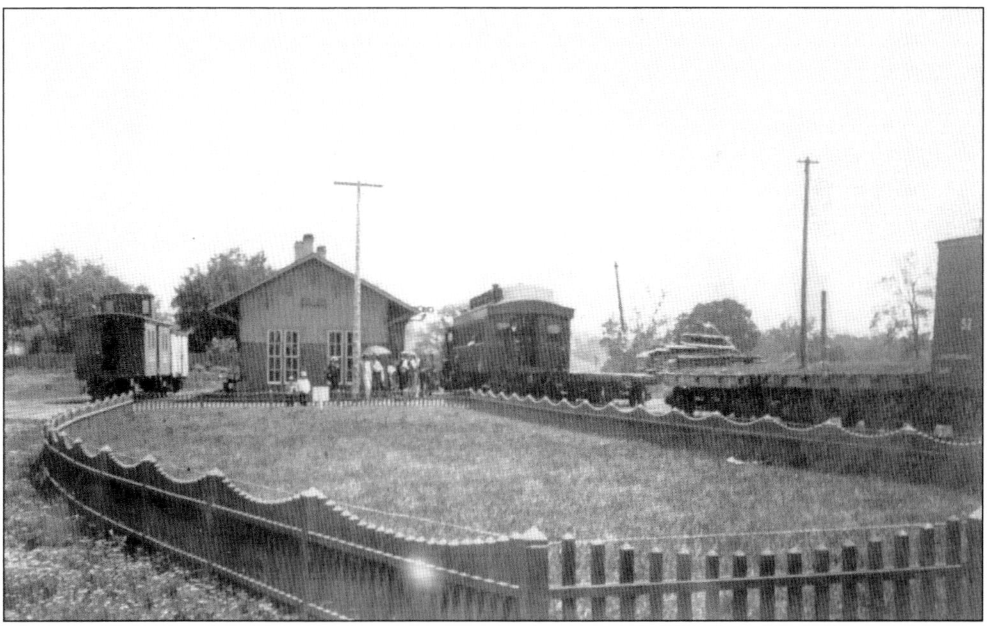

In addition to the Shops, the expanding railroad made another train-related visual impact on Beech Grove, as the landscape changed with construction and completion of the first Big Four Shops railroad station. Seen here in the 1920s, the railroad station was a flurry of activity as it serviced the ever-increasing transportation needs of the community with daily commuter train service to Indianapolis.

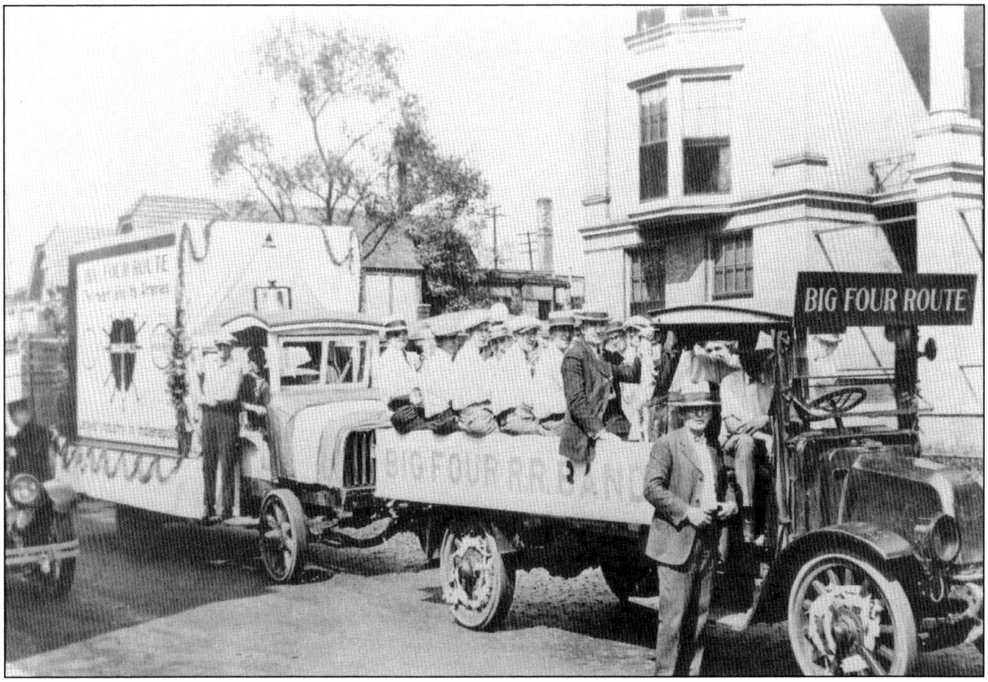

Being an integral part of the community, the Shops sponsored the busy and well-known Big Four Band. Aside from performing at Beech Grove community events, the Big Four Band traveled to other cities and towns both inside and outside of Indiana. This photograph was taken at the entrance to a hotel in Greensburg, Indiana, in 1915.

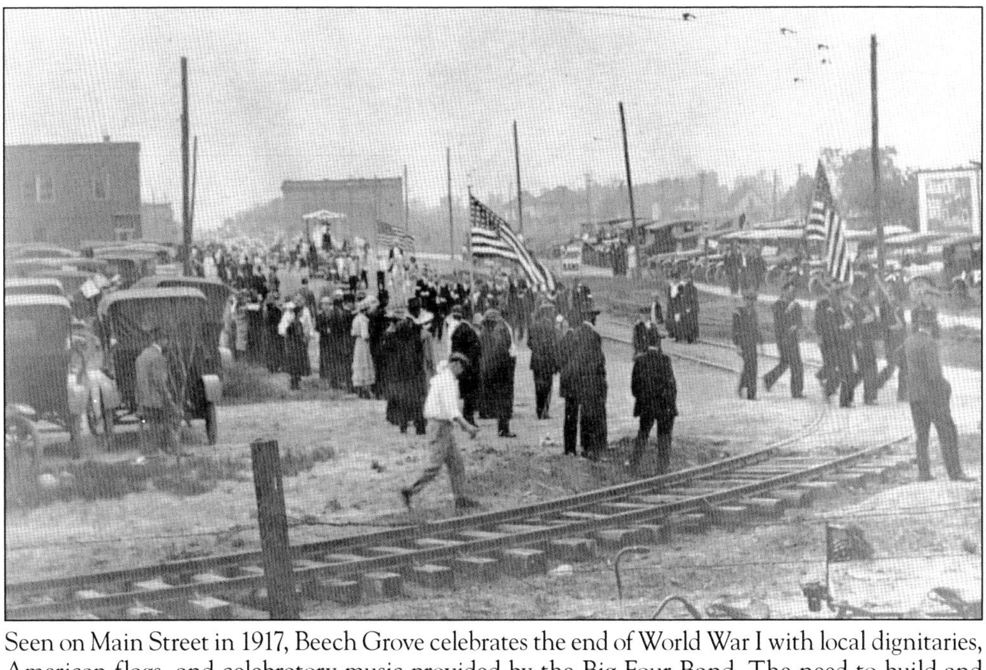

Seen on Main Street in 1917, Beech Grove celebrates the end of World War I with local dignitaries, American flags, and celebratory music provided by the Big Four Band. The need to build and service trains during the war had provided plentiful employment. The growing railroad industry continued to spur the town's growth for several decades.

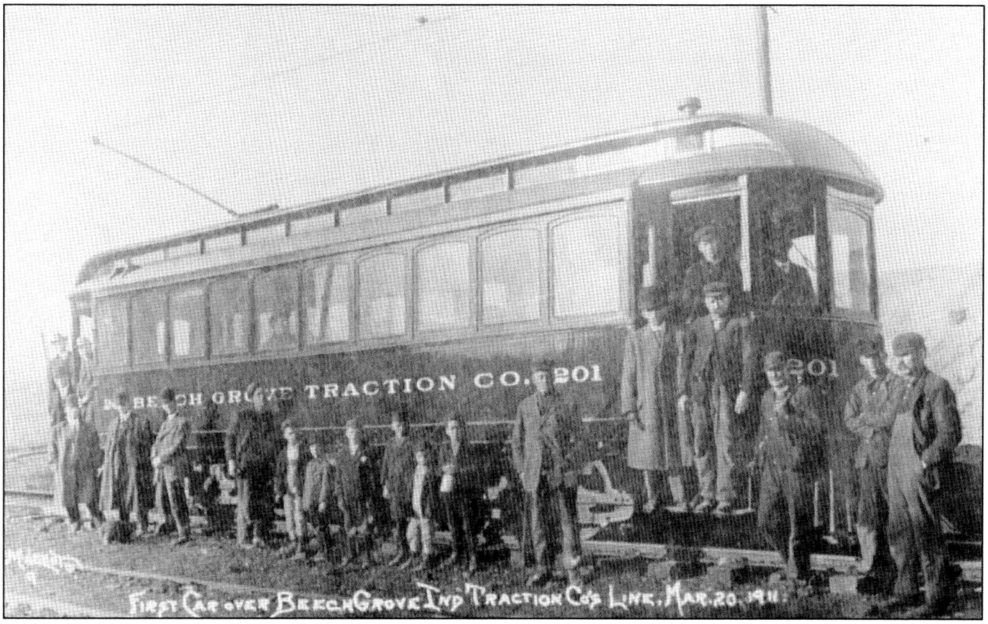

The service personnel of the Beech Grove Traction Company are posing above to be photographed with Car 201, which was the first electric-powered train placed into service on March 20, 1911, just before the train's first official run. Trolley cars, below, leave the Beech Grove Traction Company Barn at First Avenue and Alton Street for a busy day of rounds. The car barn was at the current location of Beech Grove Tire Company. The February 12, 1910, edition of the *Electric Railway Journal* announced that the Beech Grove Town Board had awarded the electric train franchise to the Beech Grove Traction Company earlier that year. Since the Beech Grove Traction Company had already acquired all necessary right-of-ways for construction, the line was ready to operate in just over a year. (Above, Joe Seiter collection.)

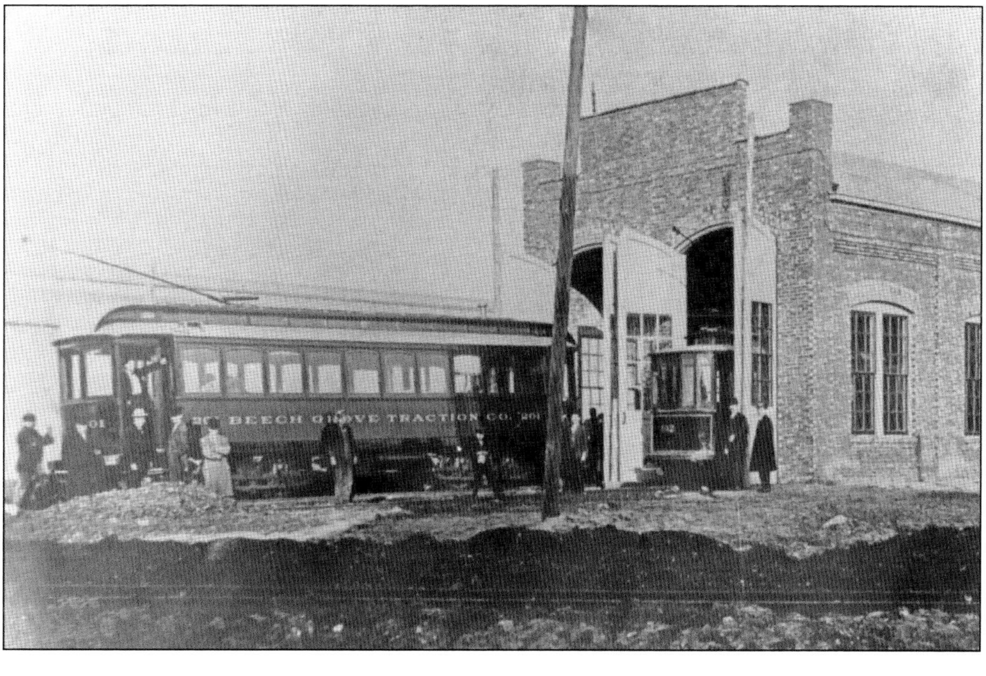

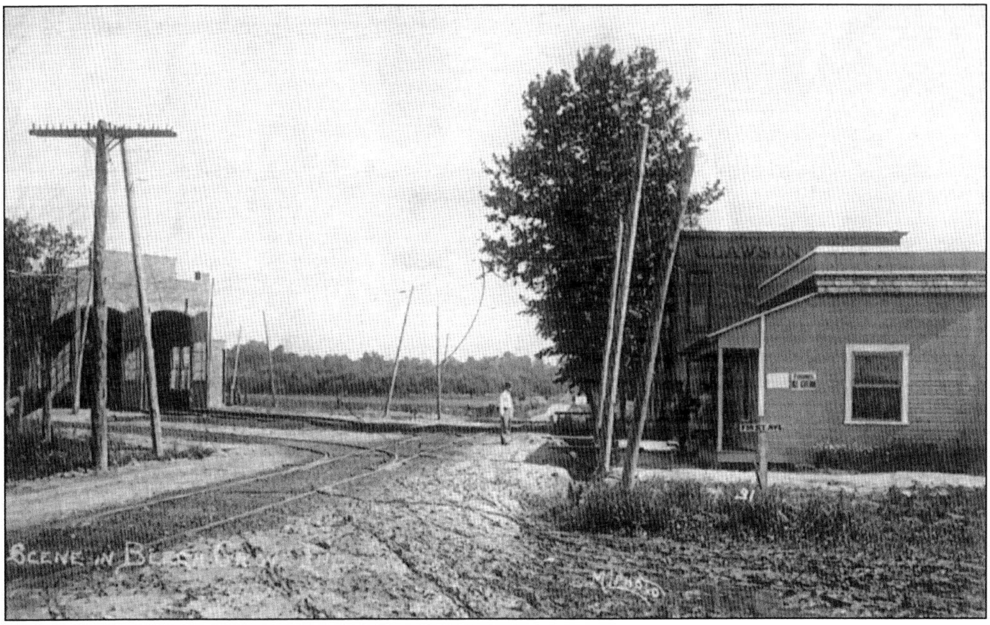

These 1911 postcards show the Beech Grove Traction Company Shed on Clawson Street near Garstang Street (above) and Car 201 traveling down Main Street (below). Some interurban historians refer to the line as a trolley line rather than an interurban, since it only ran from Beech Grove for six miles to Indianapolis, looping south of downtown, and never reaching the Traction Terminal station. The fare was 10¢ during the interurban's entire tenure of operation from 1911 until 1938. In 1938, the Indianapolis Railways Company cut power to the line due to nonpayment of electric bills, effectively ending the operations of the Beech Grove Traction Company. (Both Joe Seiter collection.)

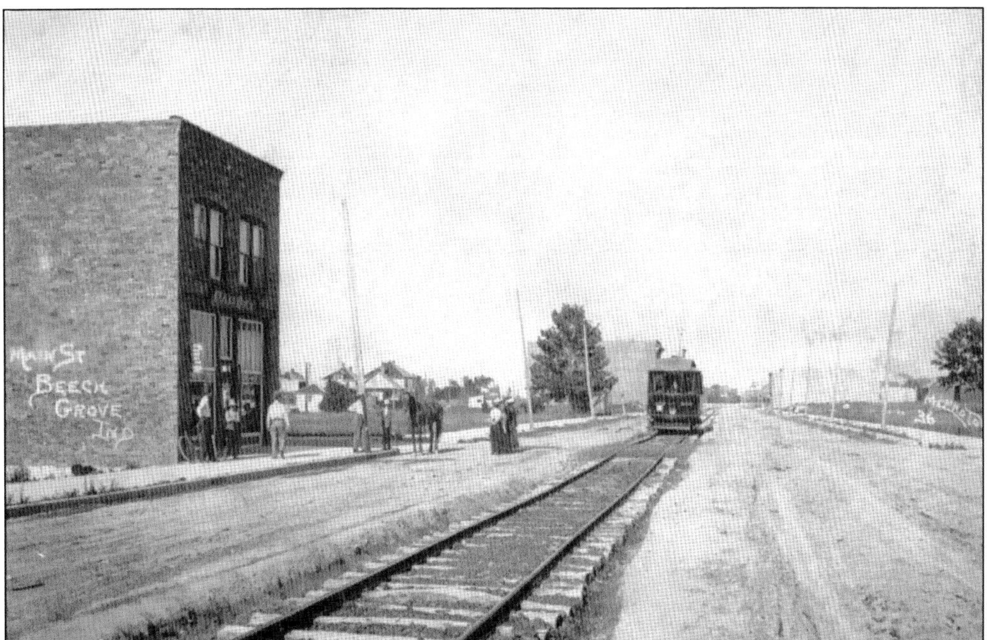

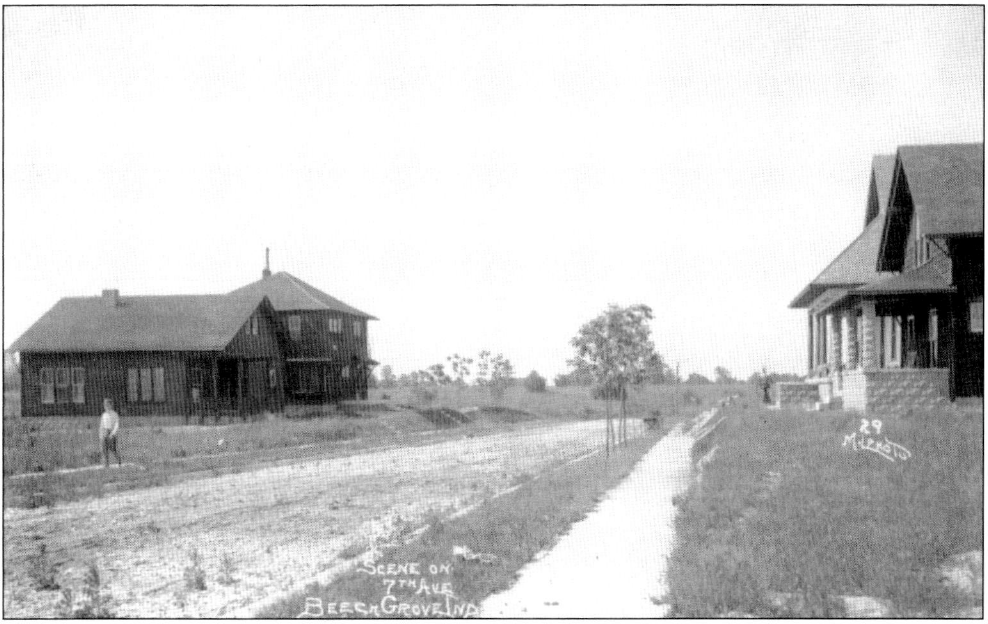

Since the Beech Grove Improvement Company shared responsibility for residential and business development with the Beech Grove Town Board, promotional efforts were enhanced by the availability of several postcards showcasing area development. These Beech Grove postcard images are among the few sources visually documenting residential growth and include professionally photographed scenes of Seventh Avenue in 1915 (above) and Ninth Avenue in 1920 (below). The two views, separated by two city blocks and five years time, depict several cosmetic improvements added between 1915 and 1920, including paved walkways and developed lawns, however, the streets are still dirt. While weeds are seen in the road of the Seventh Avenue picture, increased traffic over time has retarded green growth on Ninth Avenue. (Both Joe Seiter collection.)

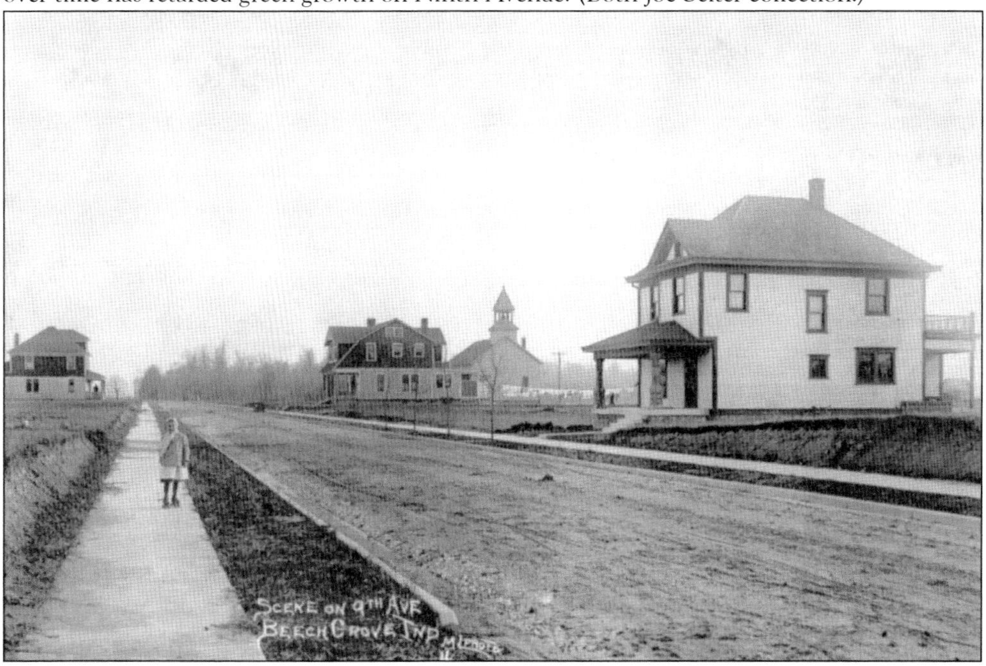

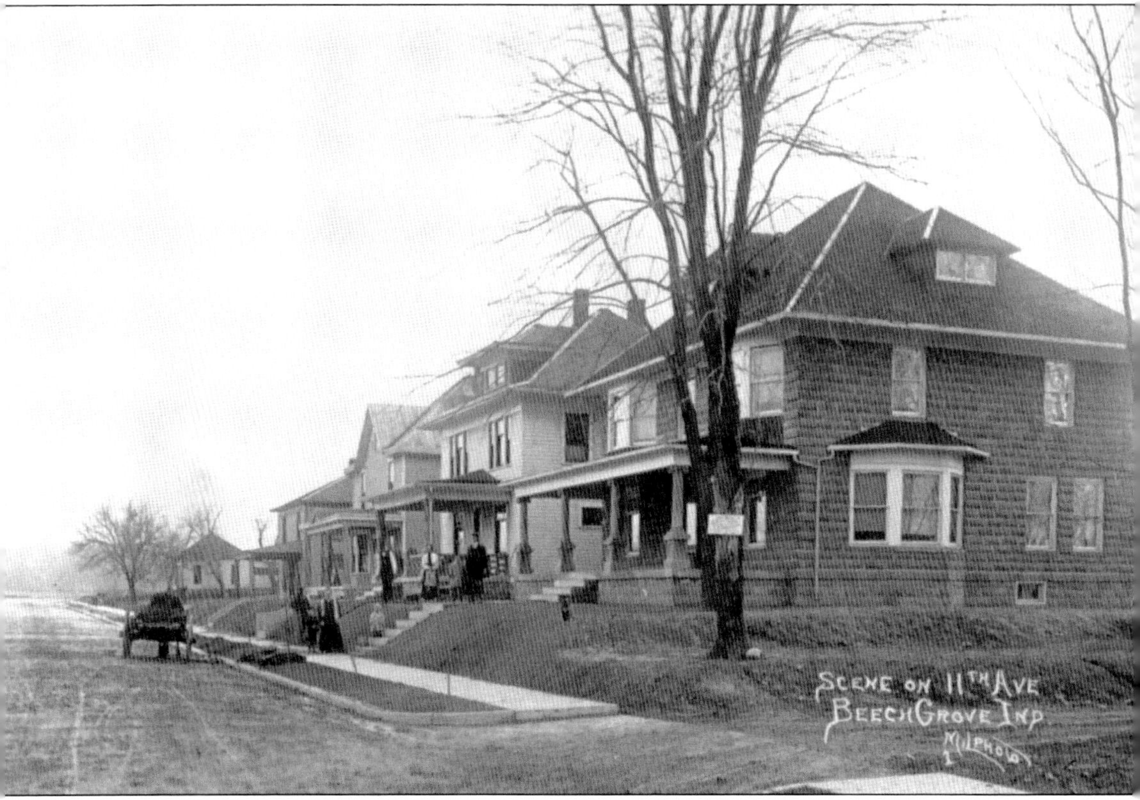

This 1920s postcard shows a close-up view of residences along Eleventh Avenue. Houses were large to accommodate the growing families of the tradesmen attracted to Beech Grove for employment in the large railroad facility. These families created additional growth in service businesses, retail stores, and construction businesses to build their houses. In addition, businesses such as the Cleveland Grain Company established facilities that were also served by the railroad. The growth of Beech Grove was driven by the high demand for skilled workers in these labor-intensive industries. The hours were long, the work was hard, and working conditions were often unpleasant; this was a young man's employment market. During the years prior to 1930, Beech Grove's senior and retired population was virtually nonexistent. The town's workforce was known to be young, hard working, family centered, and 100 percent Caucasian. (Joe Seiter collection.)

In the 1910 photograph at right, driver Pete Hunt is transporting residents down the "Old Hack Line," a route running from downtown Beech Grove, to stops along Prospect and Churchman Avenues, operating at least three times per day. The proprietor of this horse-drawn transportation service was Guy Rutledge. Because the horse-and-carriage operation charged a hefty 15¢, and less-expensive traveling options developed, the line fell to competition and closed in January 1911, just two months before the Beech Grove Traction Company began servicing the area. Over time, trains, traditional buses, jitney bus service, the interurban, horses and buggies, and eventually horseless carriages all competed to transport area residents. After the discontinuance of the Old Hack Line, Guy Rutledge managed the Beech Grove Transfer Company, seen below.

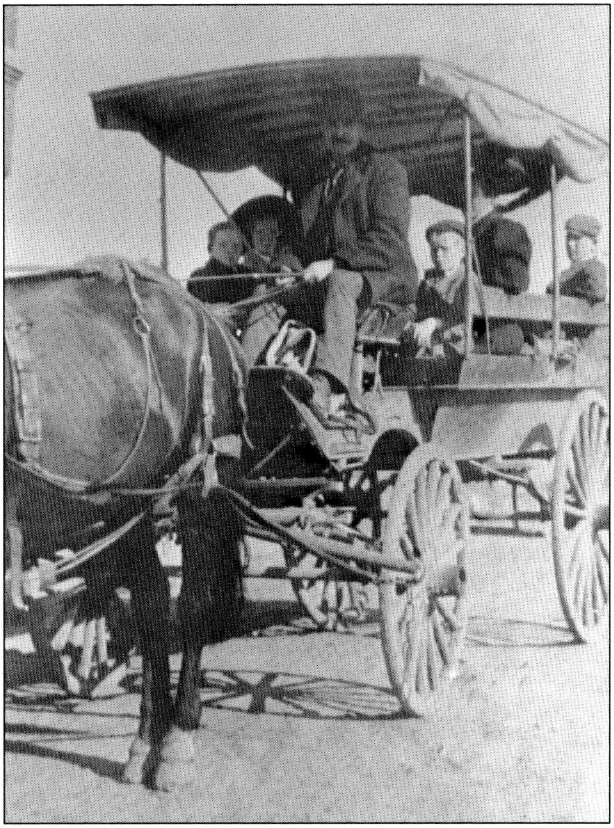

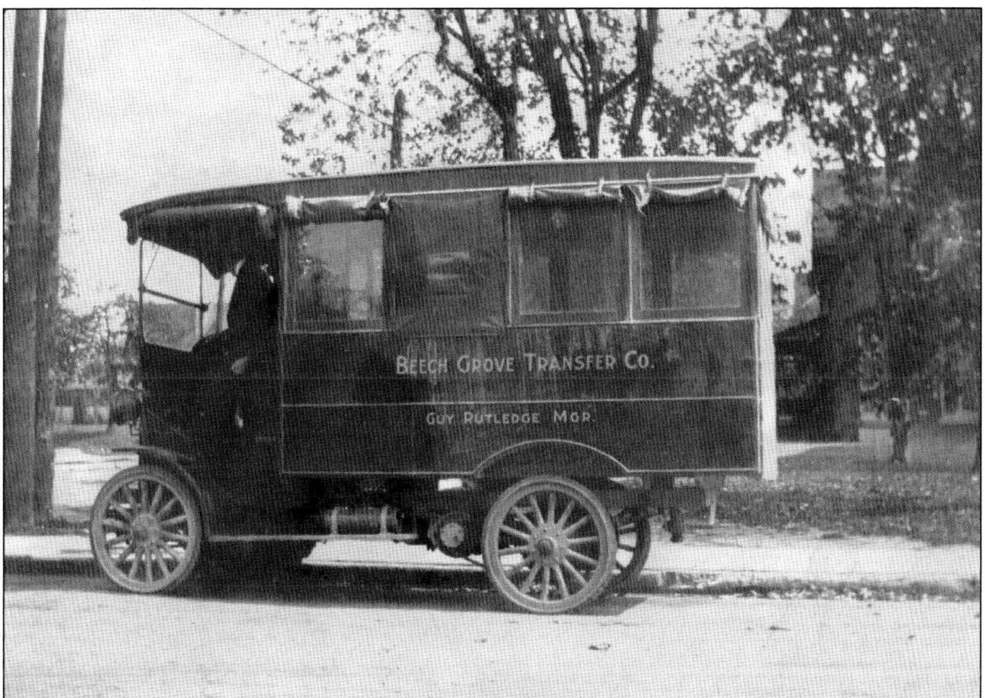

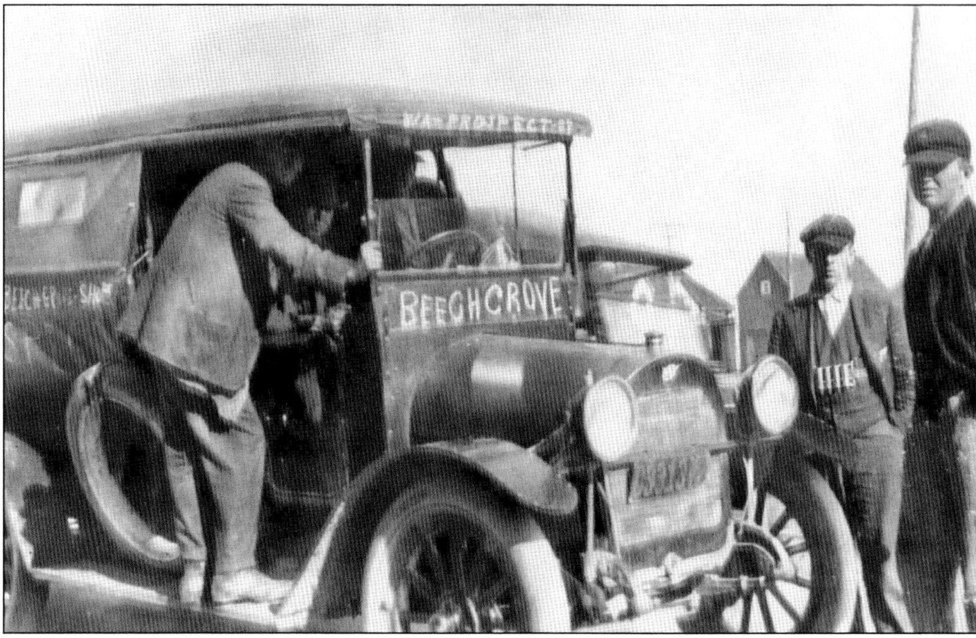

For wealthy residents, a private taxi was a great, flexible alternative to public transportation. By the 1920s, area roads were improving, easing the barriers to travel around central Beech Grove. The taxis were most used for short jaunts around town and area farms, but they could be hired, with advance notice, for personal travel to Indianapolis. This Beech Grove taxi, seen above, had a fixed route marked "Washington-Prospect," referring to streets in Indianapolis. The South Side Motor Coach below was a familiar sight in the 1920s as it moved along Sherman Avenue and Bethel Drive to the Cleveland Grain Elevators and other area homes and businesses.

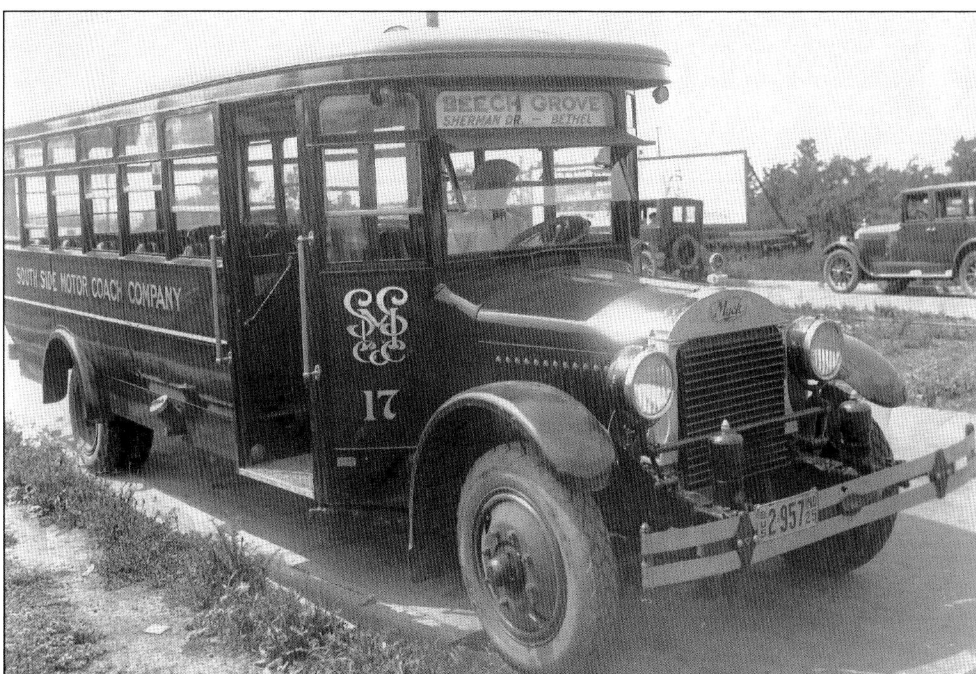

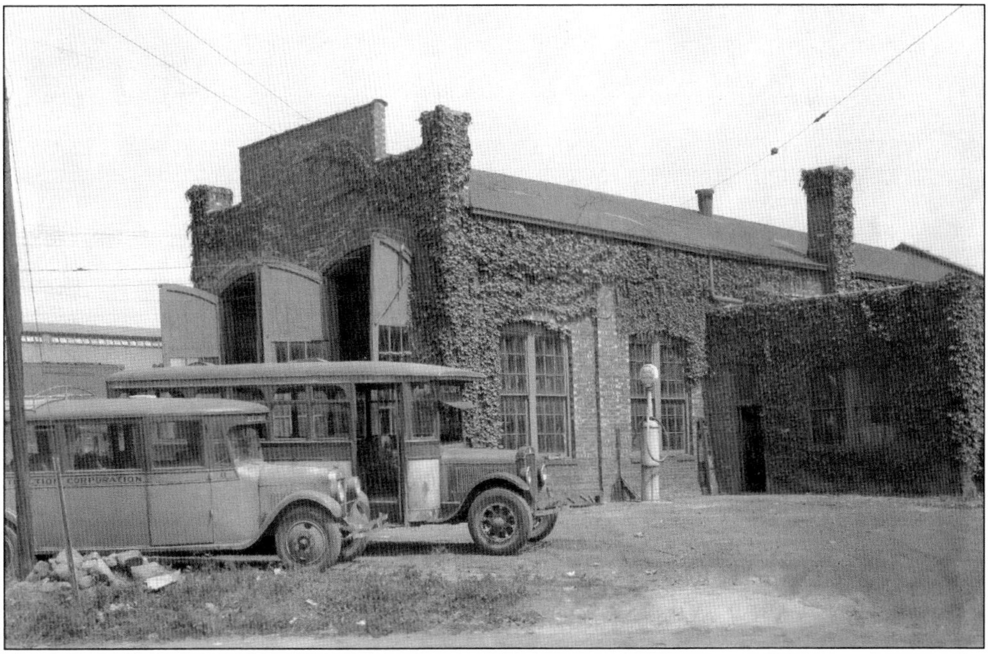

This interesting 1920s photograph represents several modes of travel, including, from left to right, a taxi, a Stanley Steamer bus, and the interurban barn, which also served as a bus pick-up point. Because Beech Grove was located over six hard miles of rough roads to Indianapolis, and there were many travelers from the city to Beech Grove employers as well as residents with business in Indianapolis, a variety of travel businesses successfully coexisted.

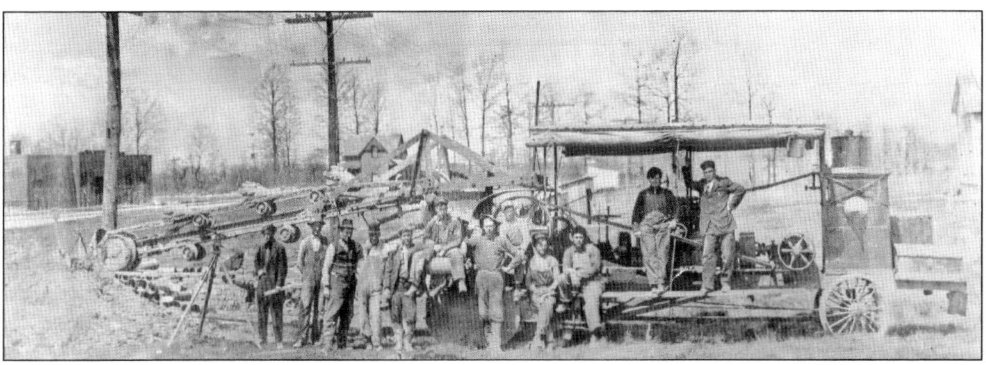

The town of Beech Grove was proud of its modern storm and sanitary sewer system. This 1920s photograph shows sewer construction workers with a steam-powered excavator. Because the town was planned from the very beginning, the work of sewer design, construction, and maintenance was greatly facilitated, although the actual construction remained grueling work.

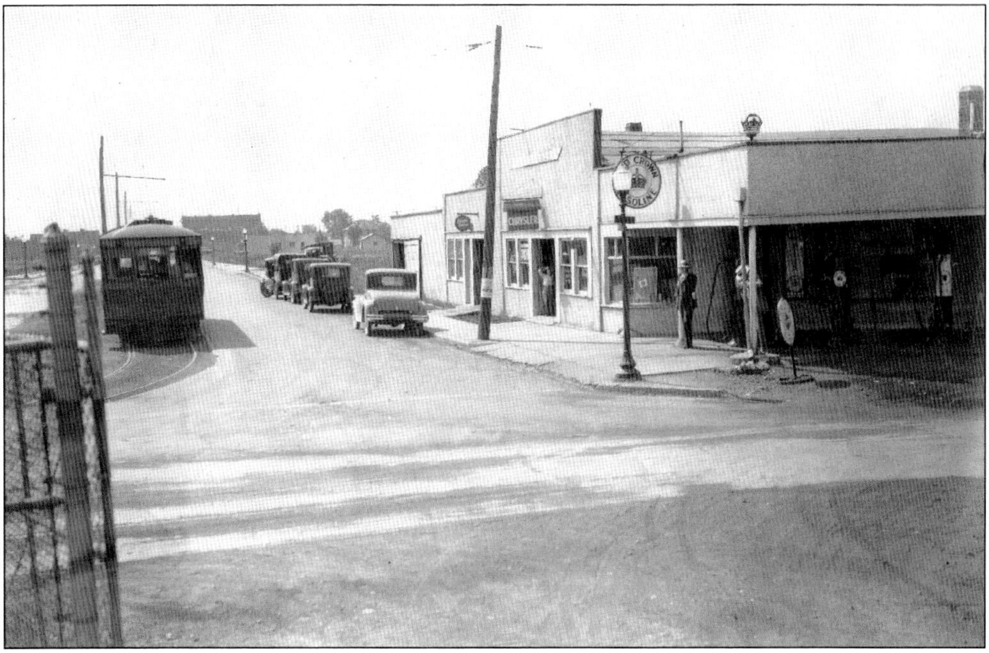

In this classic 1920s view, looking west down Main Street from the Beech Grove Shops gate on First Avenue, Bill Day's Service Station and the O. J. Sturber Chrysler Dealership are clearly visible. Automobile-related businesses began to populate the streets of Beech Grove, as did cars, sharing the road with the still popular interurban.

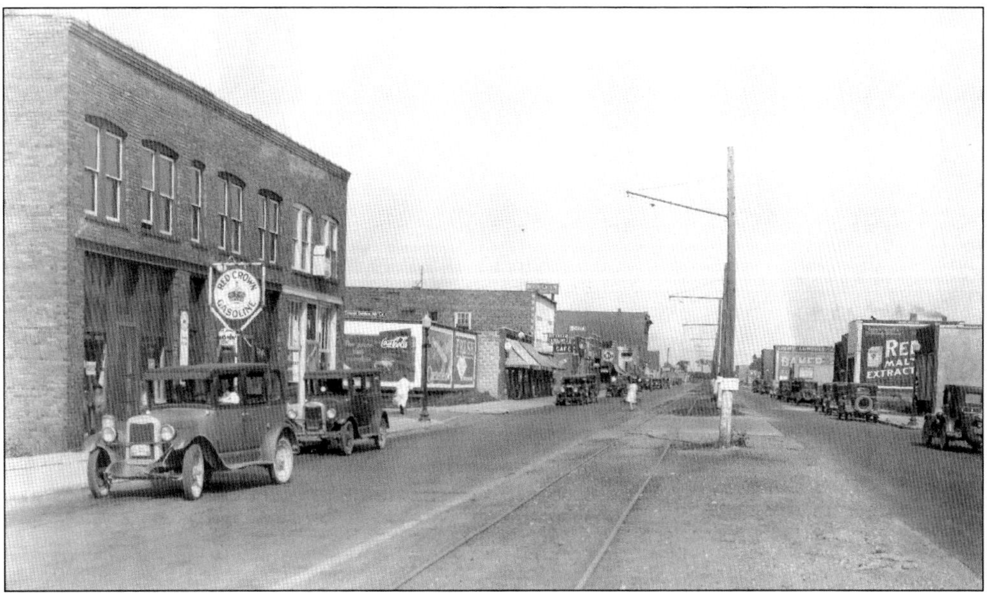

By the late 1920s, this Main Street view looking east from Eighth Avenue shows the streetcar line sharing the right-of-way with numerous automobiles. The central commercial district was both the town's central community hub and the home to the major suppliers of operational necessities to the railroad Shops. With an abundance of employers, including a growing hospital, affordable housing, safe streets, and a variety of agricultural, retail, and service businesses, Beech Grove was a self-contained community.

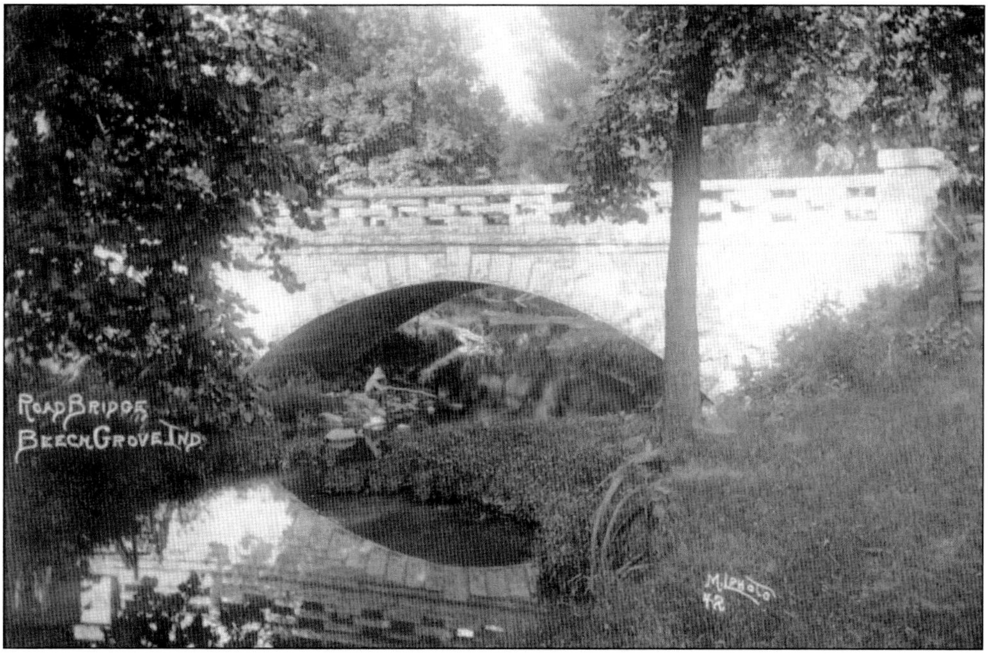

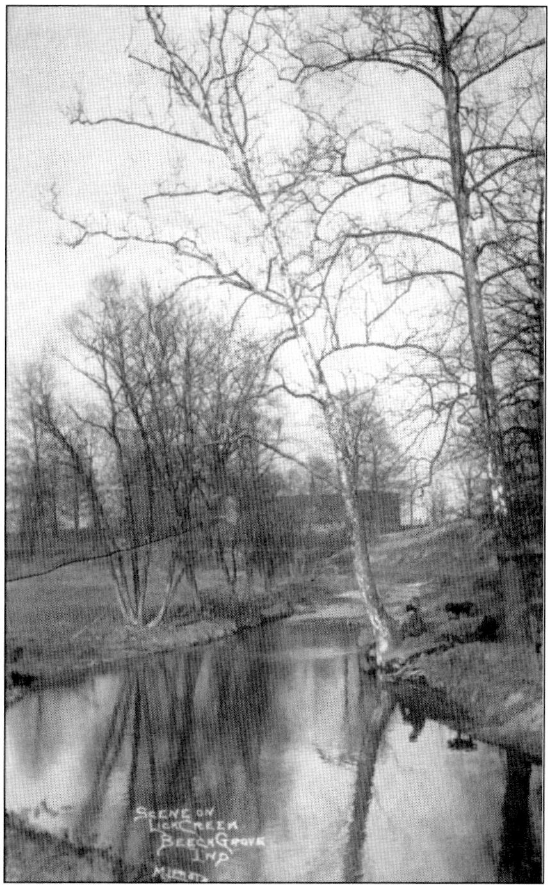

Even with the hustle and bustle of Main Street, the clanking of heavy machinery at the Shops, the distant whistle of trains, and the rumble of automobiles, the town still provided the serenity of country living. Seen under a road bridge over Lick Creek, the 1911 postcard above depicts a young boy enjoying the simple pleasures of afternoon fishing. A later, undated postcard, seen at right, shows another view of Lick Creek, now with far fewer trees and St. Francis Hospital plainly visible in the background. As Beech Grove continued to grow, the tranquil spaces were gradually eroded by the reality of building a great American city. (Both Joe Seiter collection.)

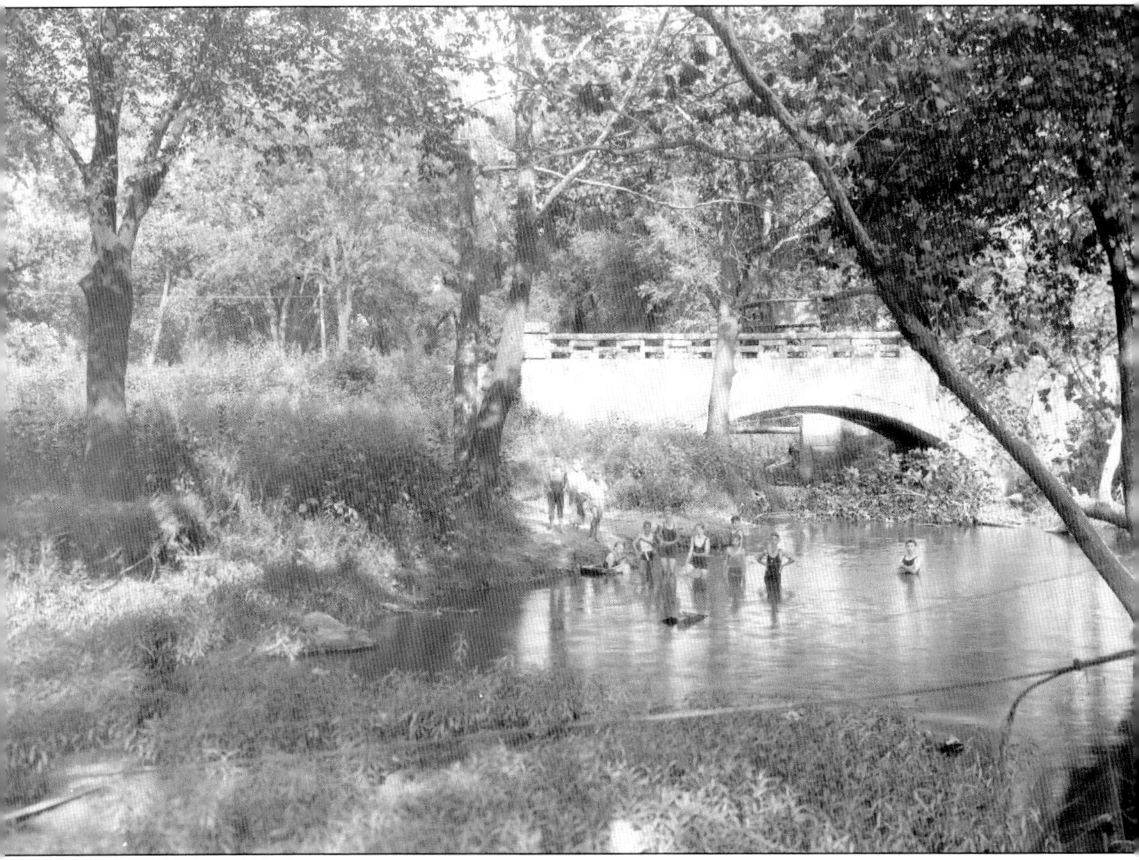

Some of the pleasures of a simpler time managed to elude the signs of progress and development, as seen in this 1930s photograph of the unofficial community swimming hole known as "8 Feet in Lick Creek." While the memories of longtime residents conflict concerning the exact location of the creek bed pool, most agree it was located within the forested area now known as Sarah T. Bolton Park. The swooping willow trees buffered the swimming hole from sight, allowing for skinny-dipping, youthful tobacco smoking, and alcohol consumption in relative privacy, eventually forcing Bolton to clear the banks so activity on Lick Creek could be monitored. Similar delinquent behavior had also forced monitoring at the Devil's Backbone in nearby Greenwood, as well as along White River, near Riverside Park, in Indianapolis. There were also safety concerns with unsupervised swimming, especially for those who enjoyed jumping from the road bridge, resulting in a difficult-to-enforce swimming ban in Lick Creek. Still, the multiple streams running through town, as well as farms and forested areas, provided respite from the constant swell of urbanization.

Four

CHUG, CHUG, CHUG

In terms of community growth, Beech Grove was like "the little engine that could." Mirroring the construction, expansion, and prosperity of the Shops, and with the impetus gained from the active Beech Grove Improvement Company, the town progressed quickly from a loose network of farms into a modern city.

Built in 1837, the Wesley Chapel, located east of present-day First Avenue, is considered to be the first religious meeting place in the pre–Beech Grove countryside. Presbyterians are often credited with holding the first formal Christian services in town in an open-air venue under an apple tree on Tenth Avenue. These enthusiastic worshippers built, then moved, a church building to the corner of Ninth Avenue and Alton Street. While other denominations were meeting in homes, the local Methodist congregation was arranged to use the Presbyterian Church for services. Before long, other spiritual communities constructed modest buildings to hold services, including the Baptists, Catholics, First Christians, and others.

The community also supported several educational initiatives. Arising from the legacy of the Poplar Grove one-room schoolhouse—the center of pre–Beech Grove social life—the first formal school in town opened in 1907, located in a second-floor space above Wheat's Grocery. Modern-day Beech Grove has award-winning public elementary schools, a Catholic elementary school, and nationally recognized middle and high schools. Beech Grove was also home to Our Lady of Grace Academy, which was operated by the Sisters of St. Benedict.

While the first governmental administrators of Beech Grove were the town board members and a clerk, steady development mandated an expansion of governmental services. To provide the added services, the town became a city in 1935 with a mayor-council form of government.

Beech Grove has a proud tradition of supporting various civic organizations, including the Beech Grove Lions Club, Moose and Masonic Lodges, and an active Promoters Club. Community celebrations include the annual July Fourth fireworks and fall festival. St. Francis Hospital, St. Paul Hermitage, the Beech Grove Senior Center, and numerous other organizations provide health care and social services. Main Street businesses remain vibrant, the library heavily utilized, and the parks popular.

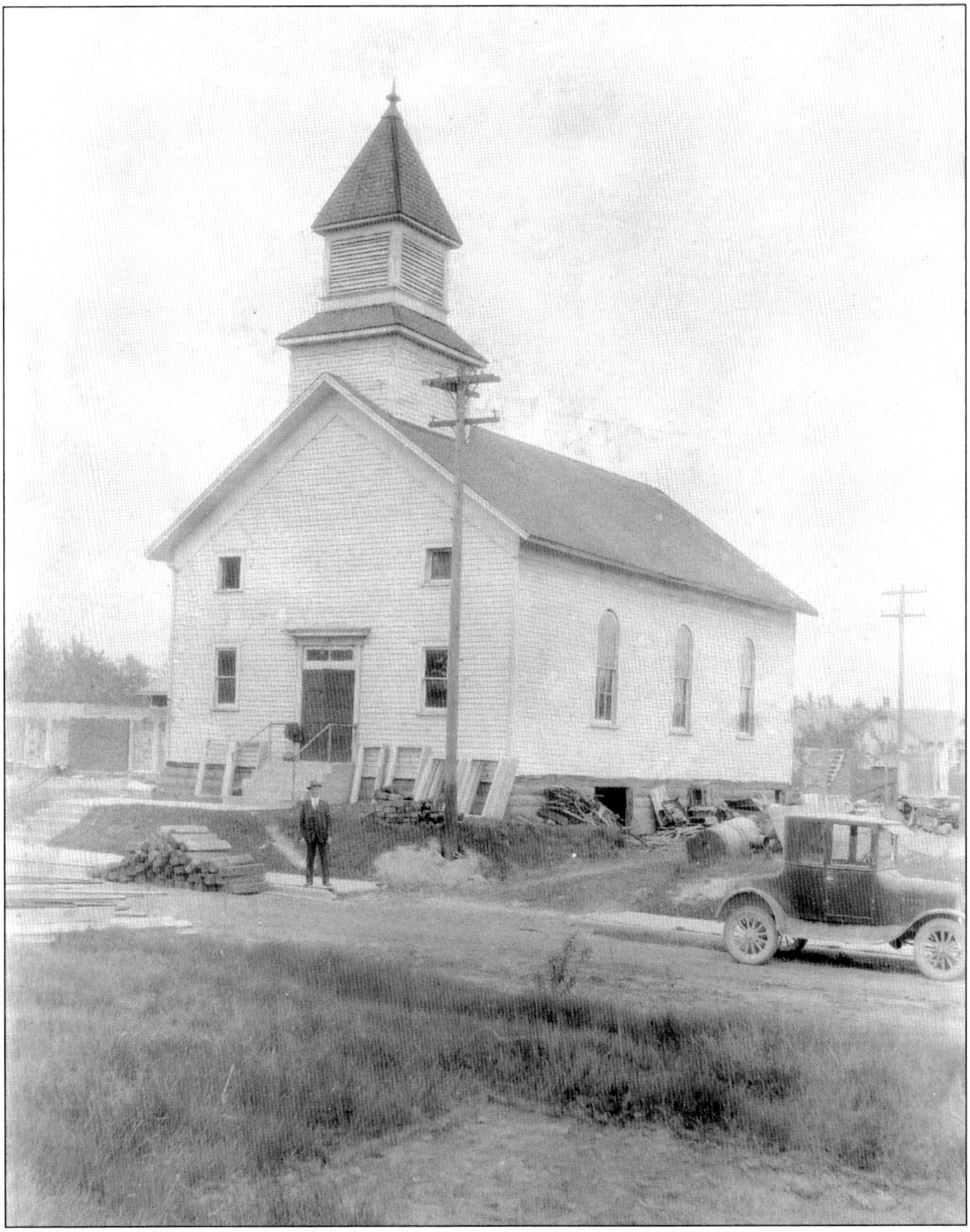

The Presbyterians relocated a church building to the corner of Ninth Avenue and Alton Street in 1908. A group of Methodists began meeting in a house on North Fifth Avenue; home-based religious services were common in Beech Grove's early years. By 1909, the Methodists were meeting in the Presbyterian Church and other locations, including the local school, but disbanded in the fall of 1910. A federation was formed between the Presbyterian, Methodist, and Christian Churches that met in the Presbyterian Church until the summer of 1912. After the federation dissolved, the First Christian Church formed after preliminary organizational lunchtime meetings occurred at the Shops. The Methodist congregation reorganized and bought the Presbyterian Church building in 1913. Although the facilities were expanded, the building did not meet the congregation's needs, and construction began for their present facility in the fall of 1926.

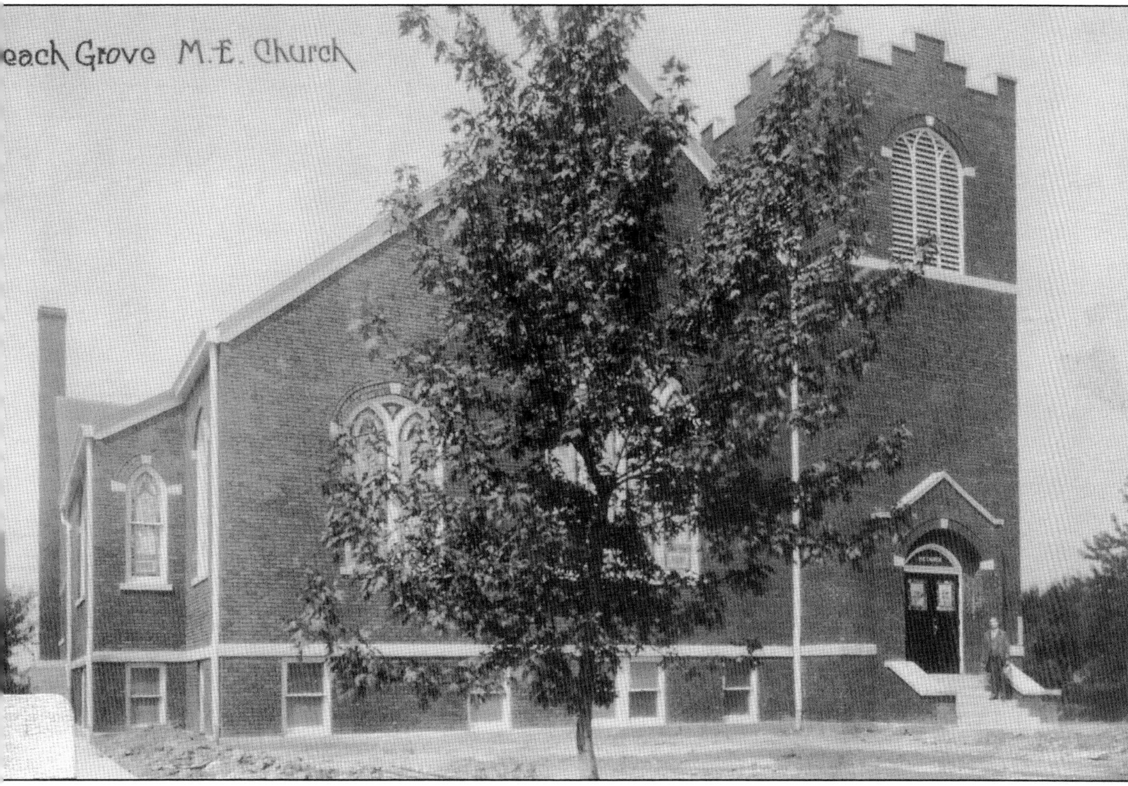

This 1940s postcard view of the Beech Grove United Methodist Church, then referred to only as the Methodist Church, depicts the home of the merged Methodist Episcopal Church, the Methodist Episcopal Church South, and the Methodist Protestant Church. The church received a large donation in 1943 and paid off all debts—the congregation's future was secure at last. Several improvements and expansion projects have occurred over the years, including the purchase of additional land and construction of an education building in 1957. Several community groups, such as the Boy Scouts and Girl Scouts, have used the church for meetings. The congregation bought the nearby home of Dr. and Mrs. Rhea in 1967, transforming the residence into the new church parsonage. Beech Grove United Methodist Church has enjoyed tremendous growth through the years and, along with Holy Name Catholic Church, has impacted the greatest number of area residents.

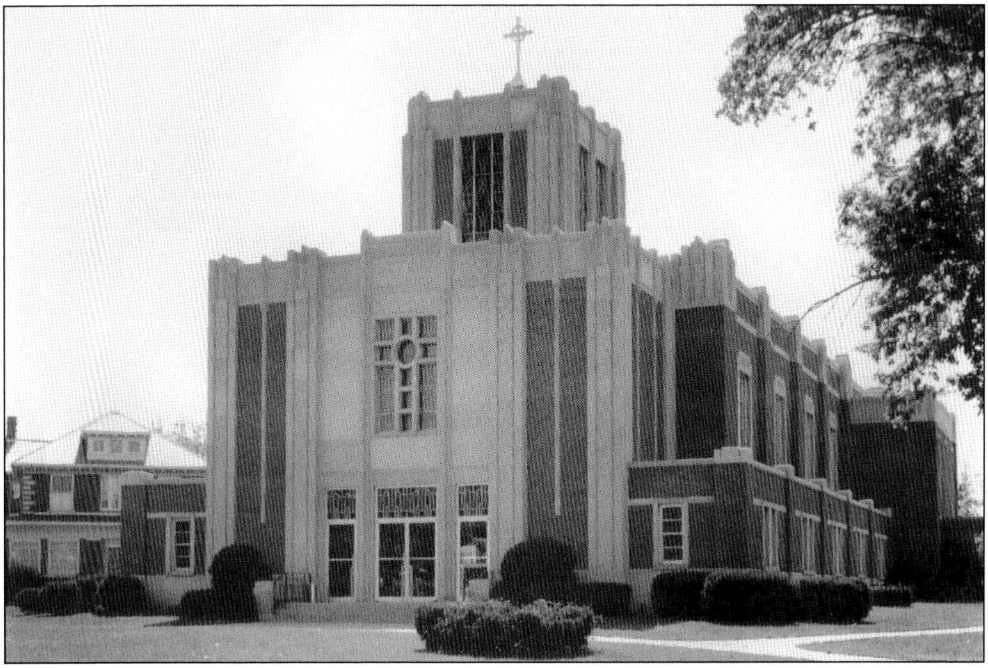

Holy Name Catholic Church has roots that reach to the very beginning of the town. While ground was purchased for the current building in 1907, services were held on the second floor of founding pastor Fr. Peter Killian's home in a small chapel. A community leader in more than religious activities, Killian oversaw the installation of the first electric lighting in Beech Grove in his home, which still serves the parish as the church's rectory. The parish was first known as Blessed Sacrament Church, but after a decade the parish name changed to Holy Name of Jesus Catholic Church. In 1922, a school was built (below), and the school auditorium space was used for parish worship. Construction of the present church began in 1953 under the leadership of the congregation's third pastor, Fr. Robert Hartman.

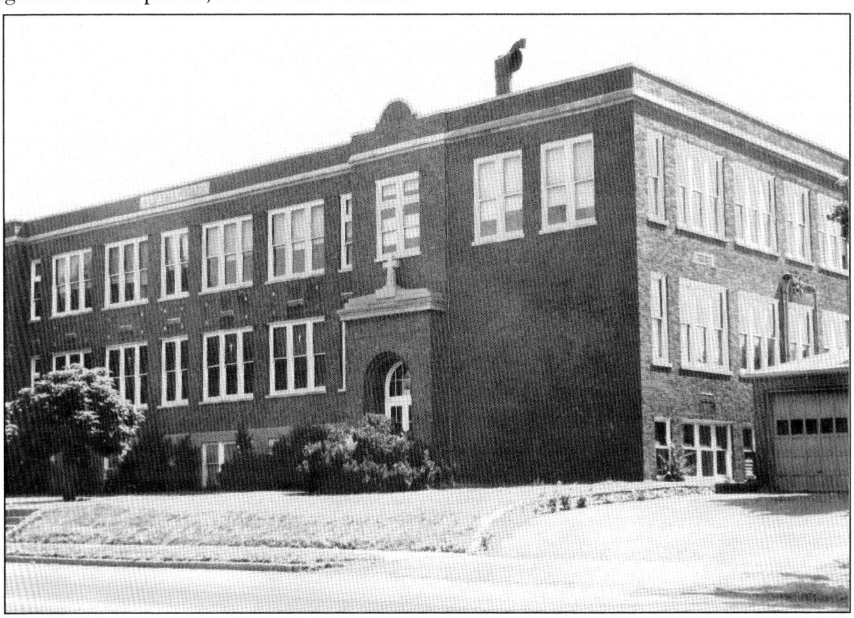

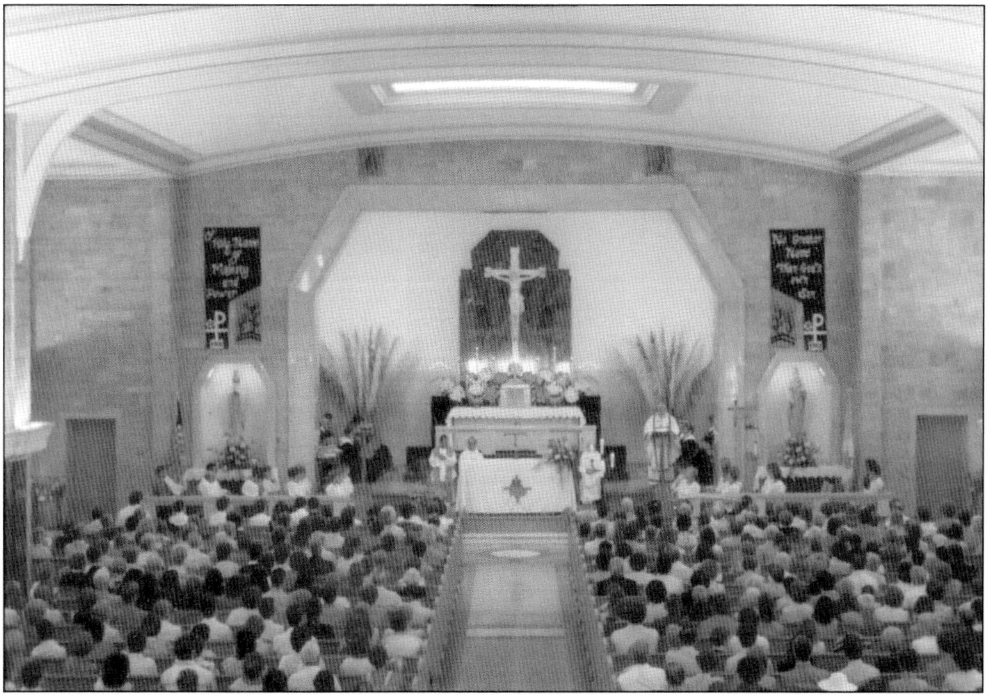

Holy Name of Jesus Catholic Church has been a center of religious and community celebrations in Beech Grove for more than 100 years. One such festive occasion in 1983 delivered packed pews as archbishop Edward O'Meara of the Archdiocese of Indianapolis presided over the parish's 75th anniversary mass. In the photograph below, acolytes, also known as altar boys, await the processional into church for Christmas mass. While firmly rooted in Catholic traditions, community outreach programs—including a popular annual festival, bingo nights, fund-raising dinners, and other events—increase awareness of the parish throughout the community. Only a third of registered parish members live within Beech Grove's city limits, attesting to the draw of this traditional Roman Catholic parish.

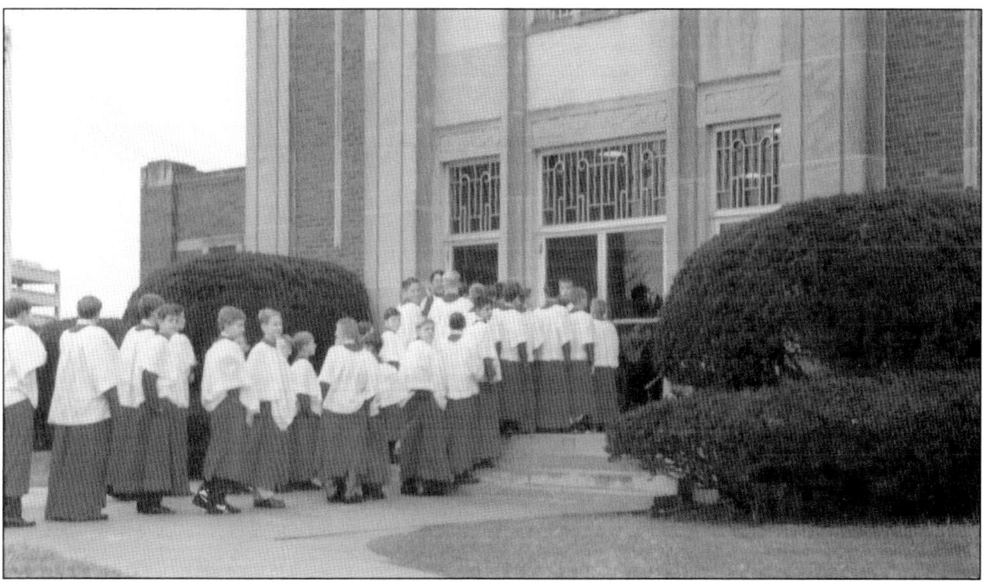

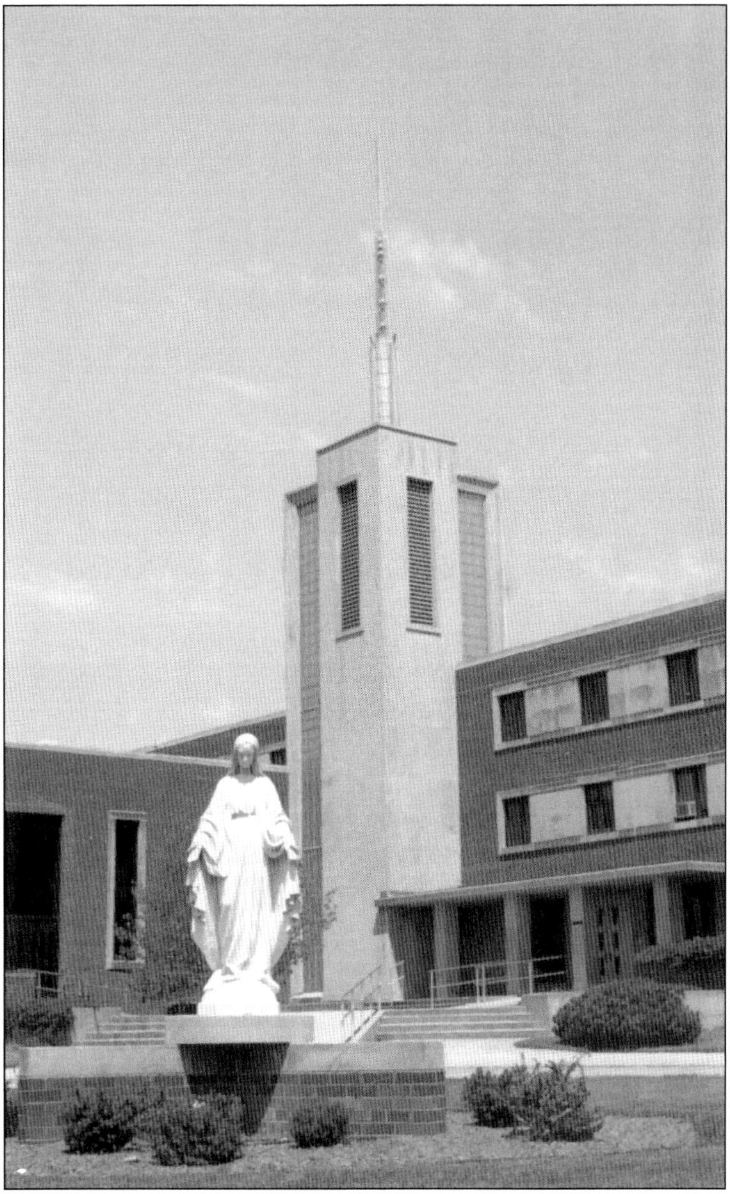

The Sisters of St. Benedict, on the invitation of archbishop Paul Schulte, sent a small group of sisters from Monastery Immaculate Conception in Ferdinand, Indiana, to Beech Grove in 1956 to establish Our Lady of Grace Monastery. They acquired acreage at Seventeenth and Southern Avenues, a few blocks north of St. Francis Hospital. The community saw rapid growth, and a Decree of Autonomy was bestowed by the Vatican in 1961, making Our Lady of Grace Monastery an independent priory. In his invitation, the archbishop requested that the sisters establish a retirement facility for Catholic seniors, including retired priests. The sisters founded St. Paul Hermitage, which opened in 1959 on the monastery grounds. The hermitage has undergone multiple expansions and renovations, and today it provides residential facilities ranging from assisted living rooms to independent apartments and has an attached nursing wing. The facility is home to several retired priests and over 100 retired lay people. The popularity of the facility is evidenced by the long waiting list of seniors wishing to move there. (Joe Seiter collection.)

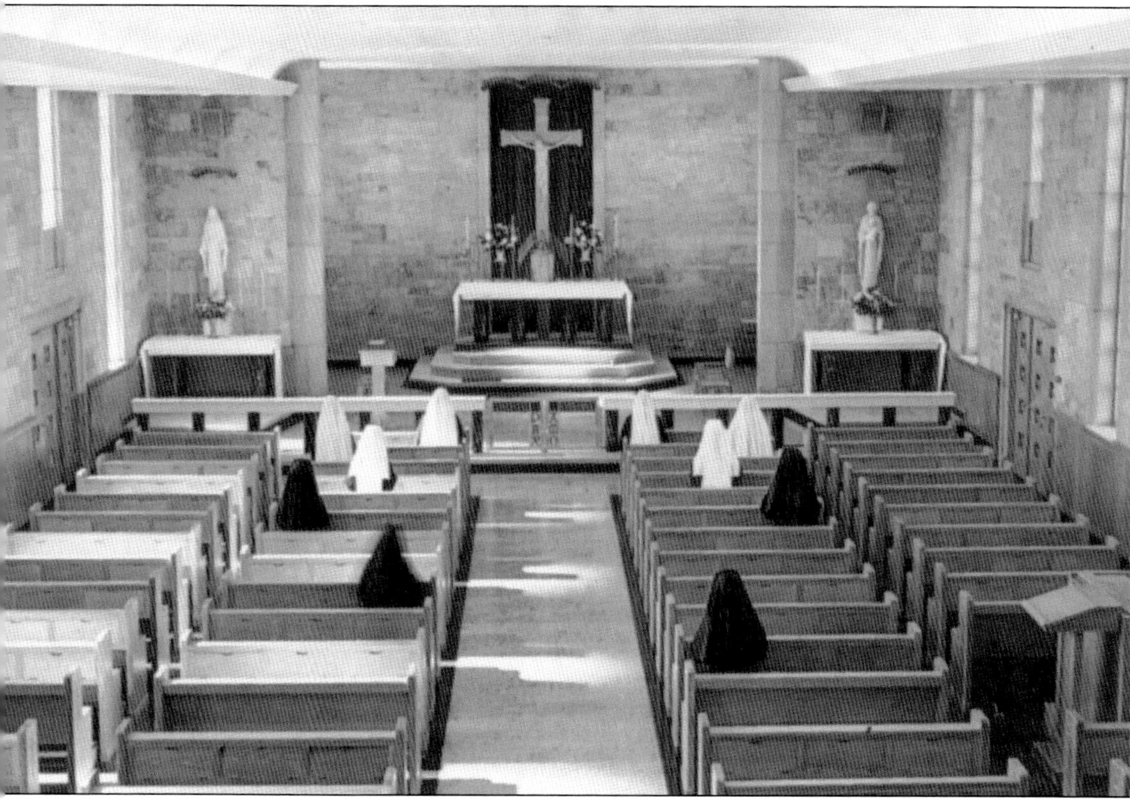

The Sisters of St. Benedict also established Our Lady of Grace Academy, a day and boarding high school for girls, on the monastery grounds, sharing some facilities (such as the chapel pictured here) with the religious community. It opened with a freshman class of 26 young ladies in the fall of 1956. The academy experienced steady growth, and in 1967 the sisters constructed a large student center. Changing social attitudes in the 1970s brought about a steady decline in enrollment at virtually all such schools, and Our Lady of Grace Academy finally closed in 1978. The sisters decided to convert the area formerly occupied by the academy and student center, complete with a gymnasium and swimming pool, into a retreat and conference center. The center, the Benedict Inn Retreat and Conference Center, hosts not only religious retreats, but it is also available for other community functions, and the gymnasium and swimming facilities are open for public use. (Joe Seiter collection.)

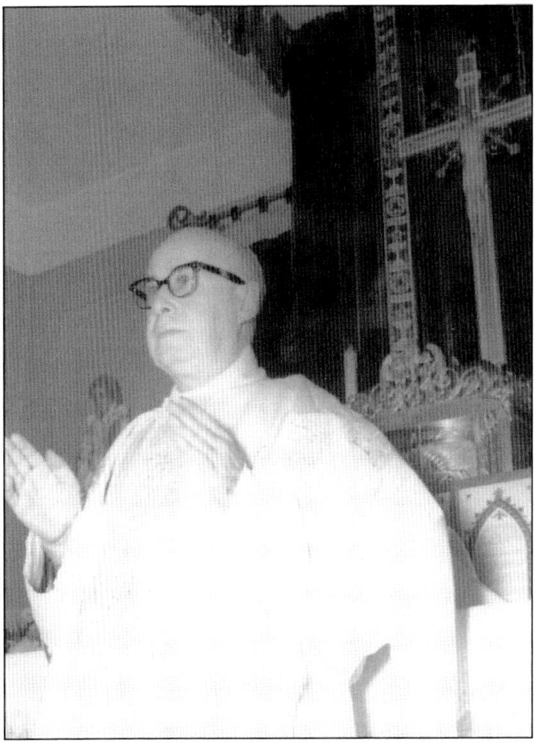

Being a small town, it was unusual that Catholic mass was conducted in Beech Grove at several different locations, including Holy Name of Jesus Catholic Church, St. Francis Hospital, and later at Our Lady of Grace Monastery. St. Francis Hospital chaplain Father O'Keefe is seen here in the early 1930s celebrating mass in the hospital chapel.

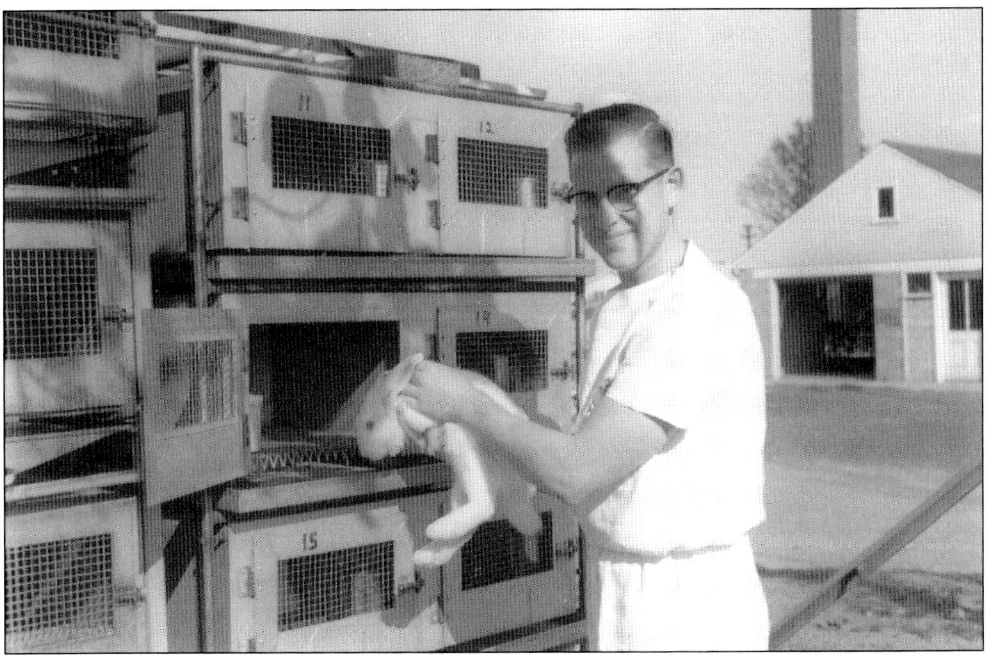

St. Francis Hospital provided not only medical care, but also employment for area residents. A hospital employee is seen here attending to rabbits for use in hospital lab testing. In addition to providing routine health care, the Sisters of St. Francis and medical staff at the facility were leaders in the introduction of new technology and techniques, drawing patients from all of central Indiana to Beech Grove for medical services.

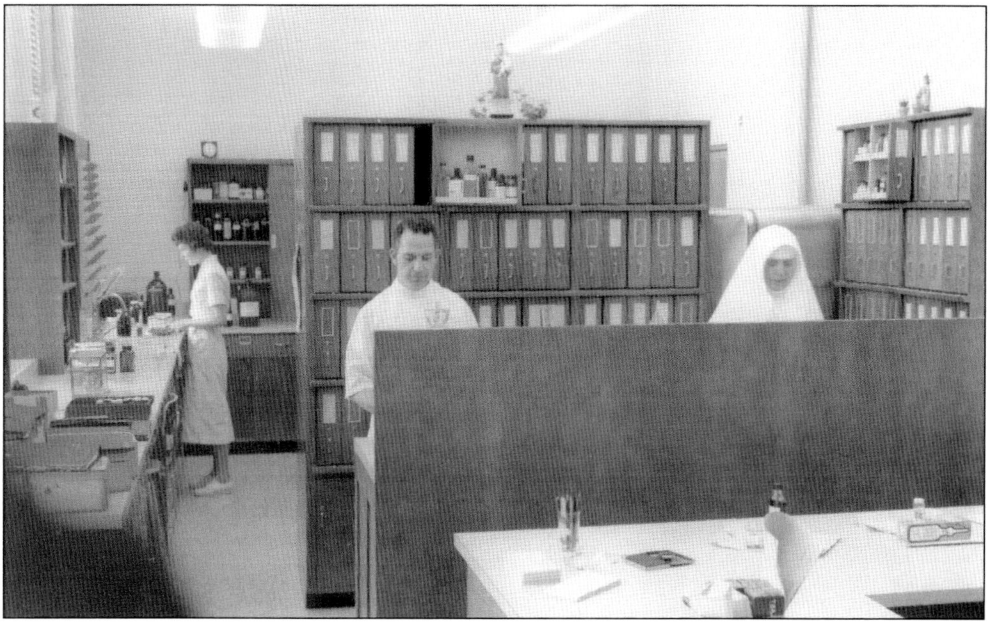

Large pharmaceutical companies and mass manufacturing of medications were not the norm, and commercially produced medications were quite expensive, so the pharmacy staff of area hospitals produced their own medications for patient use. Above, from left to right, Frances Dunn, Leo Kavanaugh, and Sister Cosma are busy readying numerous medications in the St. Francis Hospital pharmacy. Two sisters are seen with Dunn (left) and Kavanaugh in the 1930s photograph below. Although the original hospital pharmacy occupied a small space, the staff served the needs for not only the hospital inpatients, but also served the community through several physicians' offices.

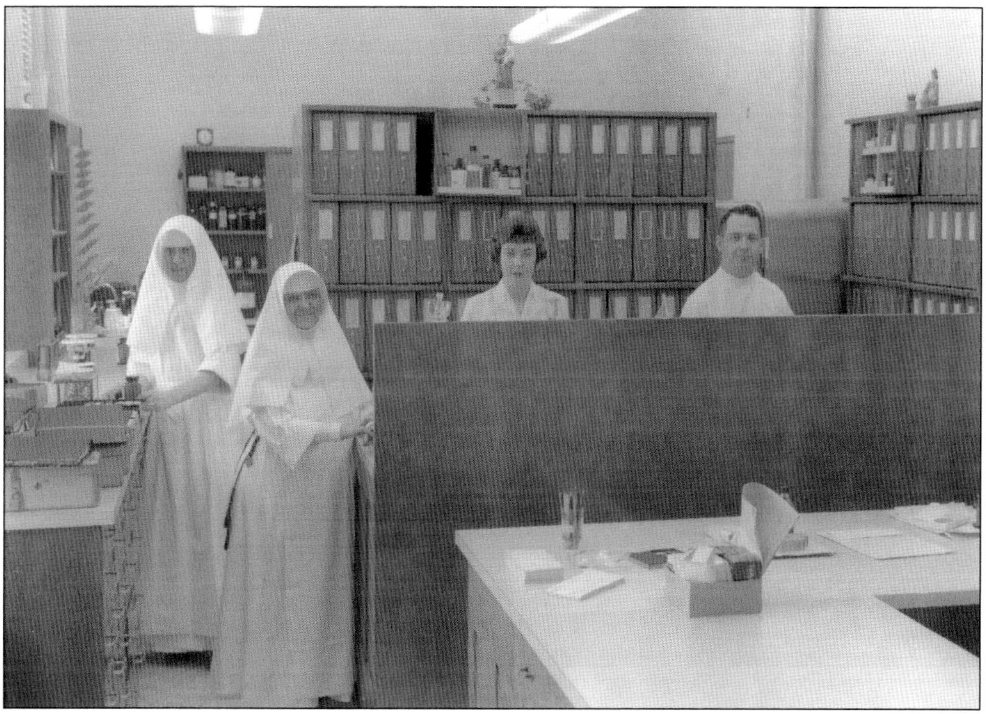

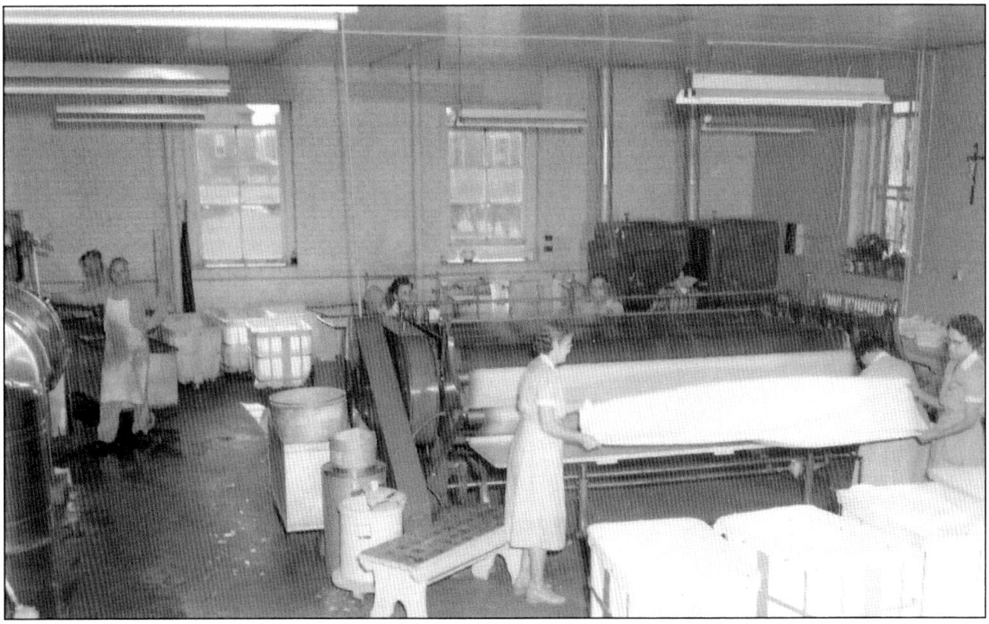

In addition to the professionals practicing medicine, nursing, pharmacy, and laboratory services, hundreds of service employees were needed to support St. Francis Hospital's growing operation. The laundry room, as depicted above in the 1940s, and the photograph below of a hospital parking lot attendant in the 1950s show the increasing variety of employment opportunities available at the hospital. Parking became a major issue for St. Francis Hospital as patients began arriving more frequently in personal automobiles and were forced to find street parking in the surrounding neighborhoods. The hospital began acquiring land to the north and west of the original building to provide parking lots. It was not long before the hospital's growth and expansion mandated the land be used for additional buildings for medical uses, so it was only a matter of time before a parking garage was built.

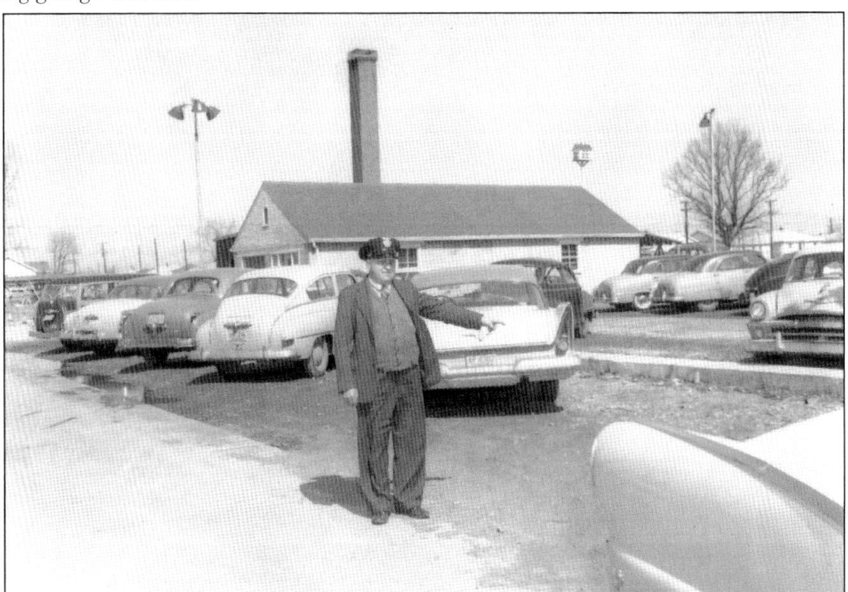

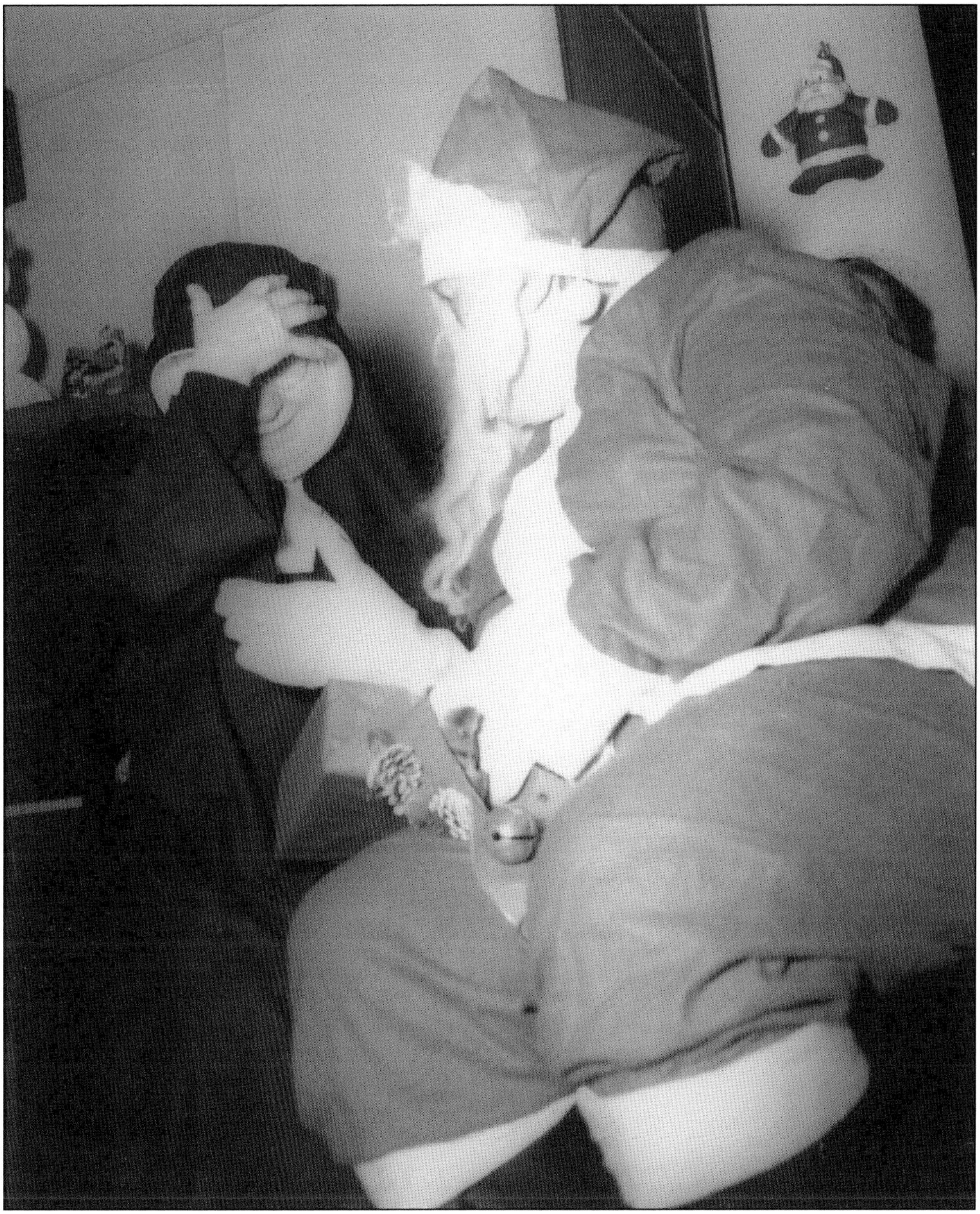

Employment at the hospital was not all work. Hospital administrator Sister Alexis takes time to visit with Santa in the 1950s. While it is difficult to tell if she has been naughty or nice, it is likely that she is asking Santa for expanded facilities. Even though a second hospital wing had been added in the early 1930s, doubling the number of beds, the hospital was overflowing by the 1950s. The Sisters of Saint Francis of Perpetual Adoration embarked on fund-raising activities for the construction of a new northern wing, again doubling the number of beds to 300. The new wing would house Indiana's first cobalt cancer radiation machine, and as the radiology department grew and their reputation for successful cancer treatment spread, a pricey $200,000 Betatron machine was purchased—the first such machine in the state. The sisters continued to lead the move to new technology by investing in a state-of-the-art computer center to assist them with management of their nine-facility health network.

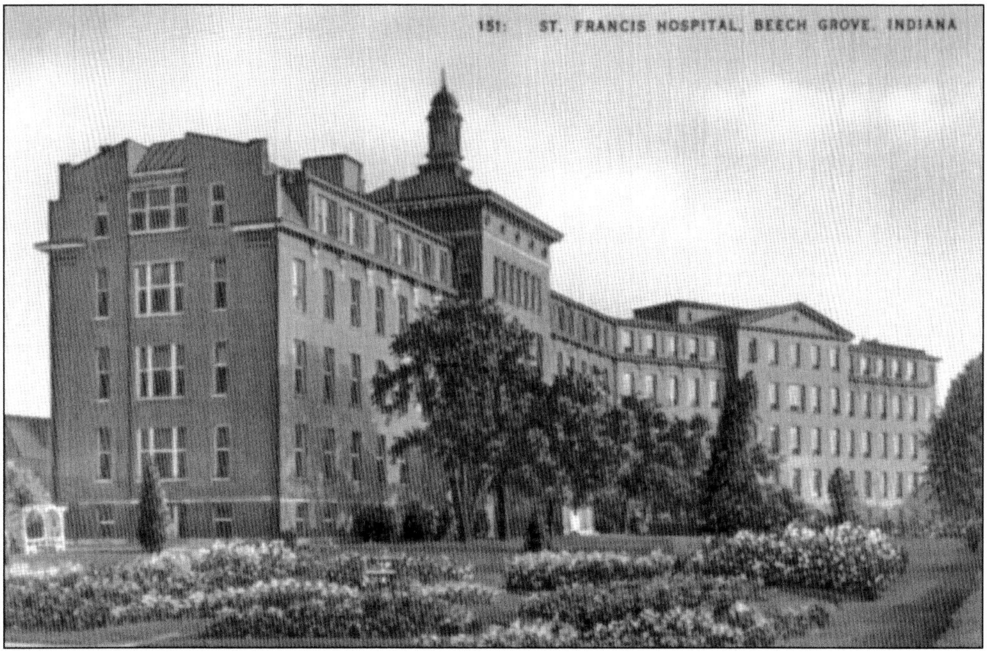

In this 1940 view of St. Francis Hospital, the original building (left) and the 1931 addition (right) are visible. The expanded facilities provided 150 general medical beds and a new obstetrics department, but the space soon proved to be insufficient as the population of Beech Grove continued to grow rapidly. (Joe Seiter collection.)

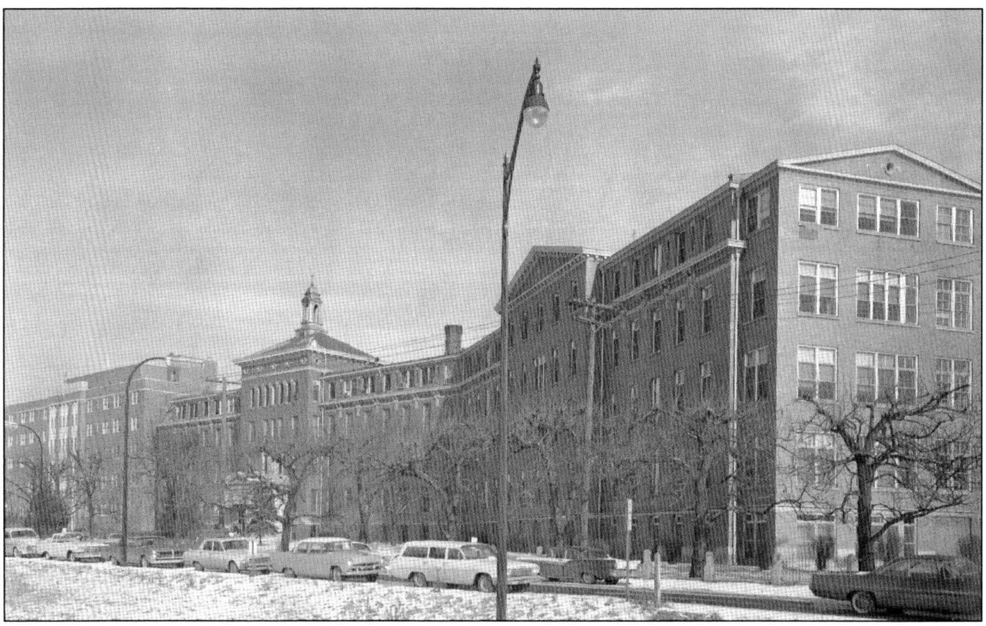

In this 1960 view of the hospital, the 1957 expansion that had nearly doubled the space is visible to the left. The hospital continued to grow to the east of the original structures and additions. Between 1931 and 1940, annual admissions had doubled, and the post-war baby boom was creating another increase in demand for services. The availability of new technology was also driving a need for additional space to house the newest treatment methods and imaging equipment.

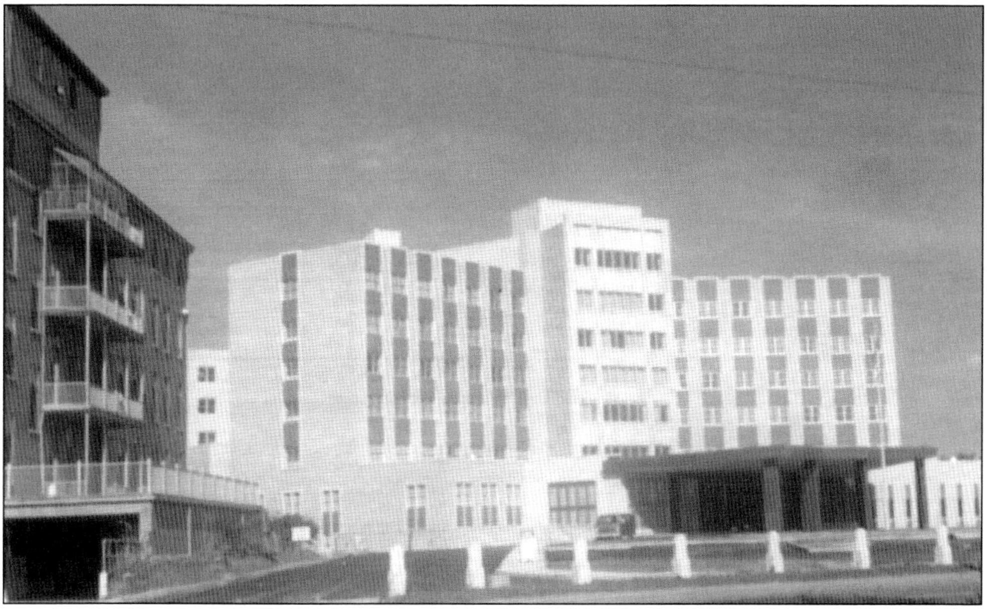

Shortly after completion, the above 1973 photograph shows the new, modern Bonzel Towers addition to the hospital. The completed six-story construction project added five floors of patient rooms with administrative and support services on the floors below. The main hospital entrance was relocated from the older building, and a special care nursery was added in 1975. The St. Francis Medical Arts Building was also constructed to the east of the towers, adding five floors of medical offices and a parking garage with space for 400 cars. In the 1983 photograph seen below, construction has begun on five additional floors to the towers. Along with the new construction, older areas of the hospital were remodeled and updated, and a new mental health department was added.

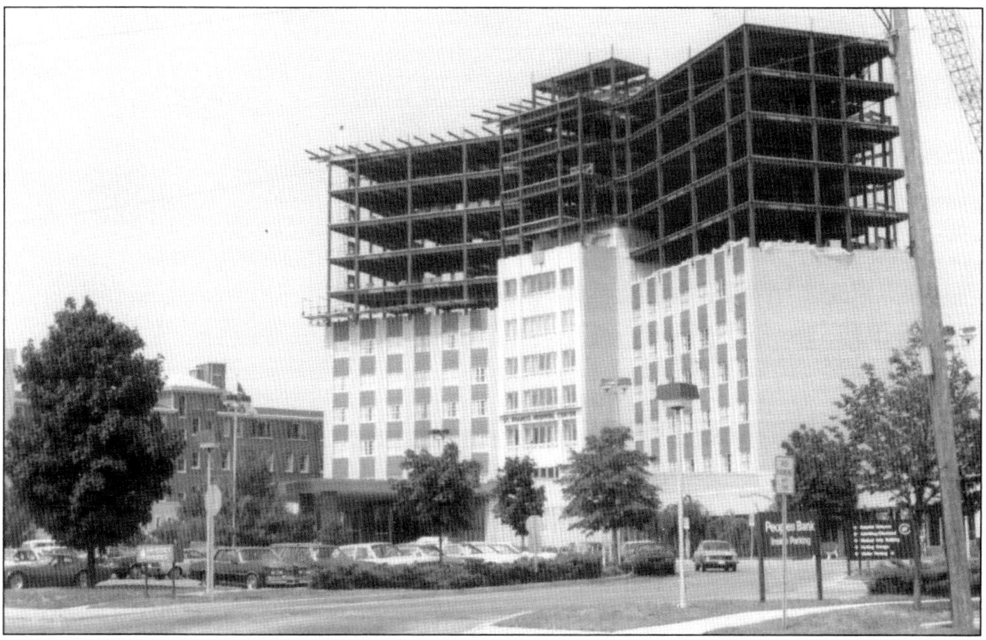

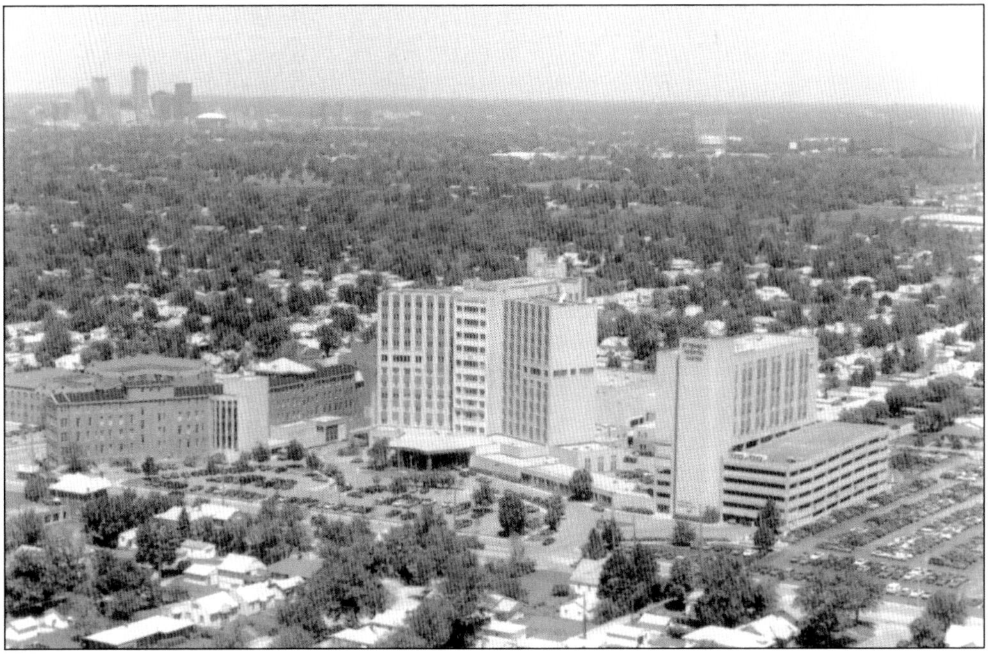

This interesting 1980 postcard offers a bird's-eye view of St. Francis Hospital. Seen are the original buildings, both Bonzel Towers additions, the Medical Arts Building and parking garage, and surrounding buildings and streets. It is impressive to note the sheer size of the sprawling complex. The skyline of downtown Indianapolis is clearly visible near the upper left corner of the card. (Joe Seiter collection.)

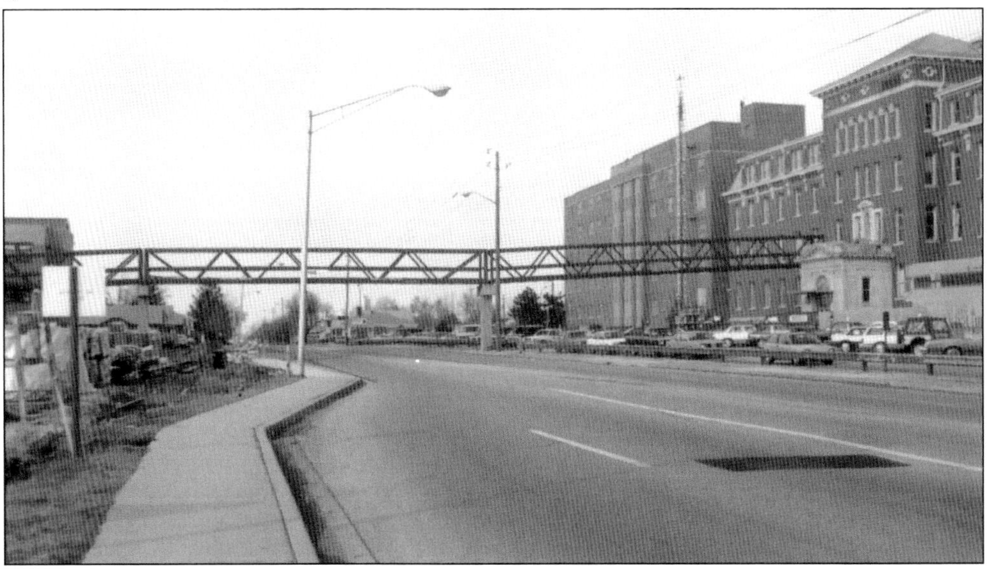

Major roadways and established neighboring development bordered the now expanded hospital on all sides, posing problems for further expansion. The problem was somewhat solved with the construction of an overhead walkway to connect the hospital itself to a new medical office and laboratory complex on the west side of Seventeenth Avenue. The bridge provided patients and staff with safe and convenient access to an added group of specialists' offices regardless of weather or traffic conditions.

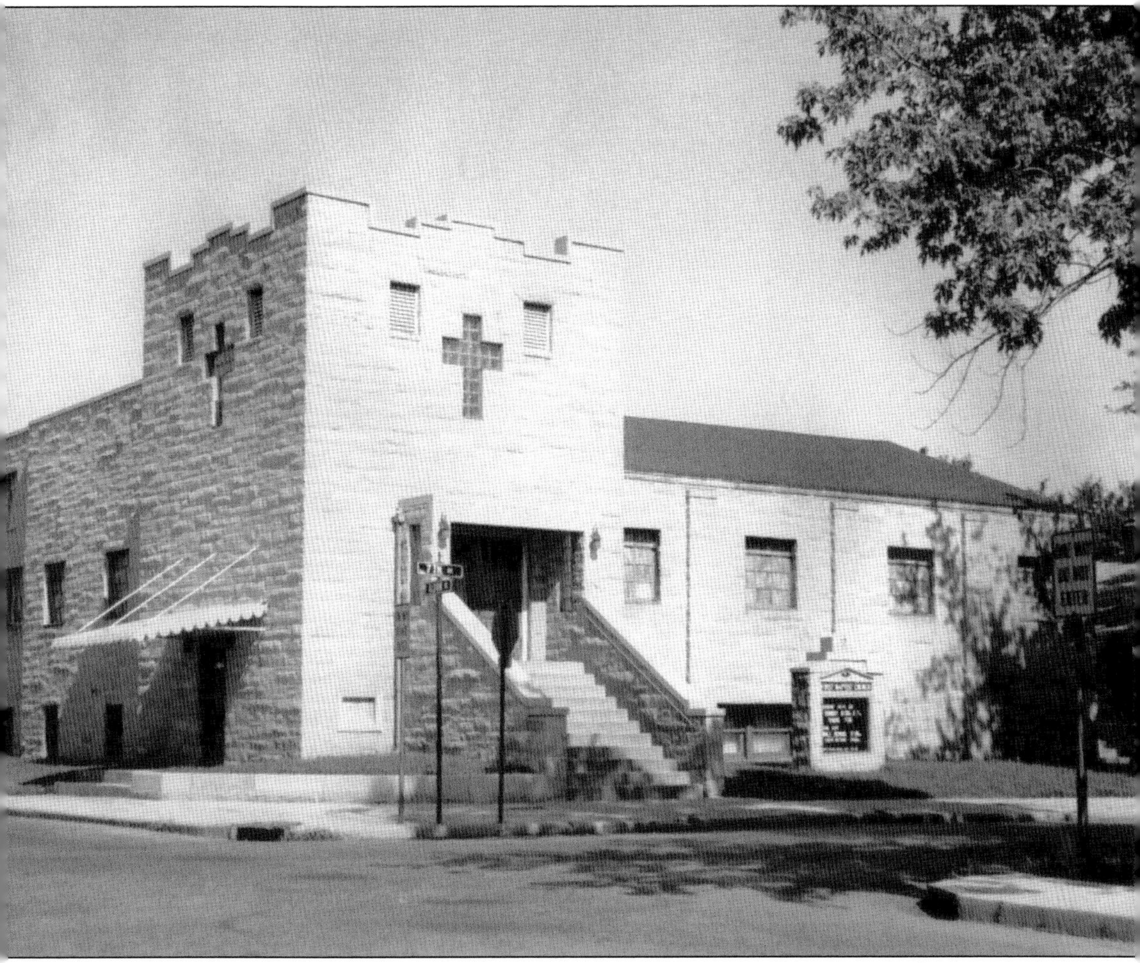

With roots dating from 1912, the First Baptist Church, located at 90 South Seventh Avenue, began with 45 enthusiastic members. The original frame building quickly became too small, and by mid-1927 a new facility was constructed. Originally associated with the American Baptist Convention, the congregation affiliated with the General Association of Regular Baptist Churches fellowship. Expanding in 1952, a new auditorium was built, followed by a new educational wing in 1956. First Baptist Church purchased land along nearby Gray Road and a new branch church was constructed. The Gray Road Baptist Church became an independent Baptist Church shortly thereafter. First Baptist continued to grow, adding a new parsonage on North Tenth Avenue in 1966. Along with the Methodists, Catholics, and First Christian Church congregation, First Baptist Church has remained a vibrant worship community serving Beech Grove. The church enjoys positive community relations with an international reach, supporting multiple missions and churches, several colleges, and other foreign ministries.

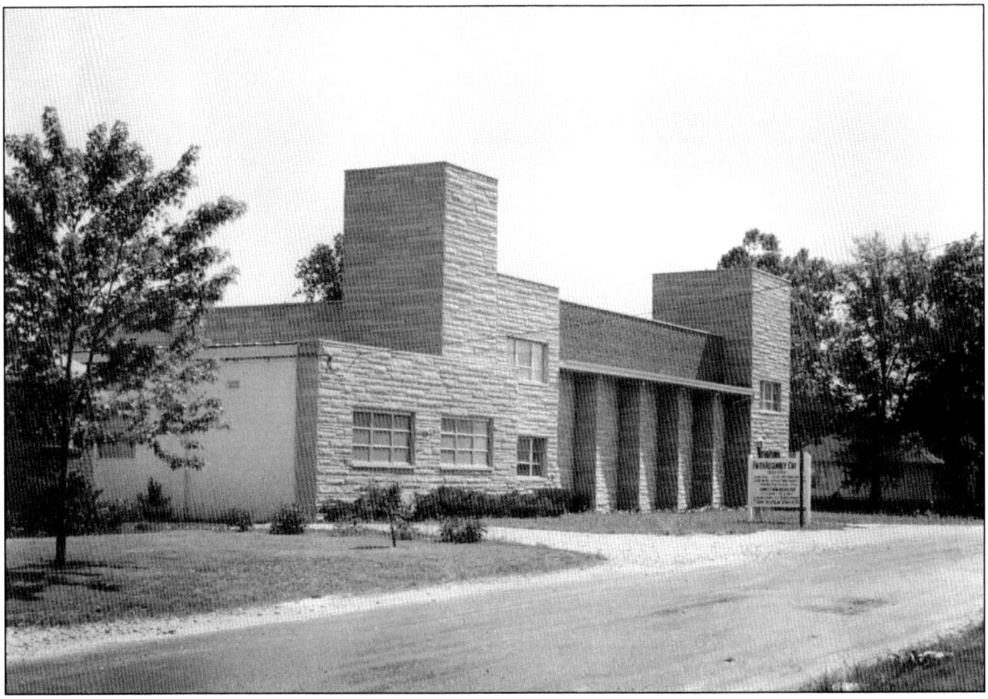

Faith Assembly Church, like so many other churches in Beech Grove, had a humble beginning. In 1958, a 33-member congregation met in the basement of the Beech Grove Public Library. Under the initial leadership of Rev. James P. Monson, the congregation and facilities grew to include a second building with a 400-seat auditorium. Many Christians remember the Challenge of Faith Hour, a Faith Assembly ministry that produced Sunday morning broadcasts on station WBRI.

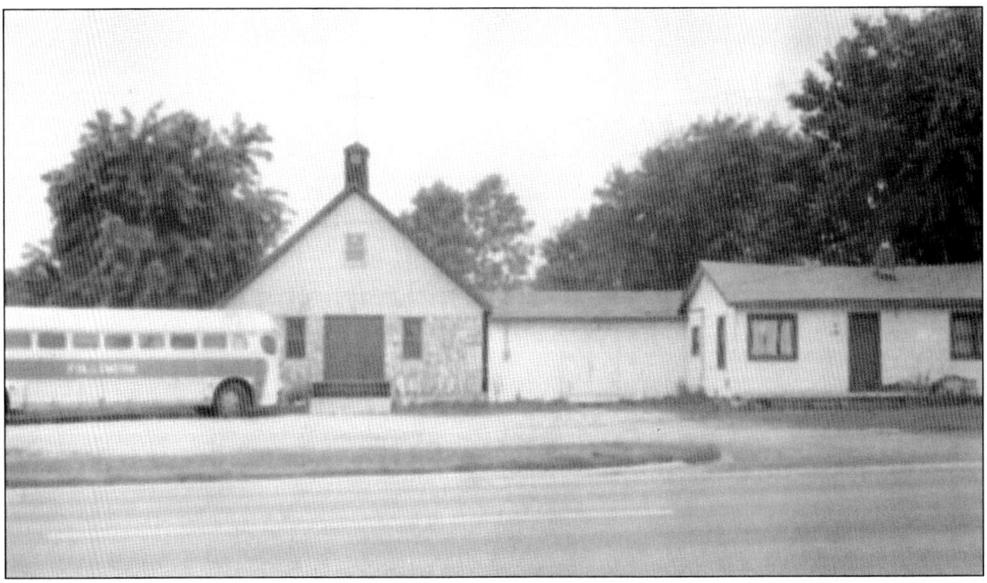

This photograph of Calvary Mission Temple, located at 4602 South Emerson Avenue, was taken in 1951 and depicts modest buildings consisting of a house with a connector to a small church. Today nearly 20 churches are located in Beech Grove, many of which are independent, nondenominational congregations. All of the permanent-location churches in the city are Christian.

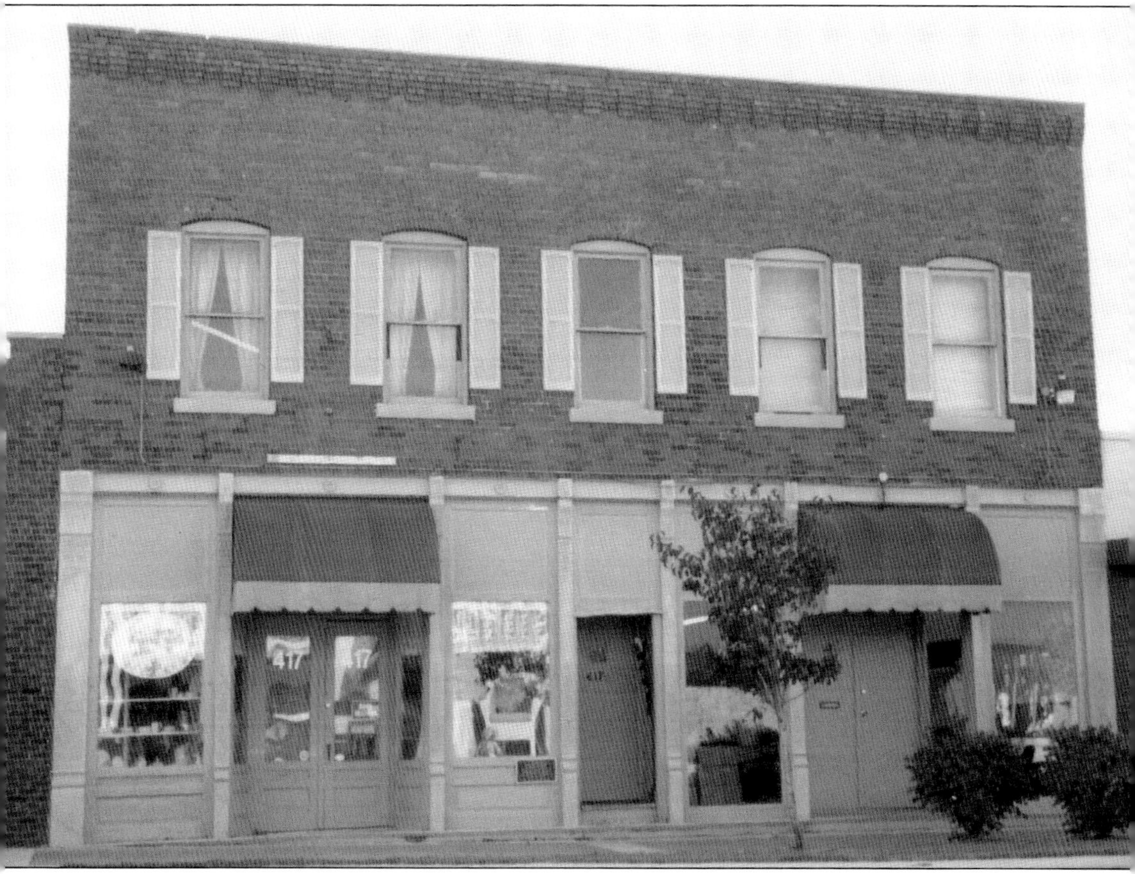

Like religion, education plays an important part in the lives of Beech Grove residents. Several documents relate that George S. Cottman, Francis Churchman's friend and neighbor, reported that early settlers' children attended classes at the Poplar Grove one-room schoolhouse. The school, which was located about one mile east of the present First Avenue, served pupils living within a mile or so radius. When Beech Grove became a town, the first formal school was located on the second floor of a new building, directly above Wheat's Grocery Store at 423 Main Street—the oldest building still standing in the city. At the time the second floor was converted into teaching space, it was already deemed inadequate, but because there were not resources available to construct a school building, the town made do. Despite the small space, the second floor was functional, and the facility was used for the sole purpose of education. The original Poplar Grove schoolhouse had often been rented for events or to house traveling salesmen, resulting in interruptions to the education programs.

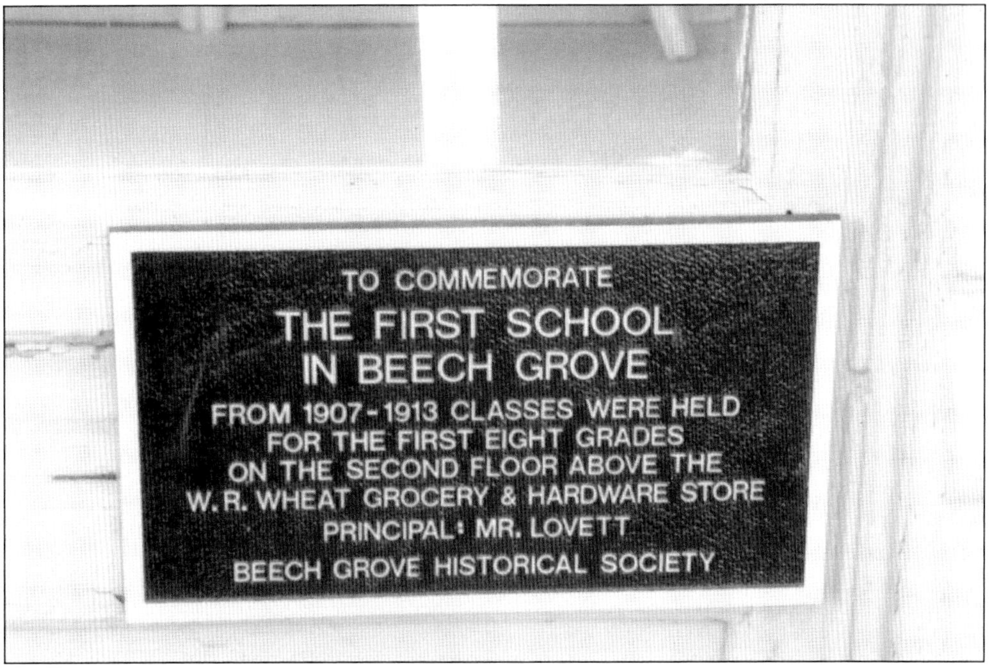

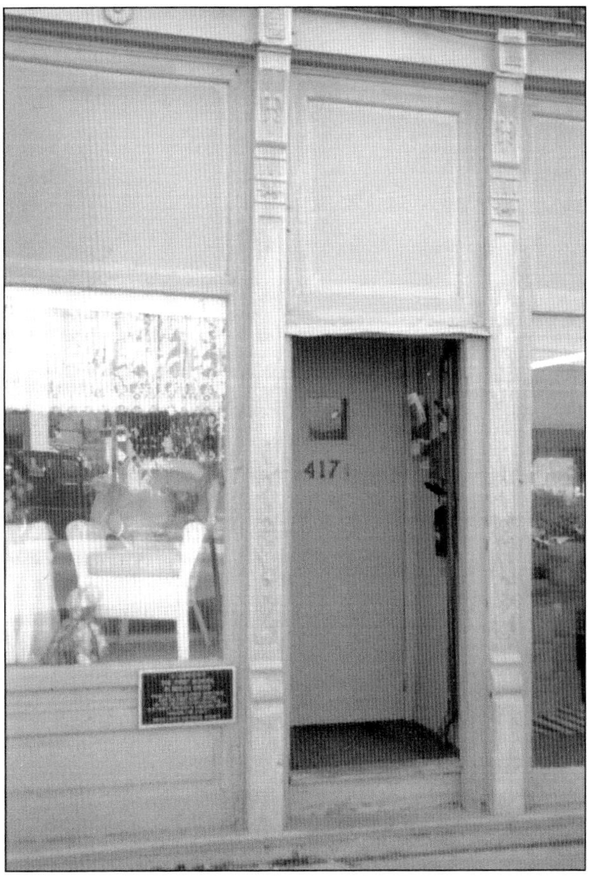

The Beech Grove Historical Society placed a plaque on the first floor that commemorates the first school in Beech Grove. According to the marker, the first eight grades were taught in this location above the W. R. Wheat Grocery and Hardware Store. Mr. Lovett is credited as being the principal. The placement of the plaque, as seen today, is to the left of the second floor entryway. A new one-floor school building was constructed in 1909, and classes were gradually transferred to the new facility. Official designation of the new building as Beech Grove's high school came in 1917, with the first class graduating in 1921.

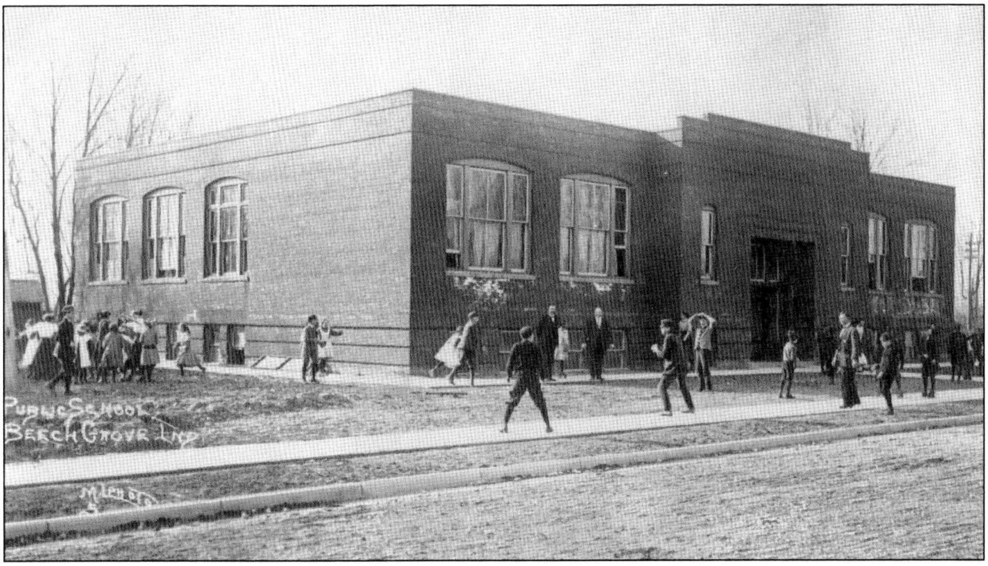

It looks like recess at Beech Grove's first public school building. This postcard from 1911 depicts the one-floor brick schoolhouse that later became the town's first high school. In 1921, Beech Grove High School's seven faculty members graduated six students. The current high school was built in 1966 on land that once was the McGregor farm, adjacent to Churchman's "Hillside" estate.

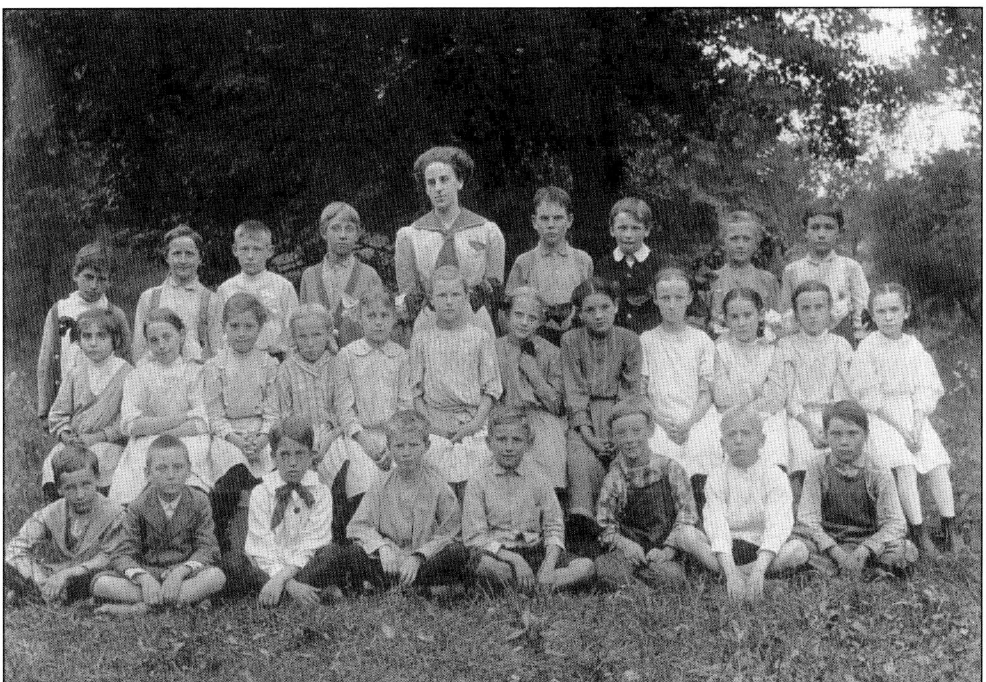

Times have certainly changed, especially in the way students dress. The girls were clearly outnumbered by the boys. This 1910 school photograph shows a combined Beech Grove public school third- and fourth-grade class with their teacher. Taken just outside the school building, students did not need to travel far to enjoy the beauty of the land.

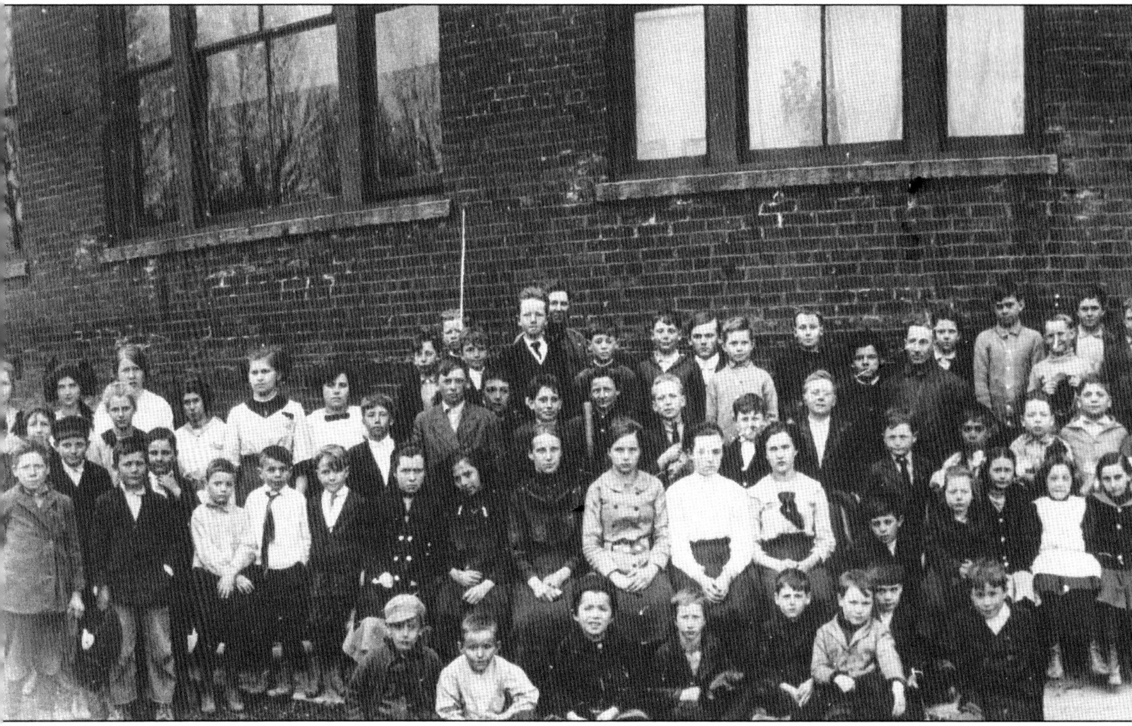

In this April 1913 picture, nearly all of the faculty and student body of the Beech Grove School are pictured. By this time, the entire student body had been relocated from the original second-floor location above Wheat's Grocery to the first public school building, located at Tenth Avenue and Main Street, seen in the background. While the original building was constructed in 1909, a separate elementary school building was soon added to the south, and a second floor was added

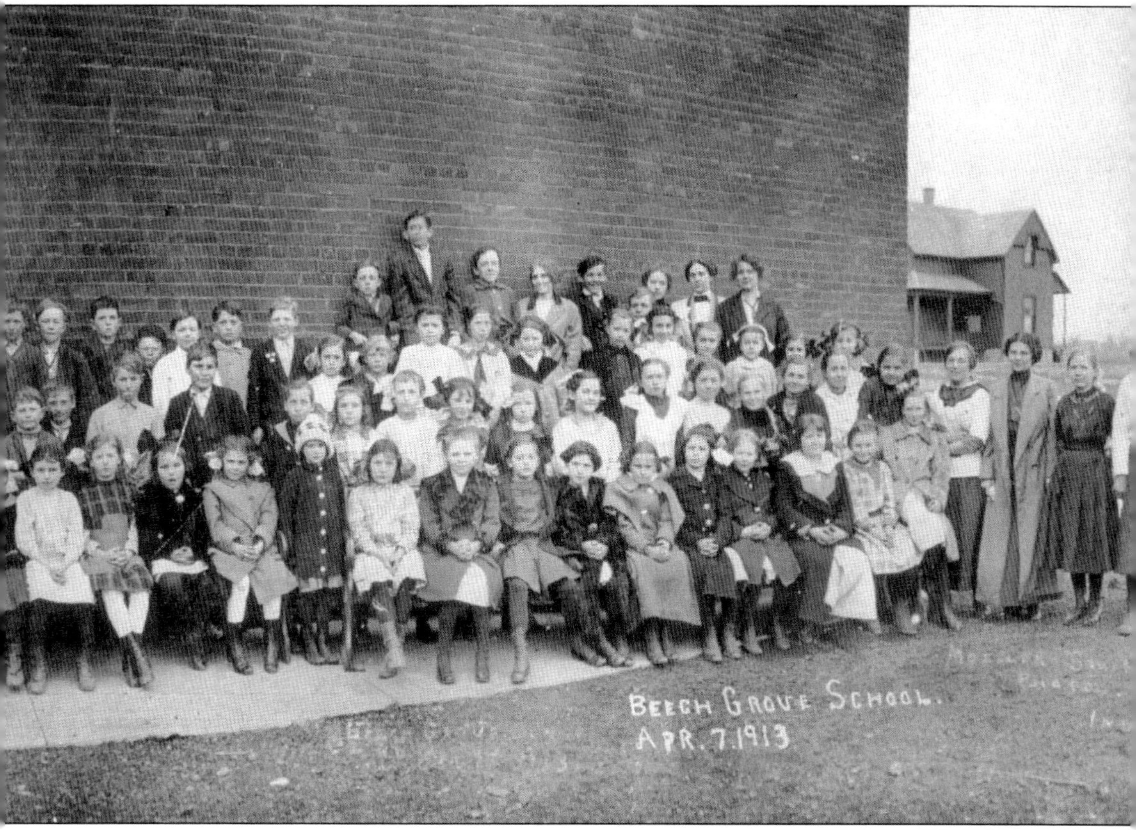

in 1918. A gymnasium that connected the two buildings was constructed in 1924. Five years later, an addition was made to the high school building to serve as the middle school. This addition was considered by many to be an eyesore; the bricks were yellow and did not match the redbrick of the existing complex.

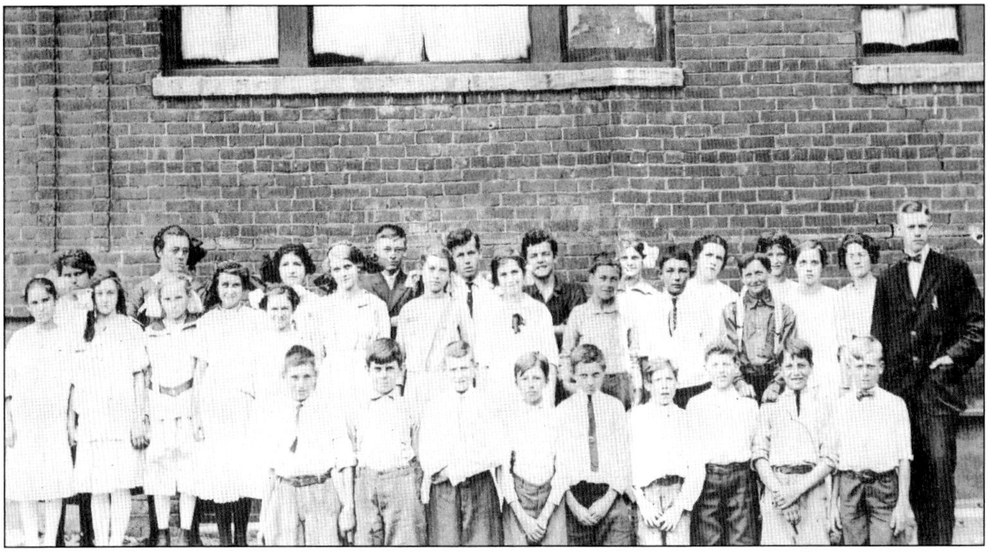

Shown here is an early photograph of seventh- and eighth-grade students, along with teacher Ralph Smith, just prior to 1920. Throughout the early history of Beech Grove public schools, grades were combined in a single room with a shared teacher. In the 1950s, junior high and high school students operated on split schedules, with high school pupils attending in the morning and the junior high students in the afternoon.

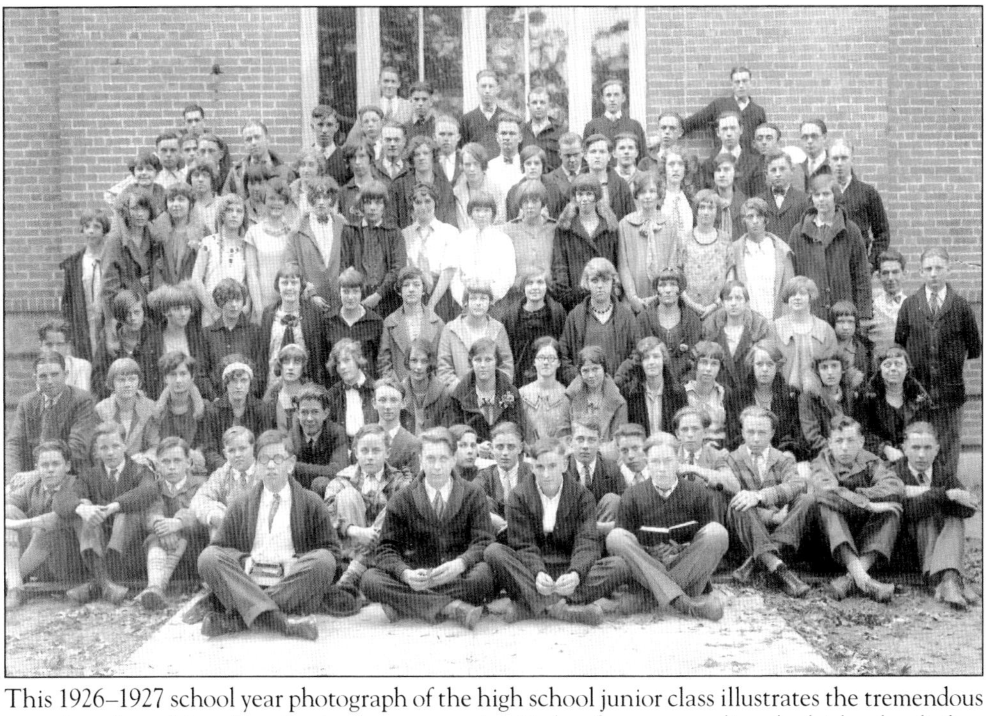

This 1926–1927 school year photograph of the high school junior class illustrates the tremendous growth and need for education in the community. Only a few years earlier, the high school's first graduating class had just a handful of students; the 1928 graduating class was several times larger. Beech Grove schools have graduated well over 10,000 students since their origination.

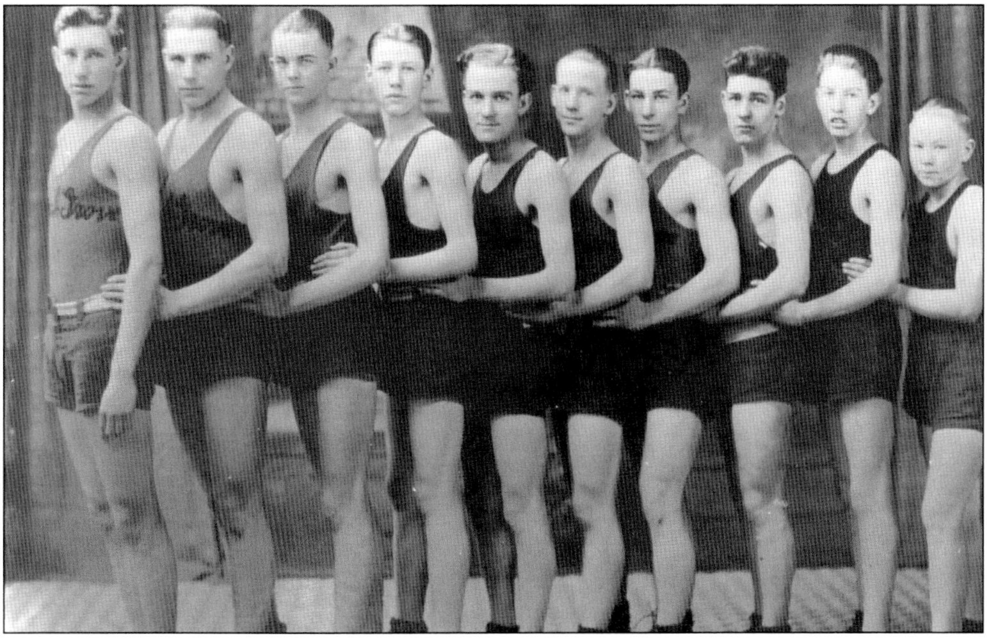

This 1924 Beech Grove High School basketball team photograph depicts a snazzy group of young athletes. School athletes were known as Yellowjackets until 1931, when teams promoted school spirit as "Hornets." Basketball teams, although informal at first, have been part of Beech Grove schools and community life almost since inception. While football and other team sports were added later, basketball remained the most popular of team sports.

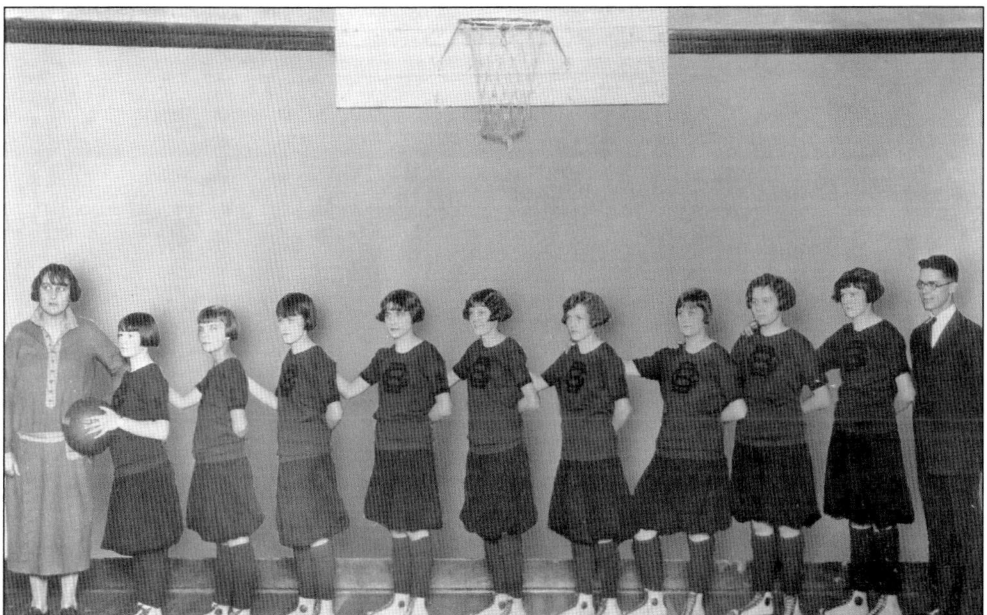

Girls were also given time on the basketball court. This photograph of the 1924 Beech Grove girls basketball team includes coach, players, and manager. Pictured from left to right are Mary Young, Jessica McClain, Mary Bodenhamer, Mary Elizabeth Kail, Erma Dunlar, Helen Burge, Edith Pierson, Joyce Bailey, Mary Herron, Marie Gilliland, and Mr. Dorsett.

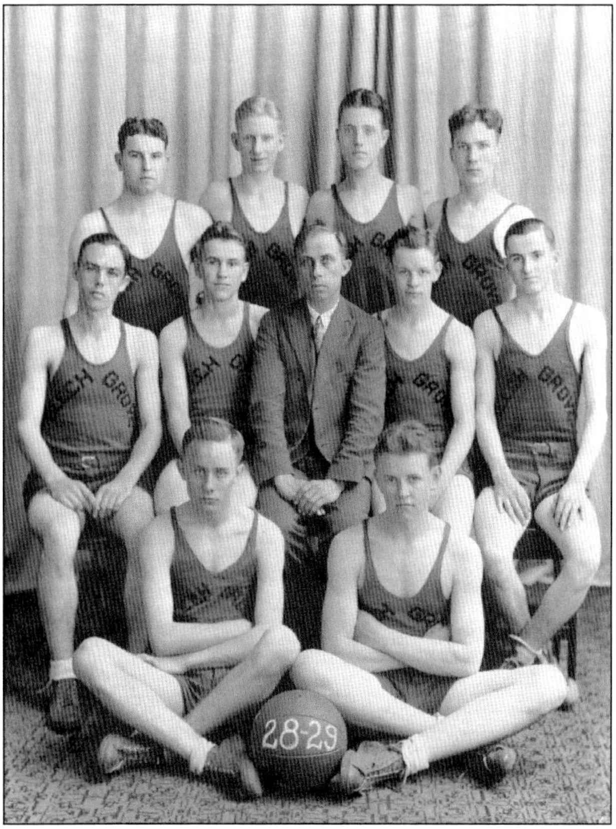

The 1928–1929 Beech Grove High School boys basketball team members are, from left to right, (first row) Elton Geshwiler and Joseph Gilliland; (second row) Howard Clark, Charles Terhune, coach Dorsett, William Gilliland, and Edward Terhune; (third row) Stanley Lawson, William Hatfield, Louis "Bud" McElroy, and Sam Brendon.

Although basketball was always an integral part of Beech Grove High School's nonacademic curriculum, a championship game was not won until the successful 1966–1967 season. This postgame celebration shows the ecstatic Hornets team, peppy cheerleaders, and smiling supporters, along with the trophy and the game-winning ball front and center.

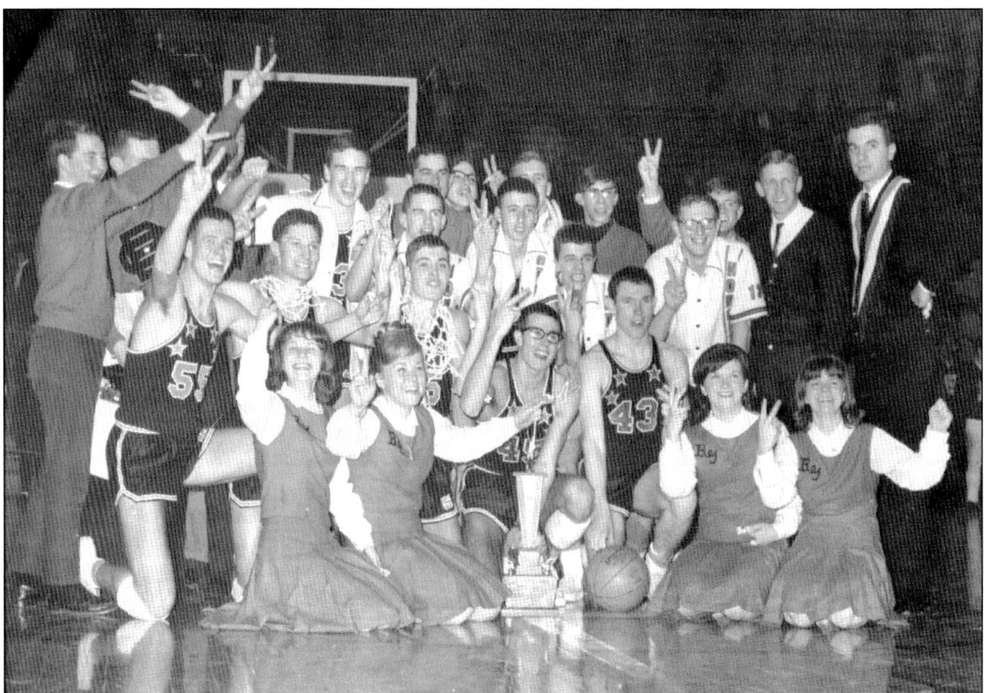

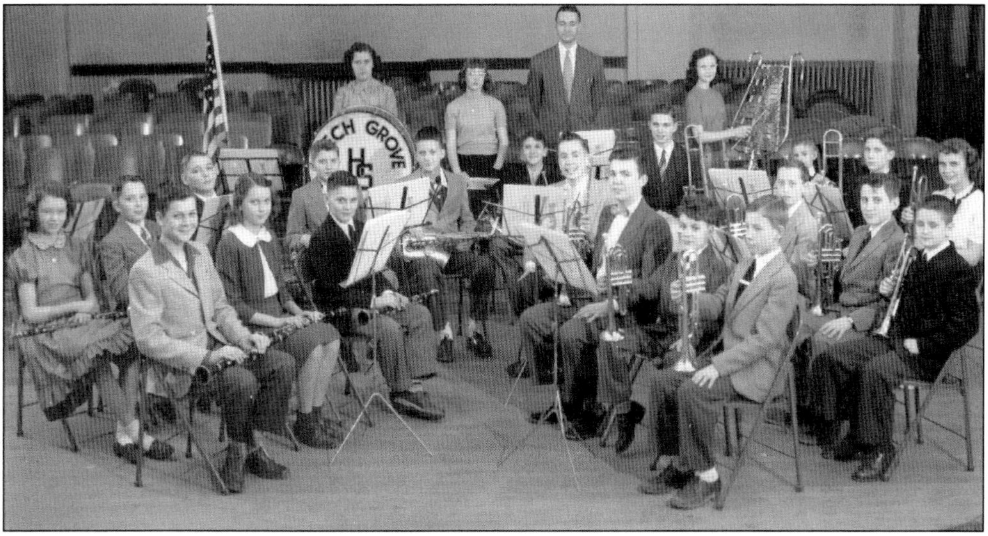

The first Beech Grove High School band is seen here at practice in 1951. The arts were slow to be offered within the schools, which instead focused on strong academics with their limited resources. While the community was considered prosperous in the early years of development, the majority of residents were hardworking, blue-collar industrial employees.

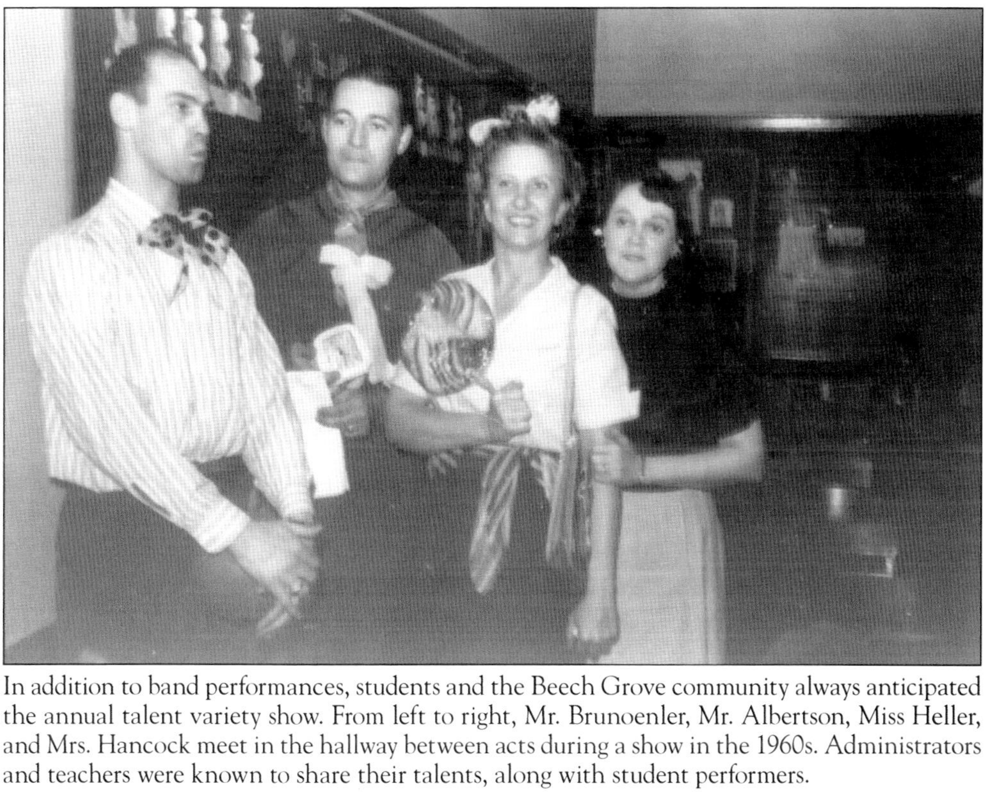

In addition to band performances, students and the Beech Grove community always anticipated the annual talent variety show. From left to right, Mr. Brunoenler, Mr. Albertson, Miss Heller, and Mrs. Hancock meet in the hallway between acts during a show in the 1960s. Administrators and teachers were known to share their talents, along with student performers.

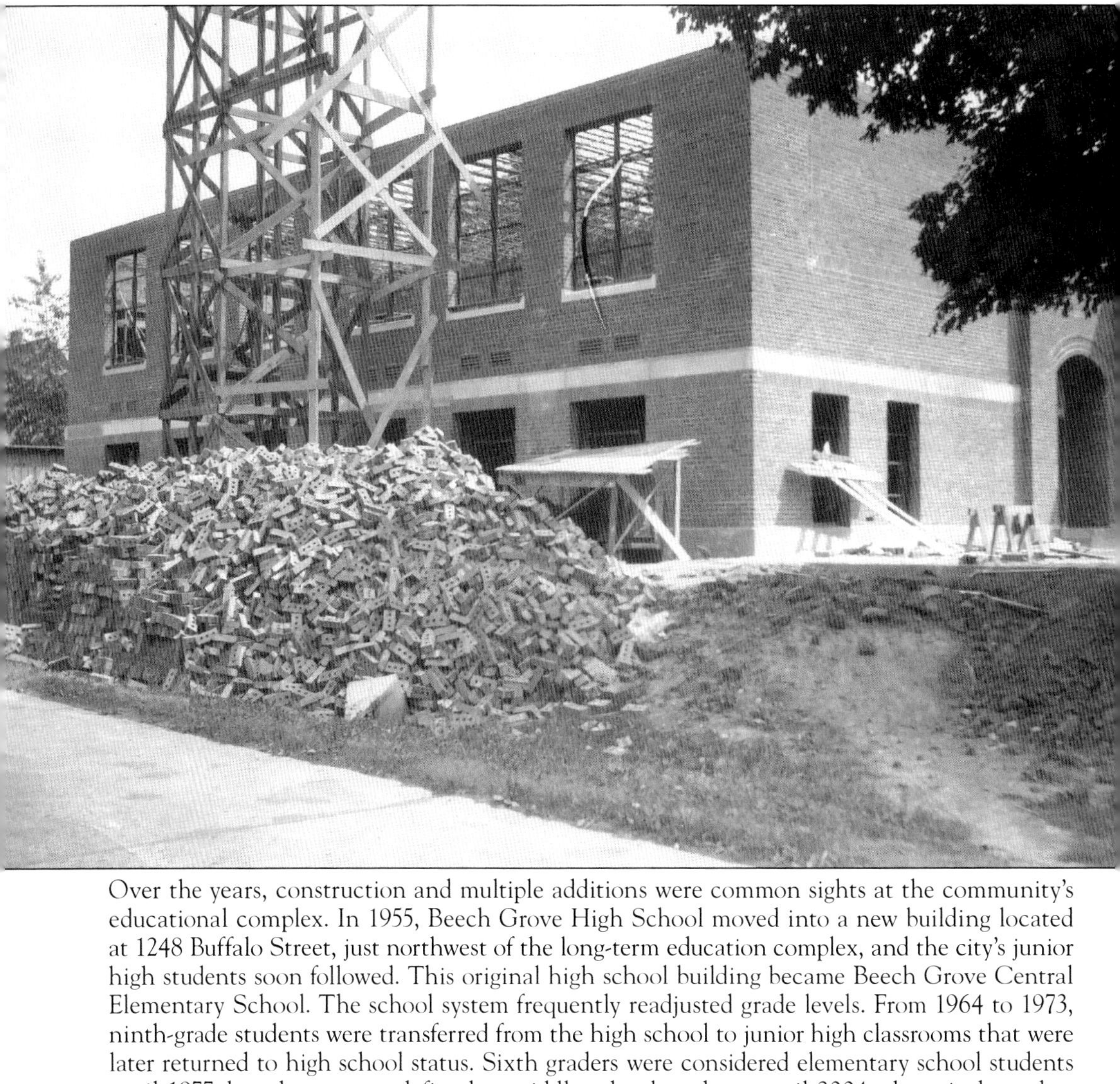

Over the years, construction and multiple additions were common sights at the community's educational complex. In 1955, Beech Grove High School moved into a new building located at 1248 Buffalo Street, just northwest of the long-term education complex, and the city's junior high students soon followed. This original high school building became Beech Grove Central Elementary School. The school system frequently readjusted grade levels. From 1964 to 1973, ninth-grade students were transferred from the high school to junior high classrooms that were later returned to high school status. Sixth graders were considered elementary school students until 1977, but they were redefined as middle school students until 2004 when sixth graders were returned to the grade school rolls. The school system currently employs more than 100 administrative and faculty members.

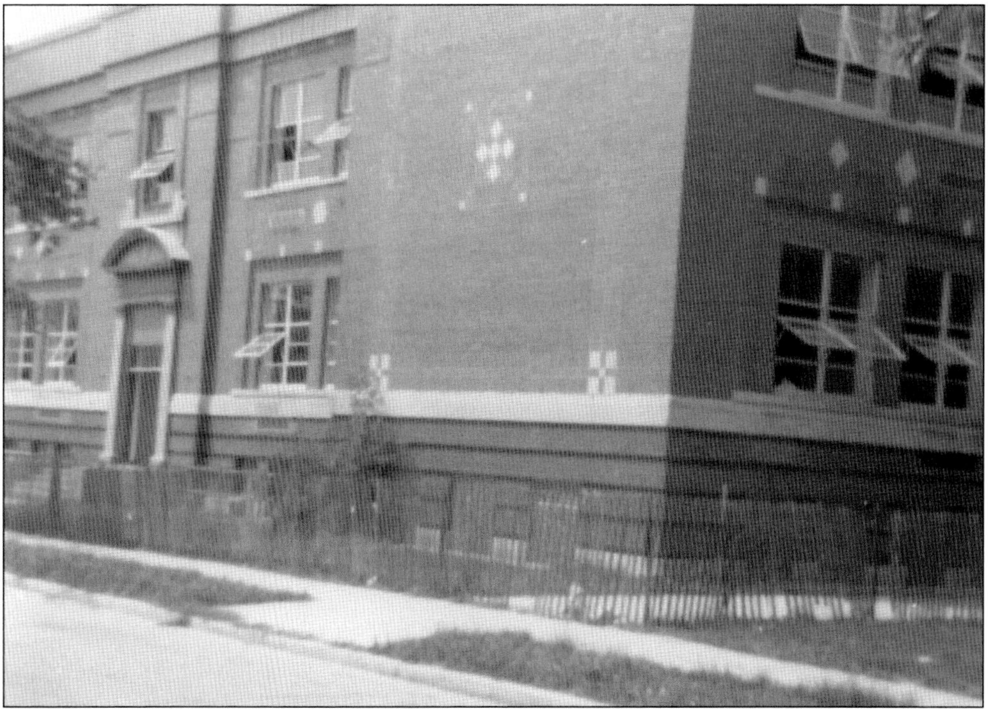

These two photographs depict pre-demolition and demolition of the original high school. Shortly after the high school section of the educational complex was removed, two additions were constructed in 1956 and 1957 to bridge the gap between the gymnasium and the 1929 yellow brick junior high addition. Just over 20 years later, 1978 saw the razing of the old junior high and elementary school buildings so they could be replaced with all new structures. Beech Grove Central Elementary School remains the city's principal elementary school. Although the building is older, the school has state-of-the-art computer labs, closed circuit television, and a multitude of updated amenities.

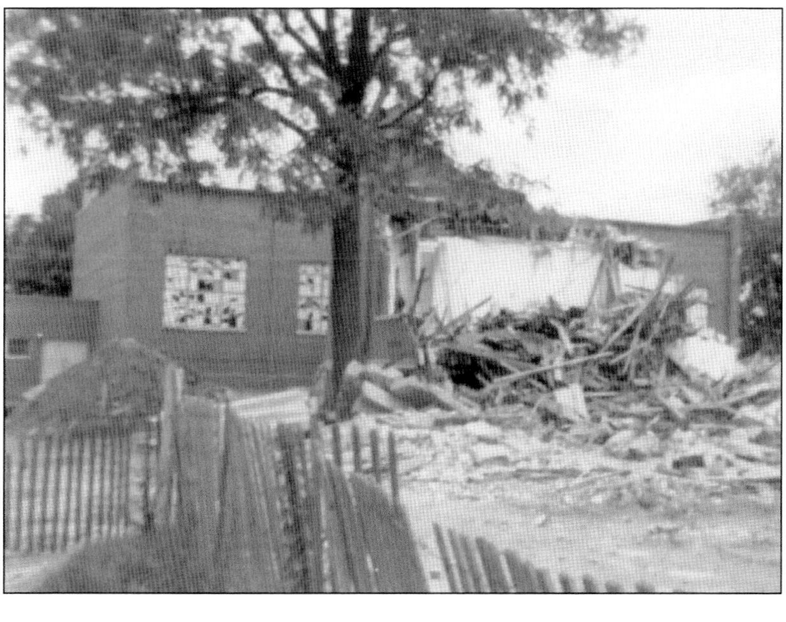

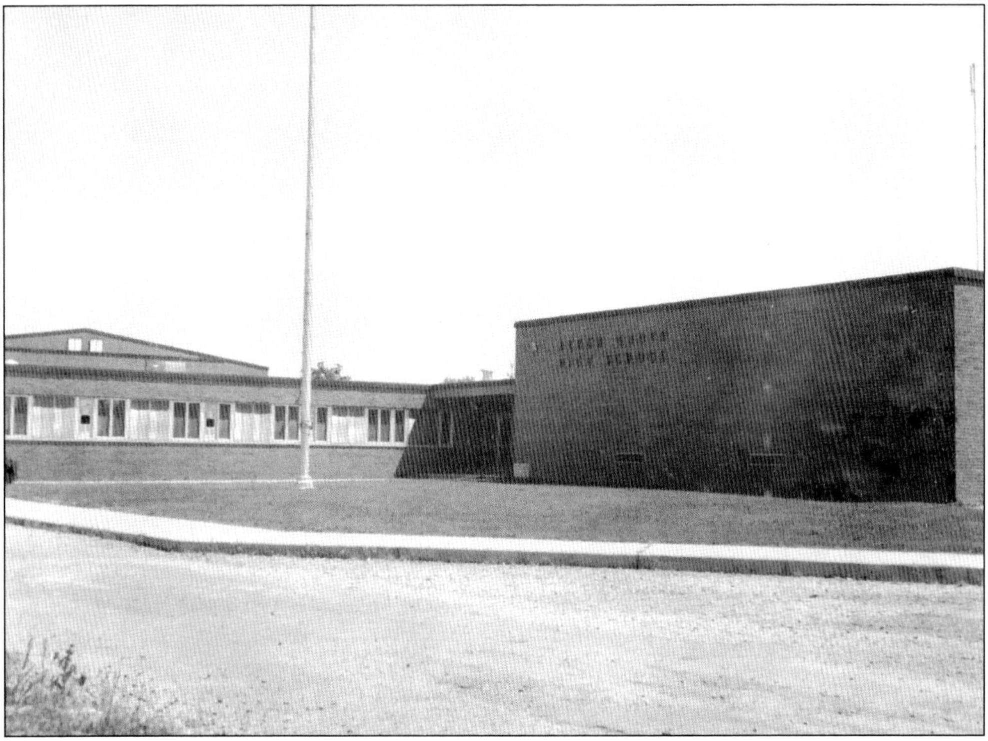

The present high school was built on a section of the old McGregor farm in 1966. The location is just east and a little north of the 4000 block of South Emerson Avenue. Adjacent to the high school is the park department's office and community center on the site of the former Olympia Club family recreation facility. The Buffalo Street facility remained in use as the junior high school. The high school (above) is seen shortly after construction. The field house (below) stands as a reminder of the school's sports legacy and as a testament to the mighty Hornets.

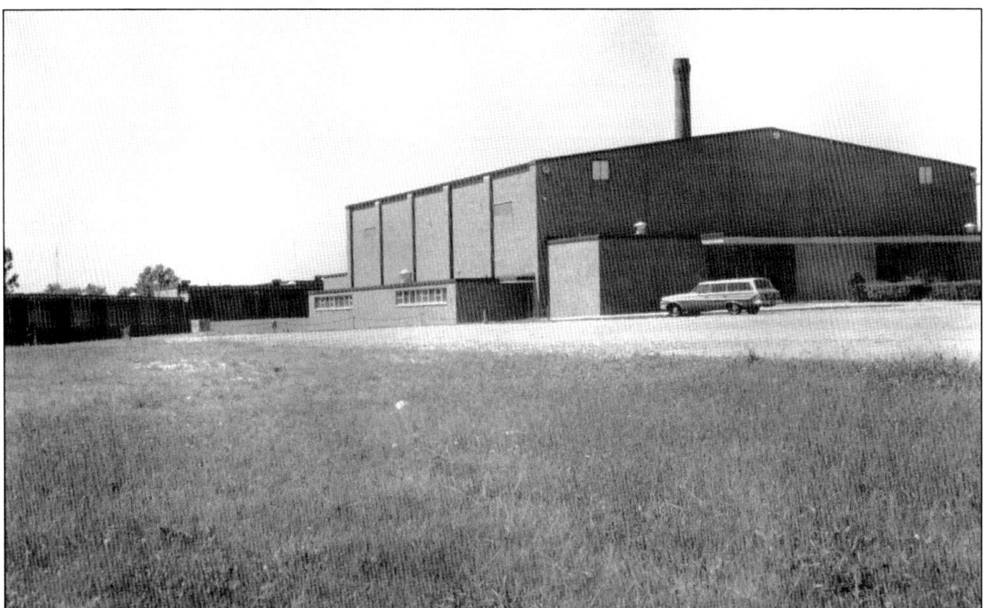

The Yellowjackets became the Hornets in 1931. This post-1945 mascot illustration depicts the stinging insect guarding his basketball and football. Beech Grove High School teams were known for their fair but very competitive brand of sportsmanship. Certainly the intensity of the Hornets mascot would cause the competition to rethink their play strategies.

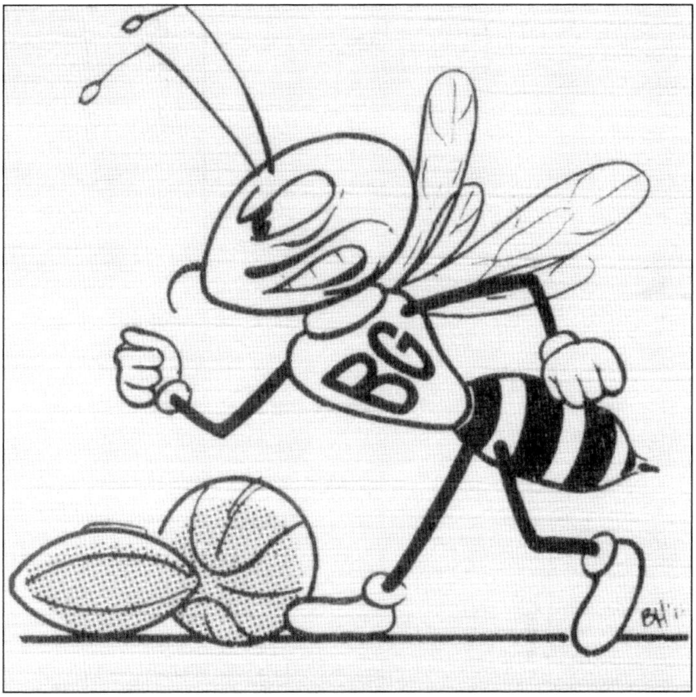

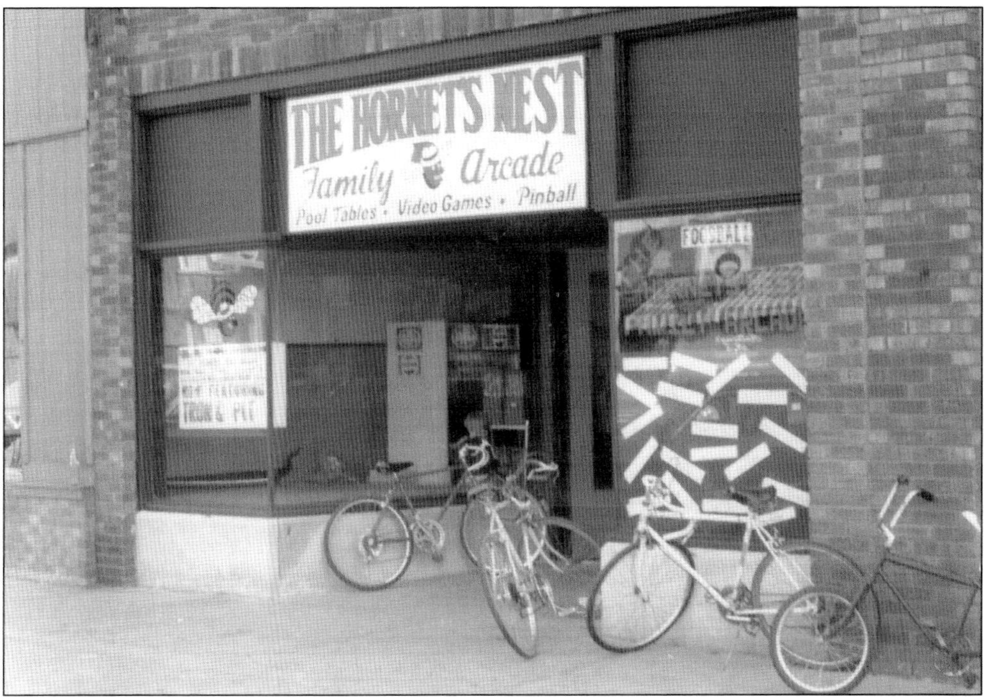

This 1982 picture shows the popular Hornet's Nest Family Arcade. This fondly remembered student hangout closed in 1983. Offering pool tables, video and pinball games, snacks, and a place to relax with buddies, the Hornet's Nest was a fairly sedate downtown business that caused little disturbance to Beech Grove's quiet streets. The Nest could become rowdy after school events, but nostalgic patrons remember the large crowds as very manageable.

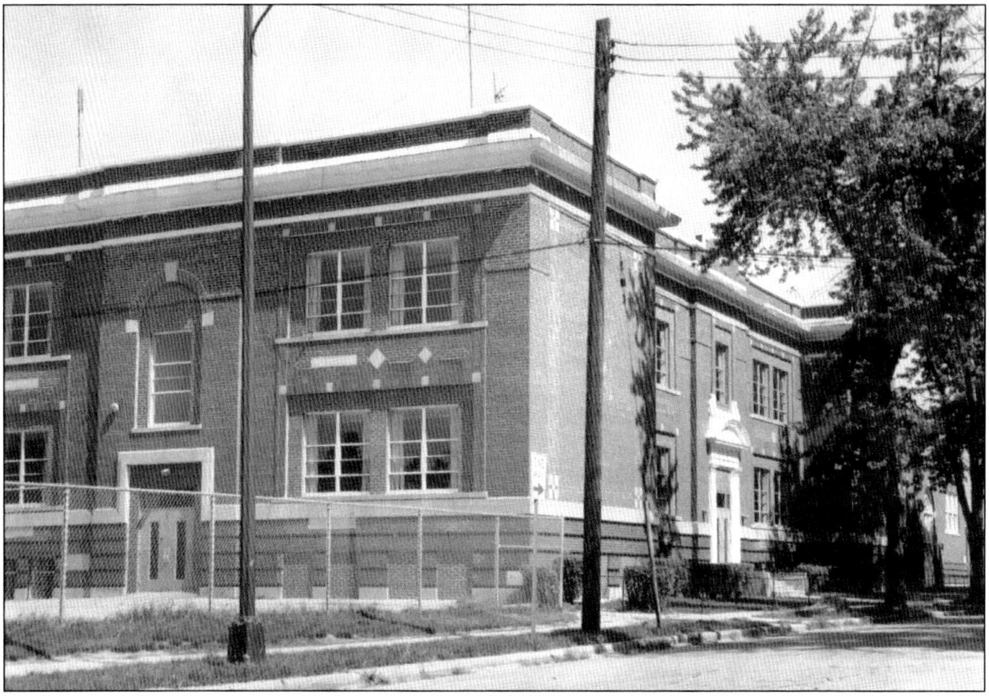

This is a 1964 photograph of Beech Grove Central Elementary School. The school system reconfigured the educational grade sequence in relation to the buildings in the district. Hornet Park Elementary School offers all-day kindergarten and first-grade classes, while Central Elementary School serves second and third graders. Non-graded curriculum is structured on a continuum, allowing for students' needs to be met on an individual basis.

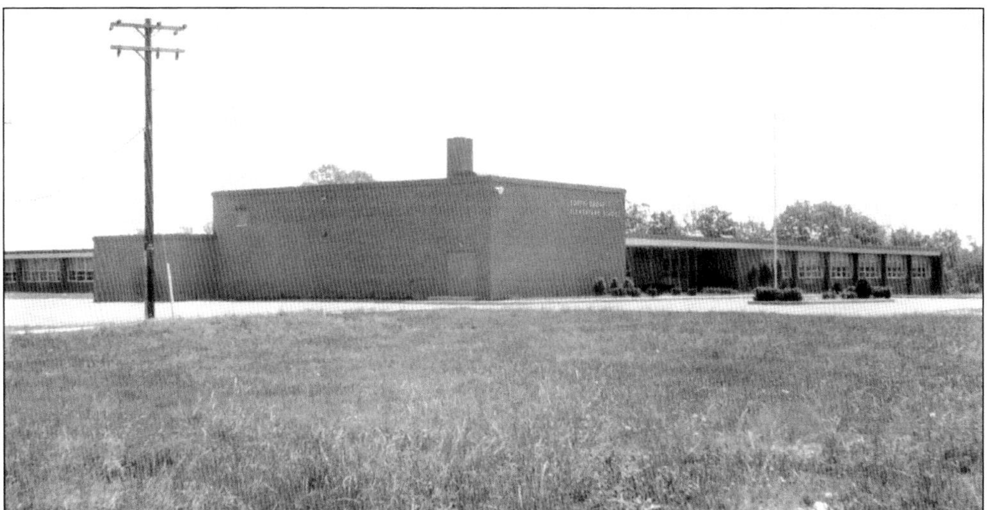

This is a 1964 photograph of South Grove Elementary School, which currently offers intermediate classes for pupils in fourth, fifth, and sixth grade. South Grove students then transfer to Beech Grove Middle School for seventh and eighth grade before going on to the high school for four years. In adapting to the changing student population and needs, the Beech Grove school system has restructured to provide more grade-specific schools throughout the system.

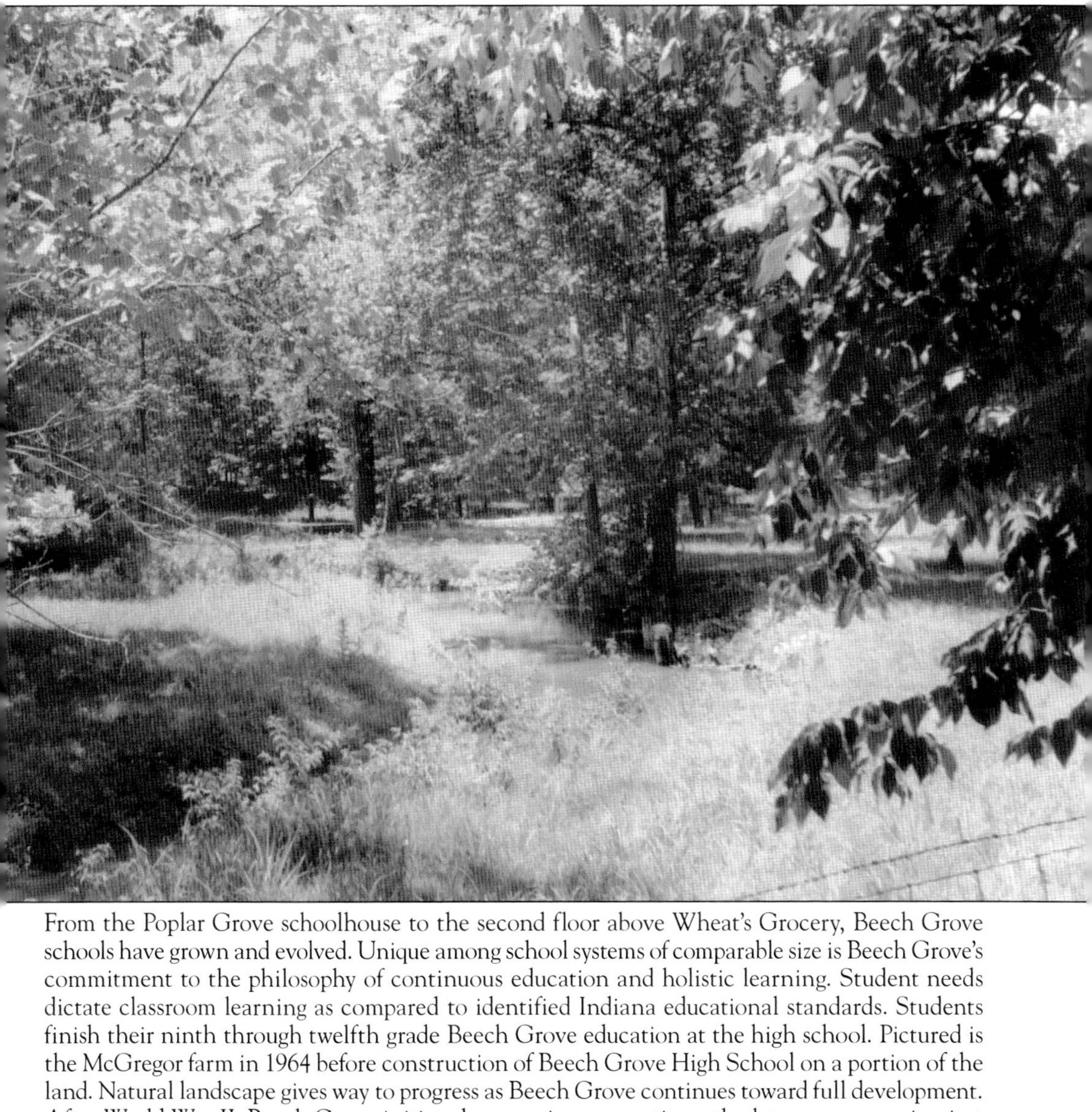

From the Poplar Grove schoolhouse to the second floor above Wheat's Grocery, Beech Grove schools have grown and evolved. Unique among school systems of comparable size is Beech Grove's commitment to the philosophy of continuous education and holistic learning. Student needs dictate classroom learning as compared to identified Indiana educational standards. Students finish their ninth through twelfth grade Beech Grove education at the high school. Pictured is the McGregor farm in 1964 before construction of Beech Grove High School on a portion of the land. Natural landscape gives way to progress as Beech Grove continues toward full development. After World War II, Beech Grove initiated two major annexations, the later one occurring just prior to the 1969 government restructuring that expanded Indianapolis to include most of Marion County, effectively preventing future annexations.

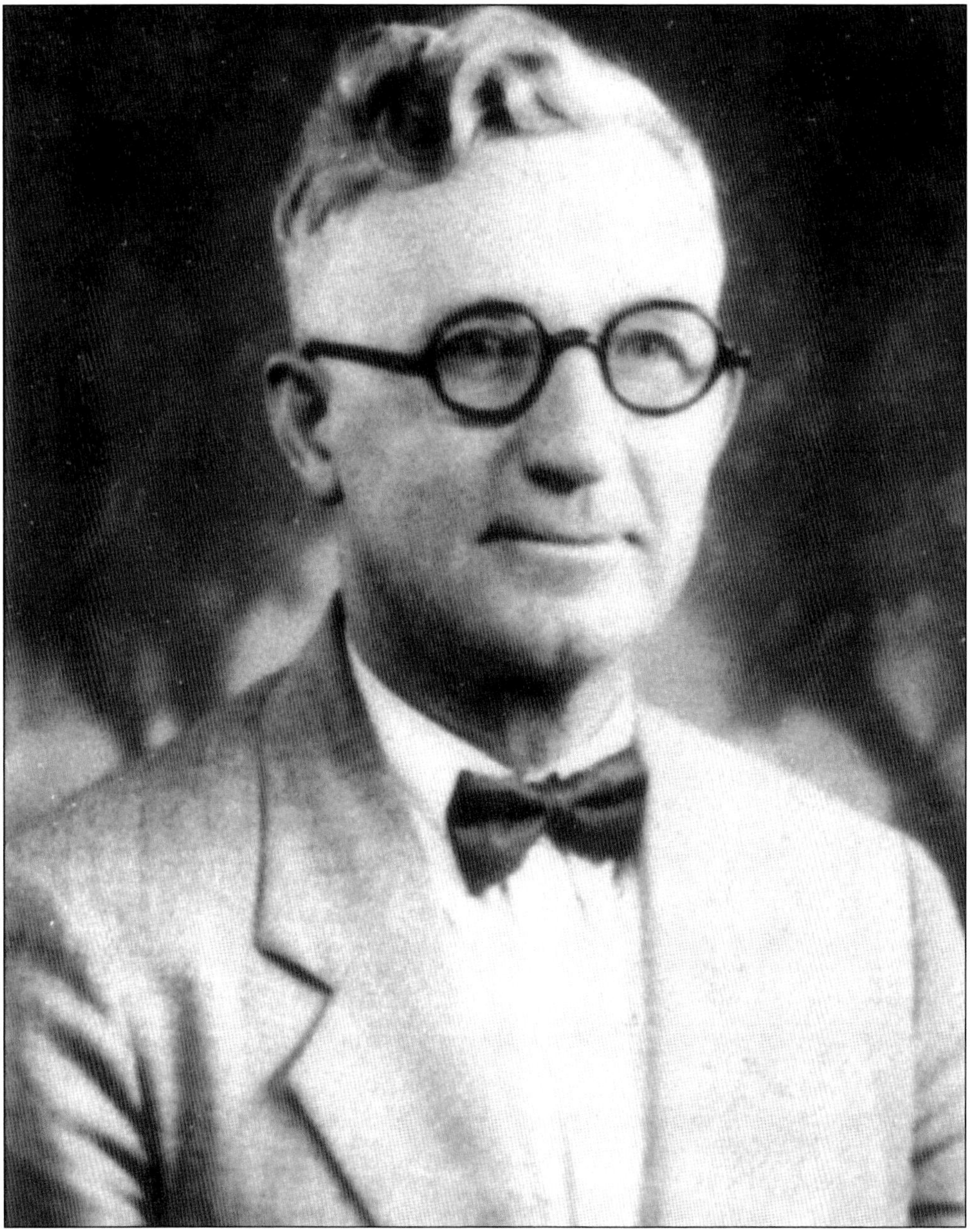

Indianapolis geographically surrounds and landlocks Beech Grove. Beech Grove remains an independent city, complete with a school system, police and fire departments, parks, a library, and public works operations. Originally a town board governed the community, from incorporation as a town in November 1906 through 1935, when the three-ward representatives and clerk treasurer relinquished their positions to a new mayor and staff. The first trustees were president John Woocher, Herbert Weelburg, and Louis McMains. Harry E. Marsh was the first elected clerk-treasurer. The board members were elected from local political parties, including the People's Ticket and Progressives. Pictured is Charles Adams, Beech Grove's first mayor, who was originally elected as a Progressive. He served from 1935, when the town became a fifth-class city, until his retirement in 1942.

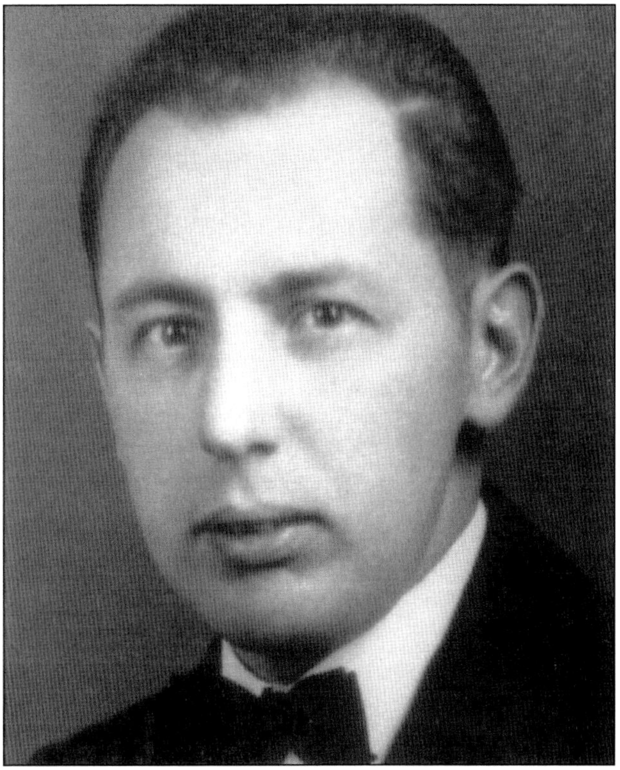

In 1935, Beech Grove was reorganized from three wards to four districts with councilmen. One councilman was elected from each district, and one additional councilman was elected at-large. After Charles Adam's tenure as mayor, Republican E. Allen Hunter (right) served from 1943 to 1948, then again from 1952 to 1955. Hunter's first term was extended an additional year due to a "skip-election" year. Richard S. Byland (below) was Beech Grove's third mayor. As a Democrat, he was elected to serve between Hunter's two terms. Byland's term was considered uneventful, and the focus was maintaining the integrity of city services as Beech Grove grew.

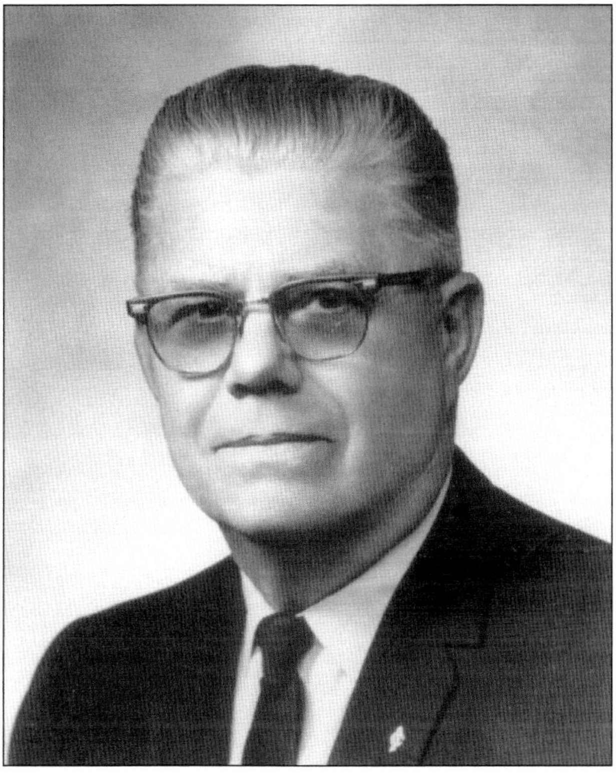

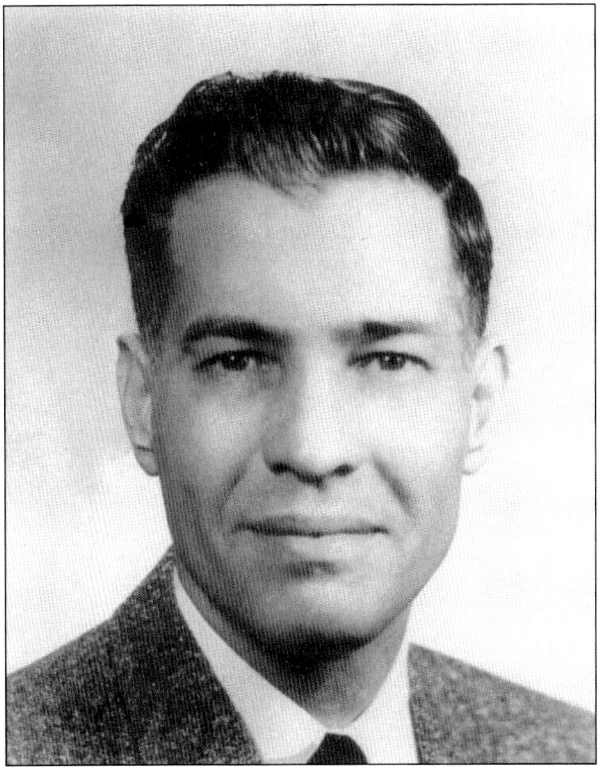

David D. Finney (left) became Beech grove's fourth mayor and served between 1956 and 1958; he was unable to complete the fourth year of his term. In 1959, Elton Geshwiler (below) became the city's fifth, and longest-serving, mayor. He continued his Democratic governance of the city until 1991 when J. Warner Wiley, another Democrat, was elected and served until 2003. Republican mayor Donald "Joe" Wright is Beech Grove's seventh mayor. Under Geshwiler's leadership, Beech Grove became a fourth-class city in 1961. Geshwiler, a longtime Beech Grove resident, was well liked and respected in local, state, and national political circles, effectively bridging the partisan gap between Democrats and Republicans.

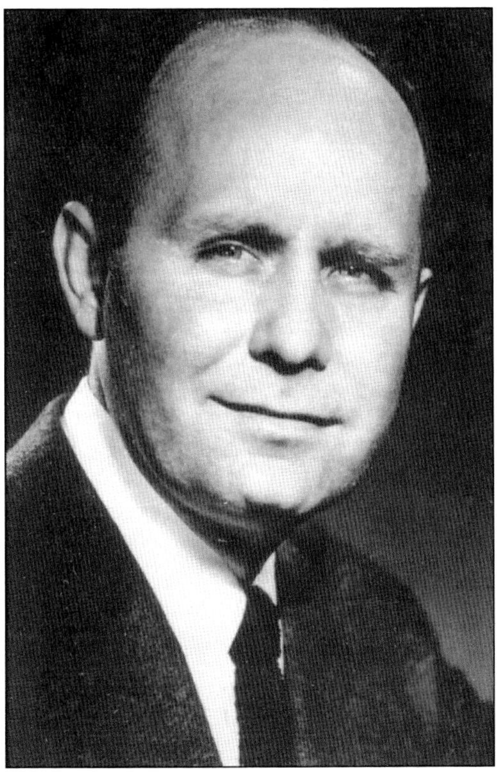

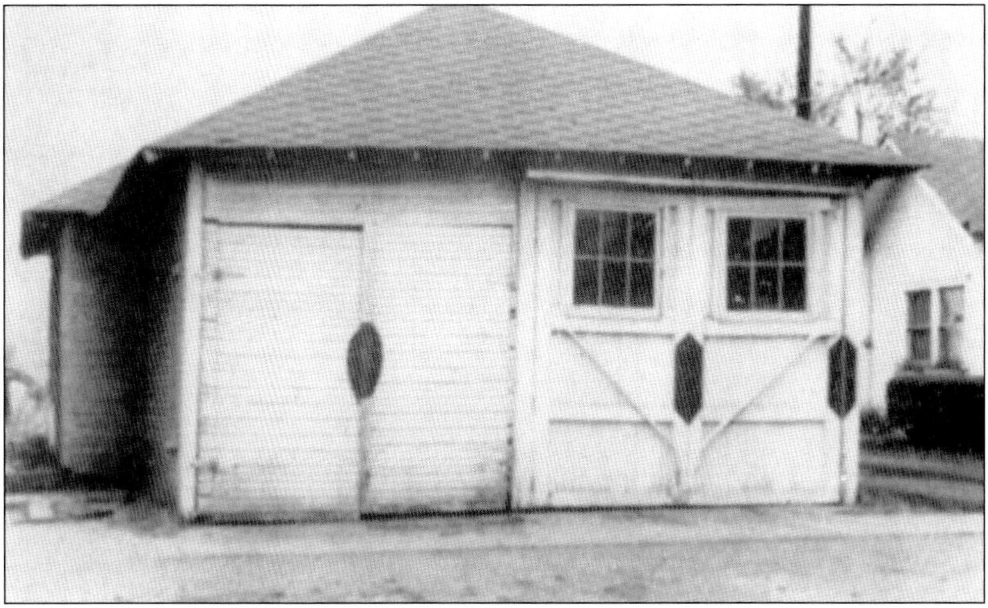

Beech Grove City Hall and fire station was located at the rear of the corner of Eighth Avenue and Main Street. This postcard view is extremely rare according to local collectors. The card offers the most complete view known to exist of Beech Grove government facilities in the late 1920s. What this image lacks in reproduction clarity is balanced by historic importance, and if not included would not otherwise be seen.

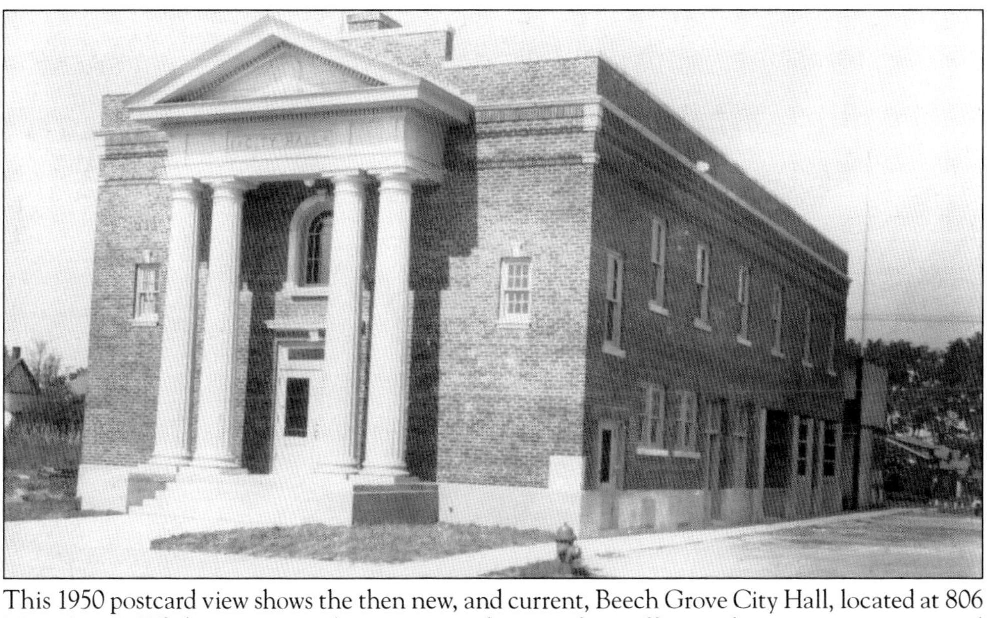

This 1950 postcard view shows the then new, and current, Beech Grove City Hall, located at 806 Main Street. While at one time the entire complement of city offices and services were contained within the building, now only the clerk's office, sanitation office, chamber of commerce, and city court remain. The mayor's office is now located at 340 East Churchman Avenue behind the police station on the public safety campus. (Joe Seiter collection.)

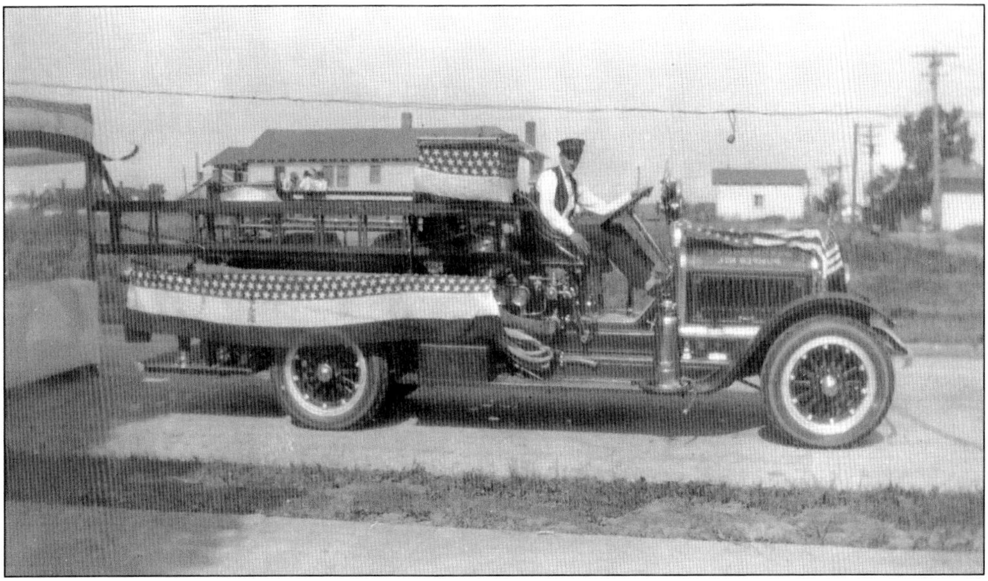

The first fire station, located at Eighth Avenue and Main Street, served the town for many years. Horse-drawn firefighting equipment, and the famous equine duo Nip and Tuck, assisted firefighter Billy Trusdale in protecting the community. In the 1920s, the department was expanded. Firefighter C. O. Driskell is seen on the town's new 1923 Stutz fire engine.

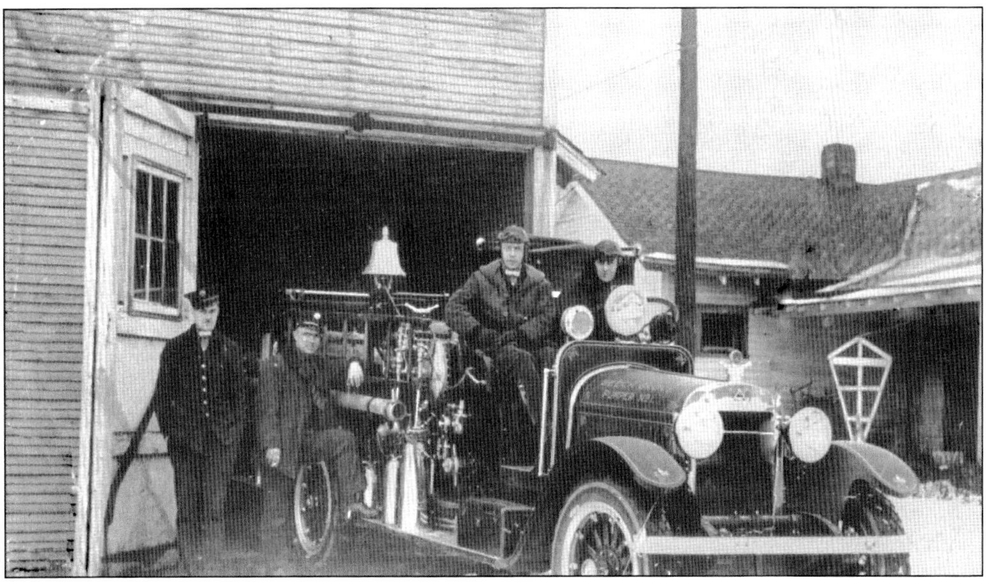

In the winter of 1926, the reliable 1923 Stutz fire truck is seen at Eighth Avenue and Main Street headquarters awaiting dispatch. Pictured at the station are, from left to right, C. O. Driskell, Raymond Adair, H. A. Terrell, and Houston Driskell. The station was replaced in 1928. Beech Grove has invested heavily in its fire department over the years.

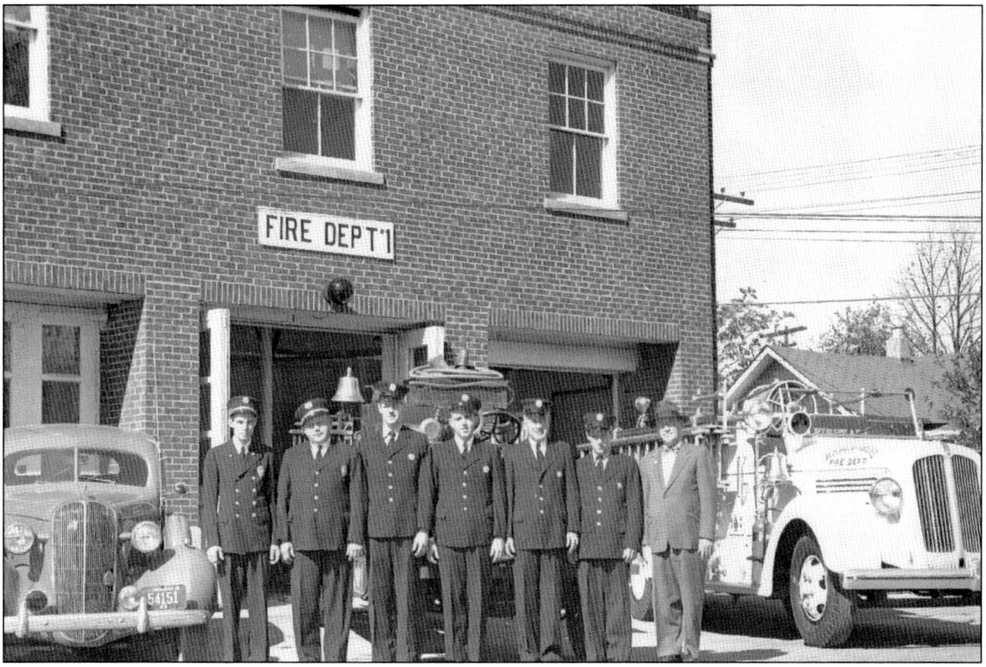

Seen here in the 1930s at new Fire Station No. 2 are, from left to right, Bob Fletcher, Paul Thompson, Mason Mackey, Gerry Klinger, Matt Wilcher, and chaplain Rev. S. Moneymaker. Even in the troubled economy of that time, the city continued to be prosperous enough to invest in new facilities, and the department continued to add the best available equipment and personnel.

In this photograph, he fire department gets new equipment. Pictured from left to right are Mayor Hunter, Joe Greenfield, Bob Fletcher, Bob Johnson, Clarence Kinsey, and Byron Sanders. The 750-gallons-per-minute Seagrave fire pumper was purchased in 1940. The Beech Grove firemen also had an aluminum, 35-foot ladder at their disposal—an amenity that even the Indianapolis Fire Department envied.

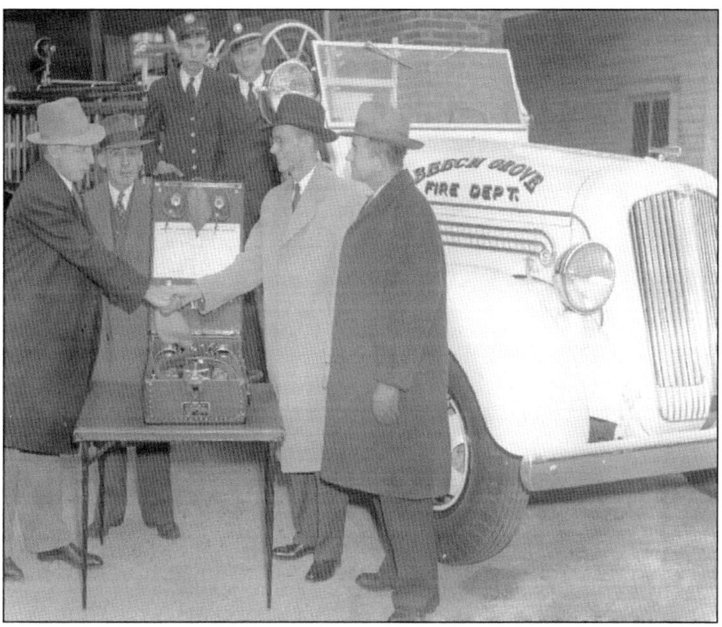

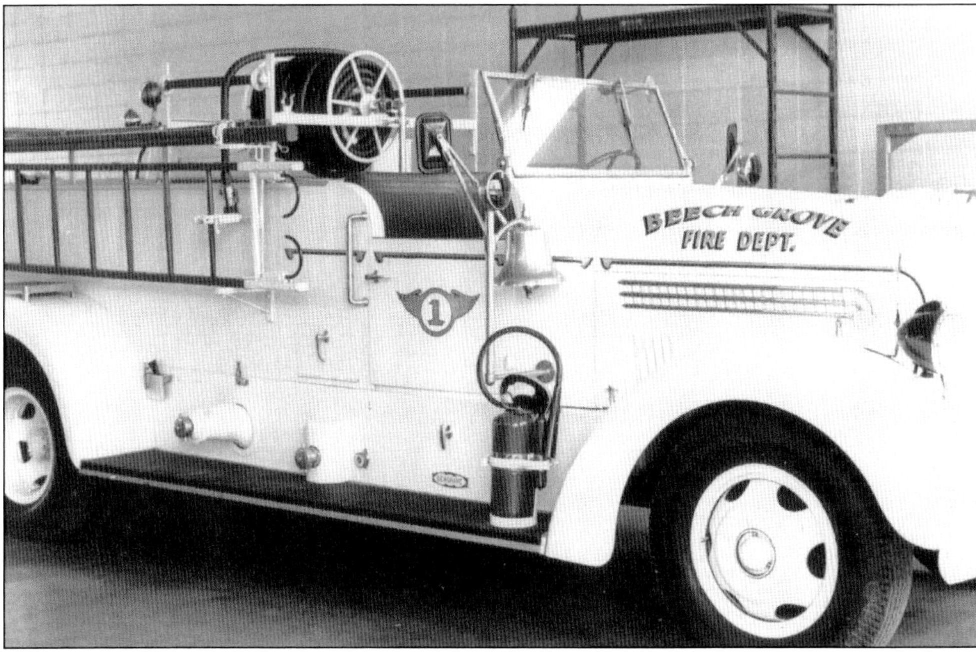

Beech Grove Fire Engine No. 1, the 1940 Seagrave pumper, is seen in this close-up photograph. The equipment also boasted a 300-gallon booster tank. The Seagrave was rebuilt in 1970 and was pulled out of storage for parades and special events. A new Seagrave engine was added to the department's equipment roster in 1953.

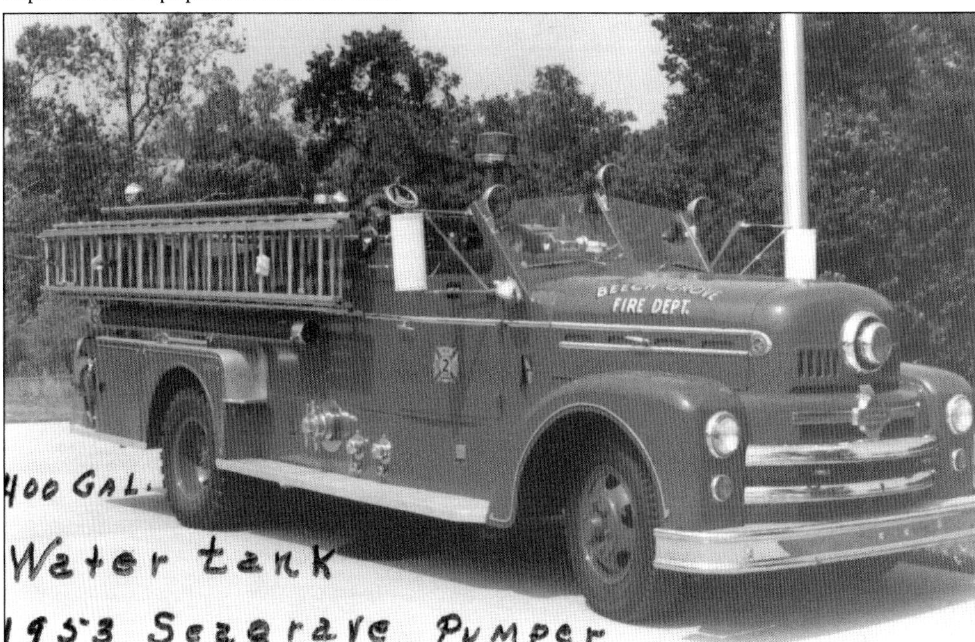

This close-up view details the 1953 Seagrave fire engine that remained in service well into the 1980s. Additional acquisitions included a 1970 Howe fire engine, complete with a 100-foot ladder attached. That apparatus performed so well that an additional Howe fire engine was purchased in 1976. The department continues to frequently add modern equipment to this day.

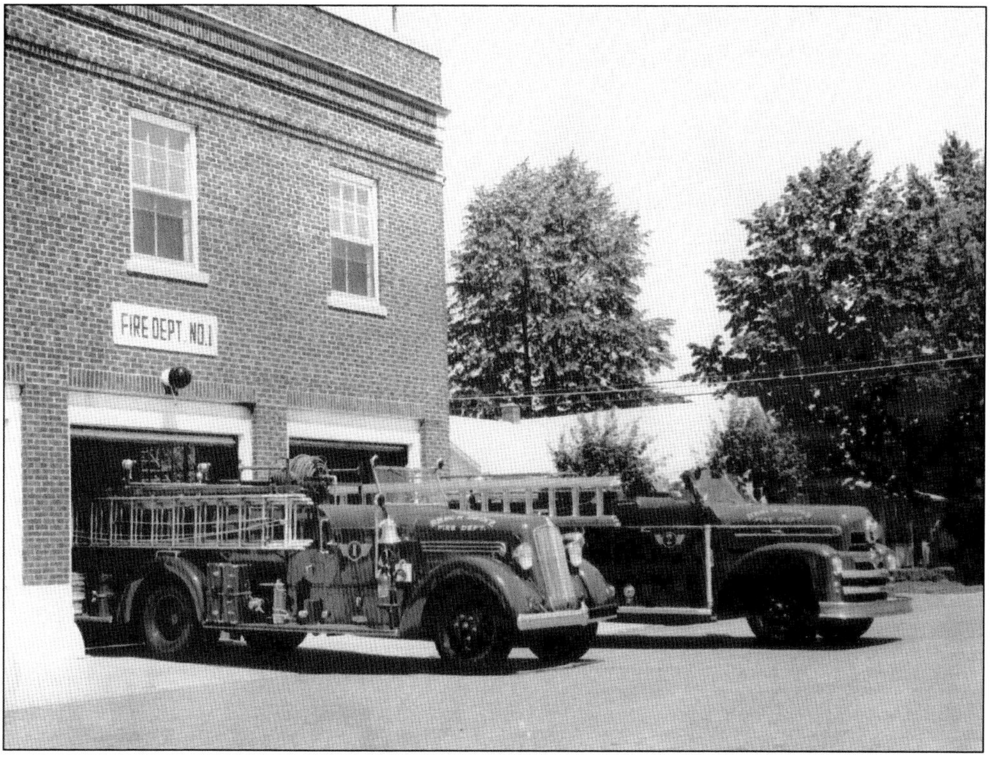

As seen in this 1964 photograph, the fire engines are poised to respond to emergencies from the city hall fire station. Soon new facilities were added to protect the swelling population. In 1970, the city acquired land at 330 Churchman Avenue and invested $158,000 in a new headquarters that became part of a public-safety campus housing both the police and fire departments.

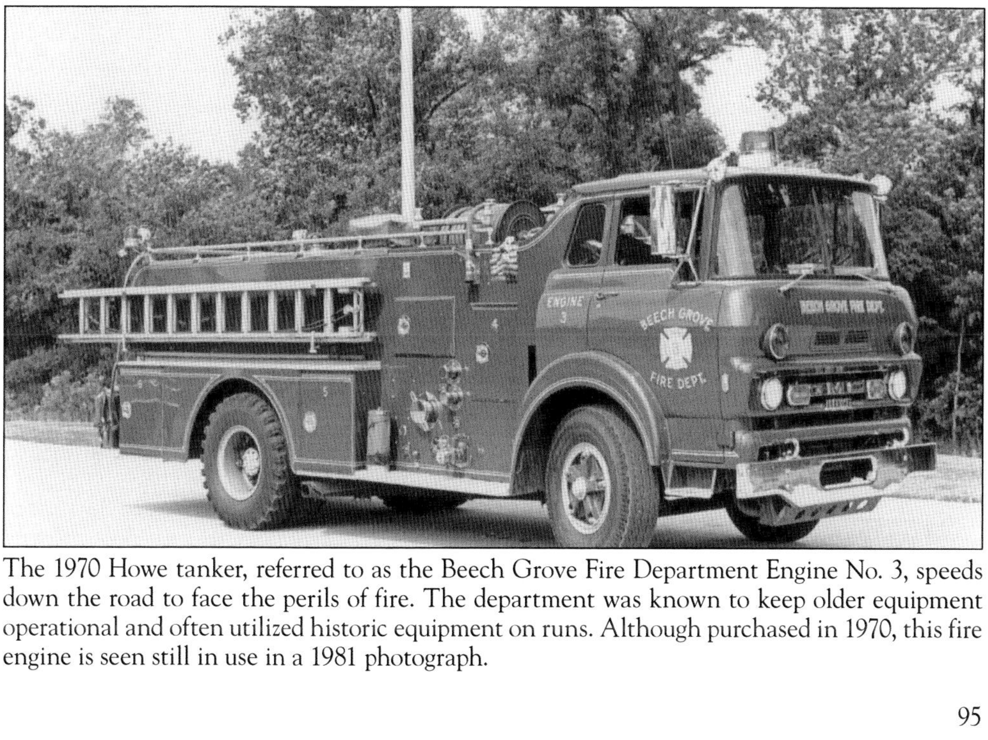

The 1970 Howe tanker, referred to as the Beech Grove Fire Department Engine No. 3, speeds down the road to face the perils of fire. The department was known to keep older equipment operational and often utilized historic equipment on runs. Although purchased in 1970, this fire engine is seen still in use in a 1981 photograph.

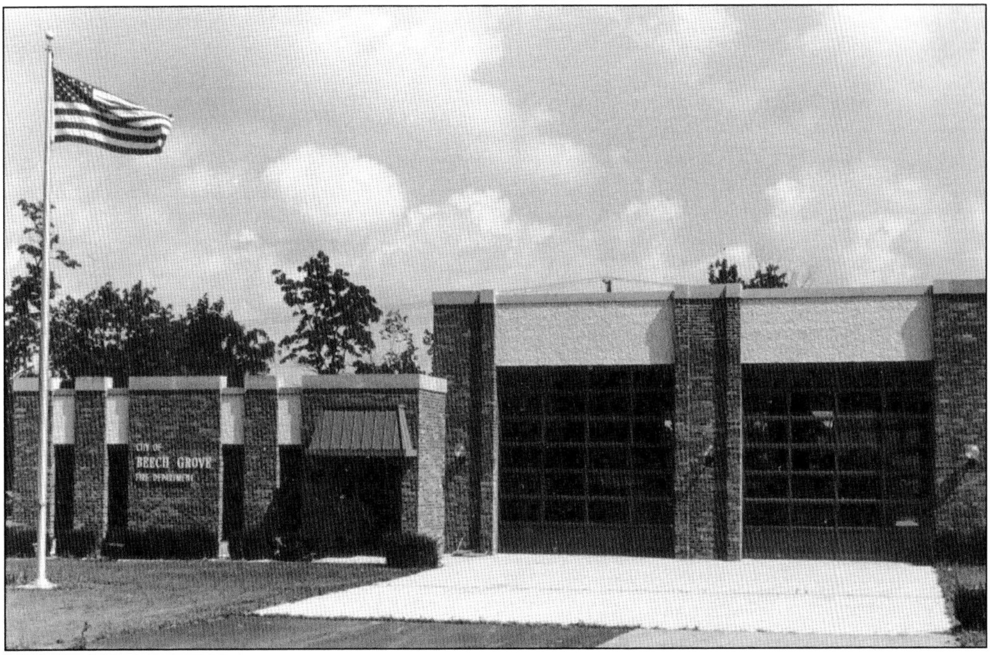

The new 1971 fire station, pictured in 1981, became the relocated headquarters for the fire department. When the new headquarters opened, 12 men were stationed for action, along with a fire chief, arson investigator, and fire prevention specialist. A four-wheel drive rescue vehicle and grass firefighting rig became operational during the summer of 1973.

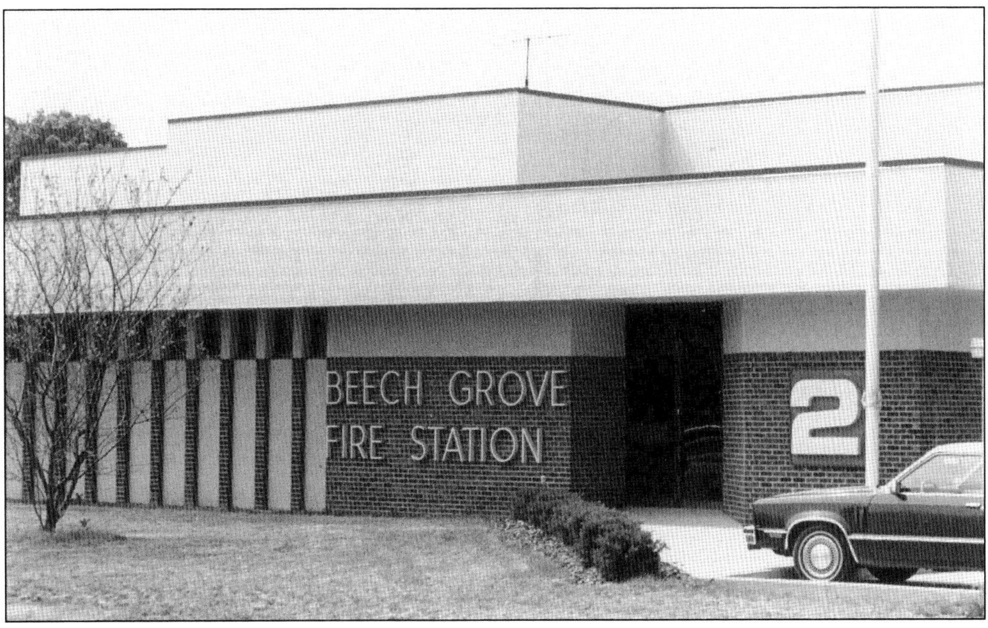

With the opening of the new headquarters, Fire Station No. 2 became the main support branch. In the early 1970s, ambulance service was initiated and was later updated in 1978 to include modular equipment. Because of the firefighters' competence and the continual updating of firefighting equipment, city residents enjoy reduced insurance rates. The low rates also save the city by reducing insurance costs on the city buildings.

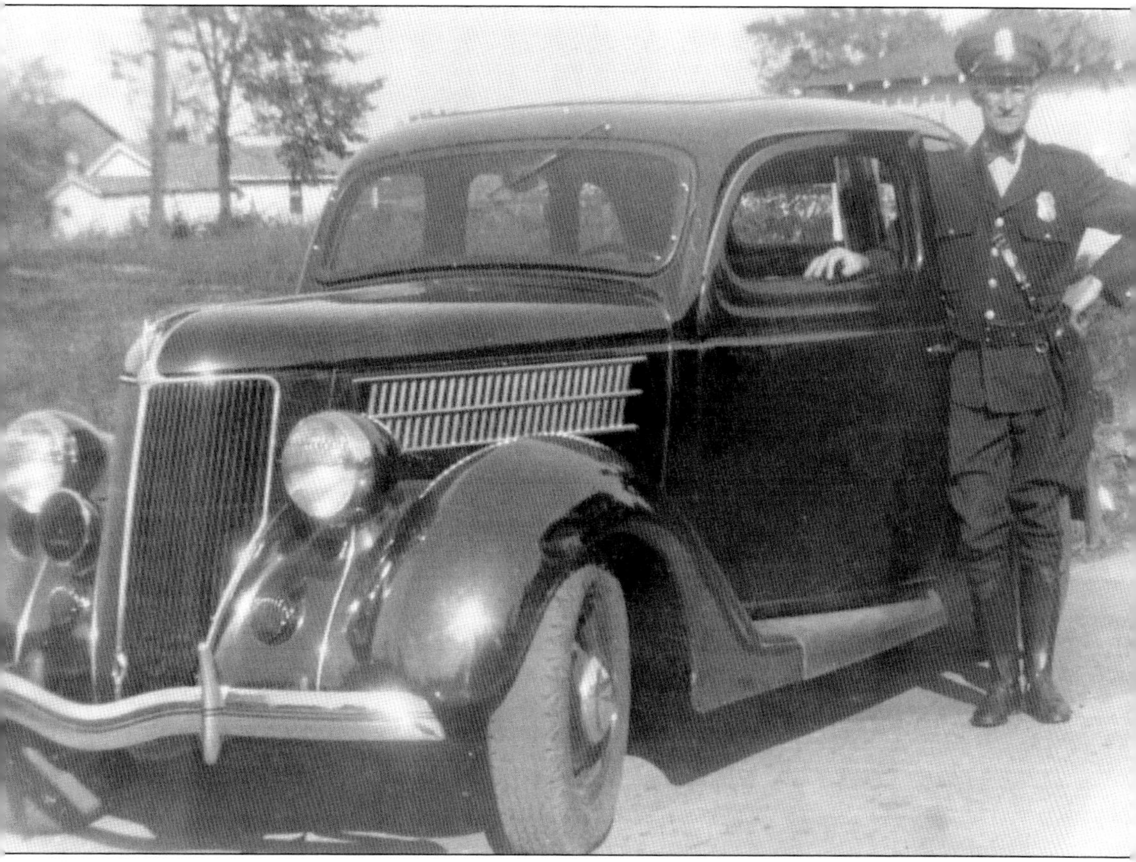

The town's first policeman was J. C. Johnson. Several law enforcement officers followed until Beech Grove incorporated as a city and Mayor Charles Adams appointed former town marshal Charles Lough (pictured) as Beech Grove's first chief of police in 1936. The city paid Lough $105 per month, and during his term the city equipped him with a $475 police cruiser. As the town grew, so did the department's arsenal of crime-fighting gadgetry, including a $30 one-way radio, fingerprinting system, and in 1946 a two-way radio. From 1924 until 1974, the police department was located in the city hall building. Under chief of police (and future mayor) J. Warner Wiley, plans were initiated to build a new, ultra-modern building at 340 Churchman Avenue named the Public Safety Campus. The building includes several modern facilities, including a pistol range, training room, library, photographic darkroom, and cutting-edge computer and communications facility.

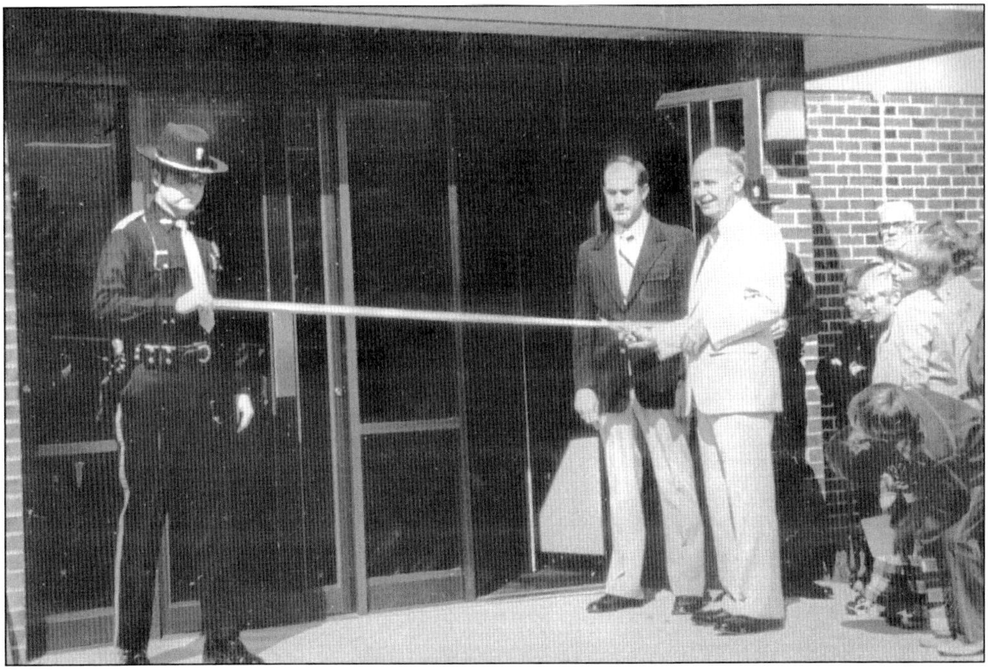

The ribbon-cutting ceremony for the new police headquarters occurred on September 22, 1974. Holding the ribbon is patrolman Dave Johnson. Mayor Elton Geshwiler performs the official ribbon-cutting honor, while police chief J. Warner Wiley observes the ceremony. Before long, the building was a flurry of activity, as community members were allowed to take tours of the building.

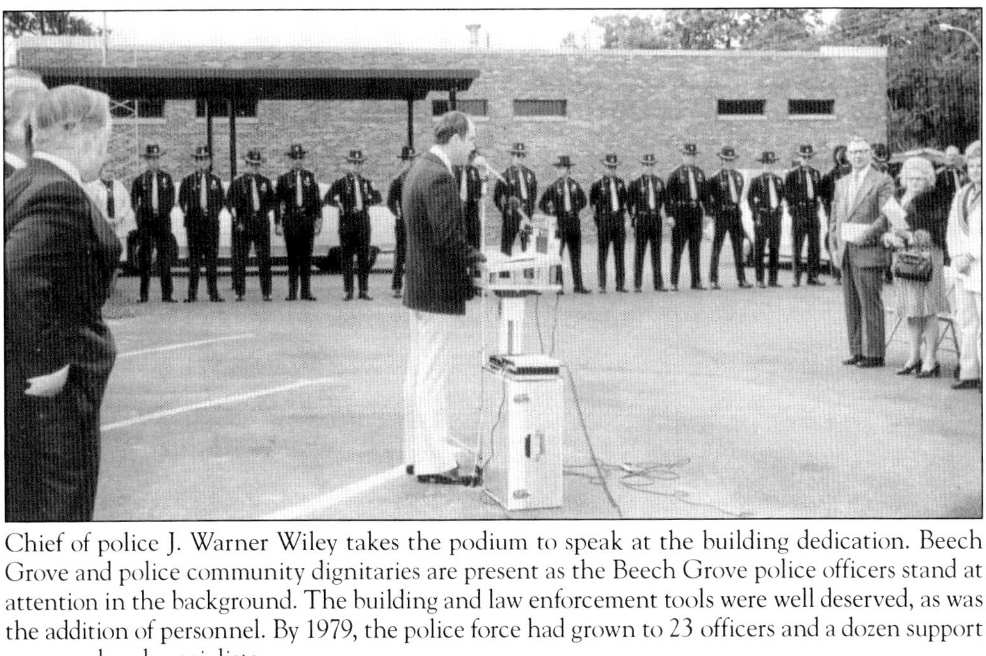

Chief of police J. Warner Wiley takes the podium to speak at the building dedication. Beech Grove and police community dignitaries are present as the Beech Grove police officers stand at attention in the background. The building and law enforcement tools were well deserved, as was the addition of personnel. By 1979, the police force had grown to 23 officers and a dozen support personnel and specialists.

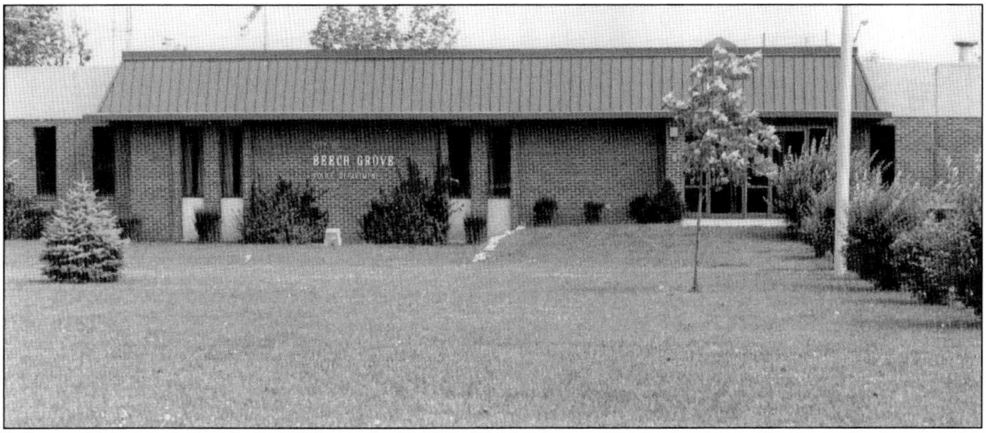

The police department's headquarters was new, modern, and the envy of departments across the state. Often recognized for being well equipped and highly educated, the Beech Grove Police Department has earned numerous awards and recognitions. During the late 1970s, the department began to invest in specialist support, including a humane officer, detectives, juvenile officers, technical dispatchers, and traffic safety inspectors. While crime has never been a major problem for Beech Grove, the police department likes to think community safety is a matter of proactive action and police visibility. A 1981 Ford police cruiser (below) was a common sight on Beech Grove streets in the 1980s, and officers were allowed to take their vehicles home.

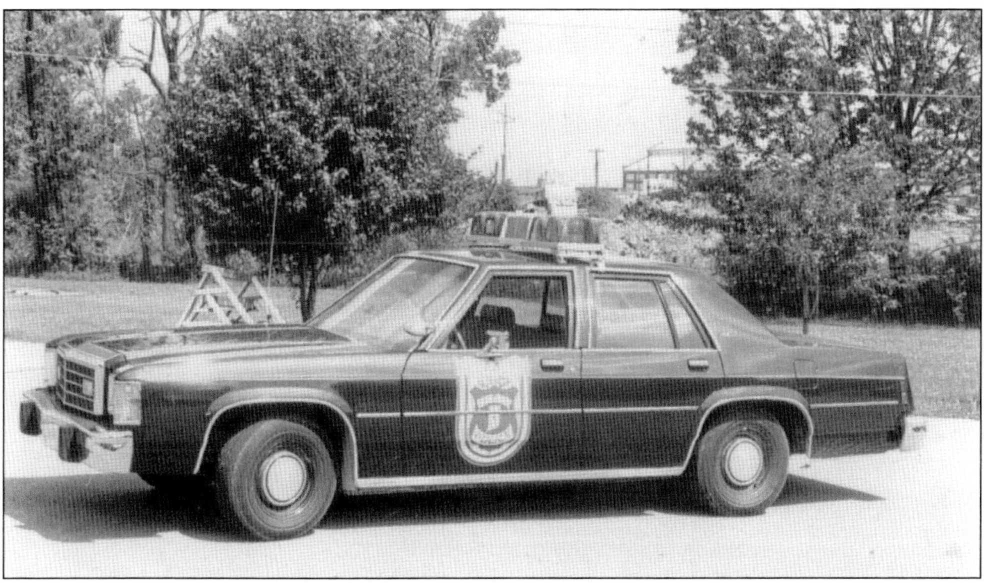

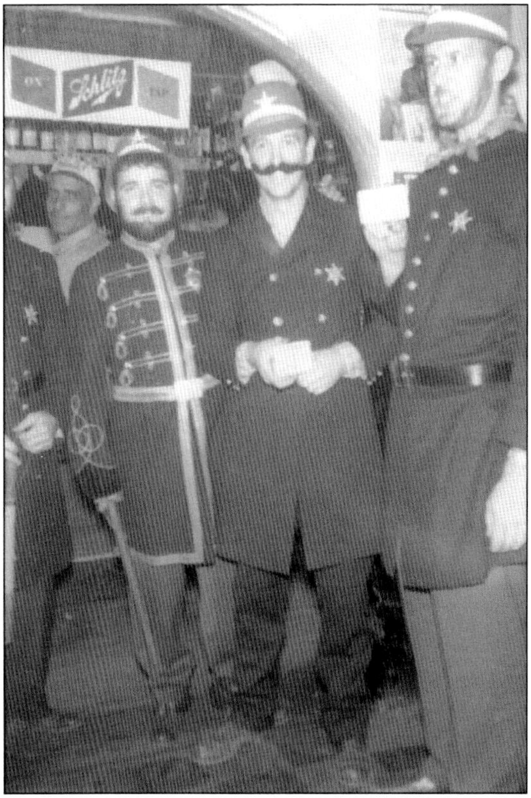

This is definitely not a photograph of Beech Grove's finest police officers. During the city's 50th anniversary celebration, a group of festival volunteers dressed as the Keystone Cops. The antics of the makeshift police force added humor to the festivities, and the "cops" even tried to arrest unsuspecting citizens in the name of fun.

Aside from the origination of a local telephone exchange, when a community gets its own post office that geographic area's independent identity is fortified. This Colonial-style brick post office building, located in the heart of Beech Grove's business district at 202 Main Street, has served the city well.

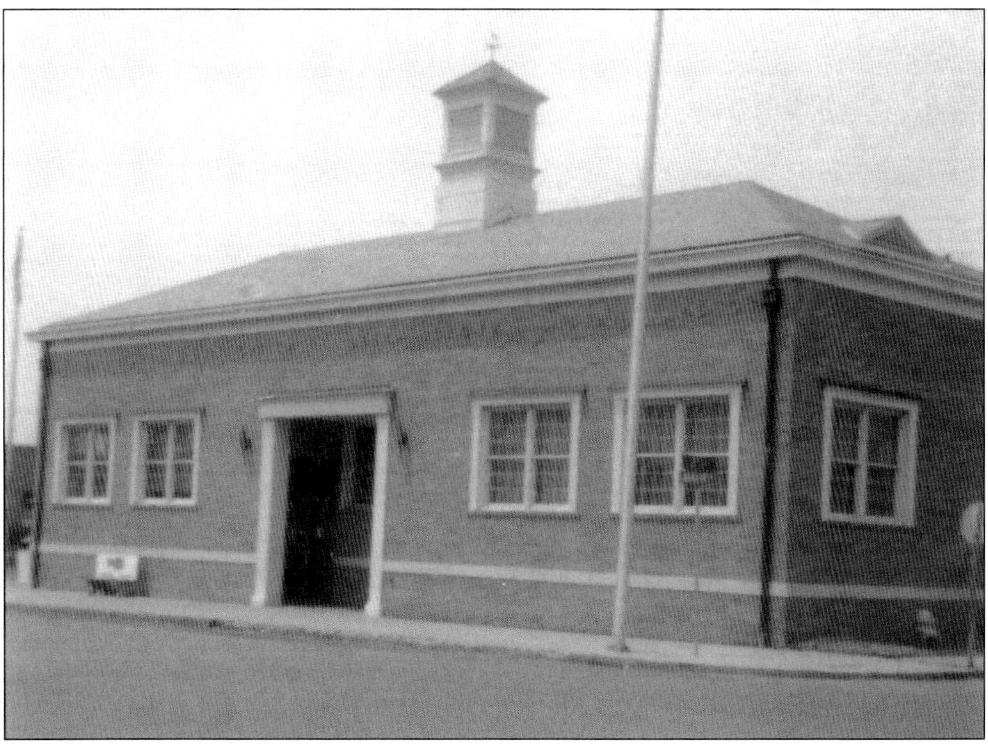

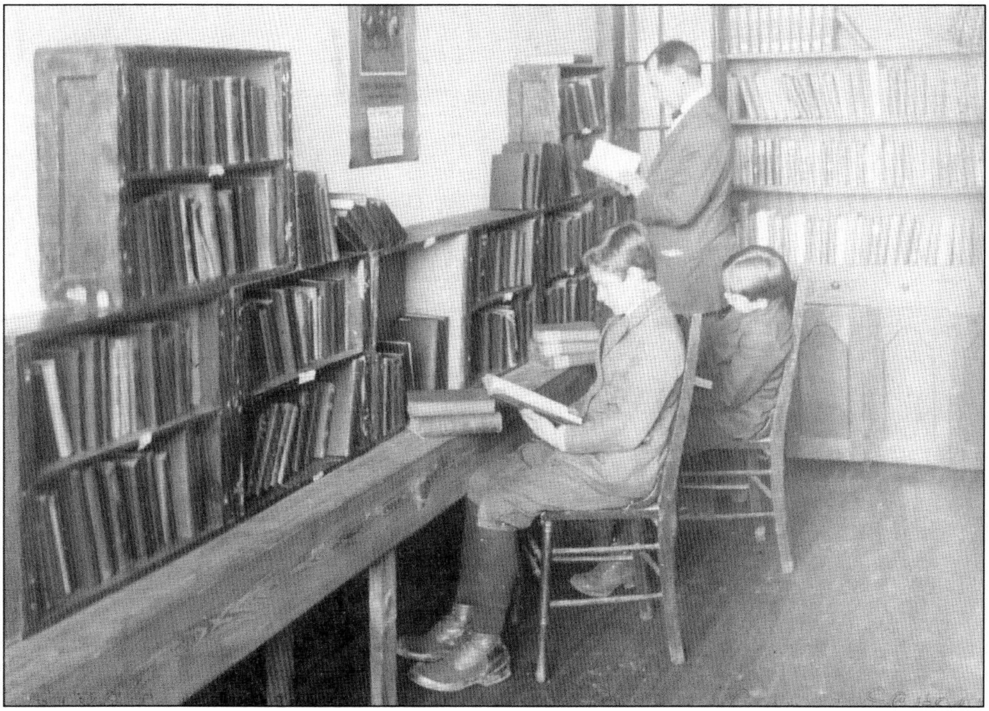

Three early patrons are seen perusing the stacks in the library located in the new high school building in 1910. Education has always been a priority in the community, so the schools had libraries, though there was no public library. On May 4, 1949, the Beech Grove City Council approved measures to establish a nonprofit library and civic auditorium, and fund-raising efforts began.

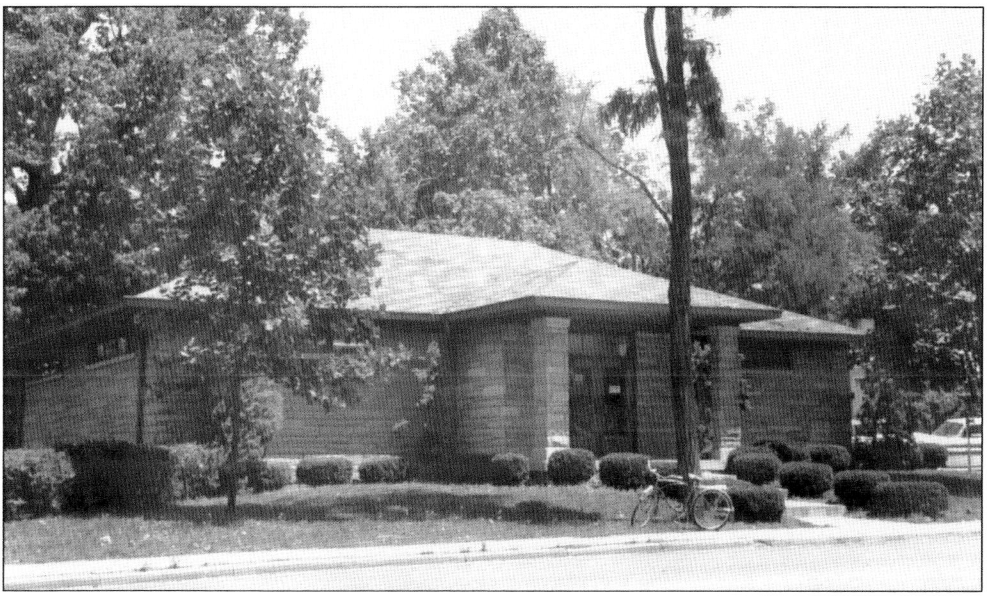

A temporary storefront location opened in 1951, and Lucille White was named the city's first librarian. Within three months, all the available space was occupied. Plans proceeded for relocation to 1102 Main Street, and ground was broken at the new site in October 1952. In a little over a year, the city had a new library that opened to great fanfare on June 1, 1953.

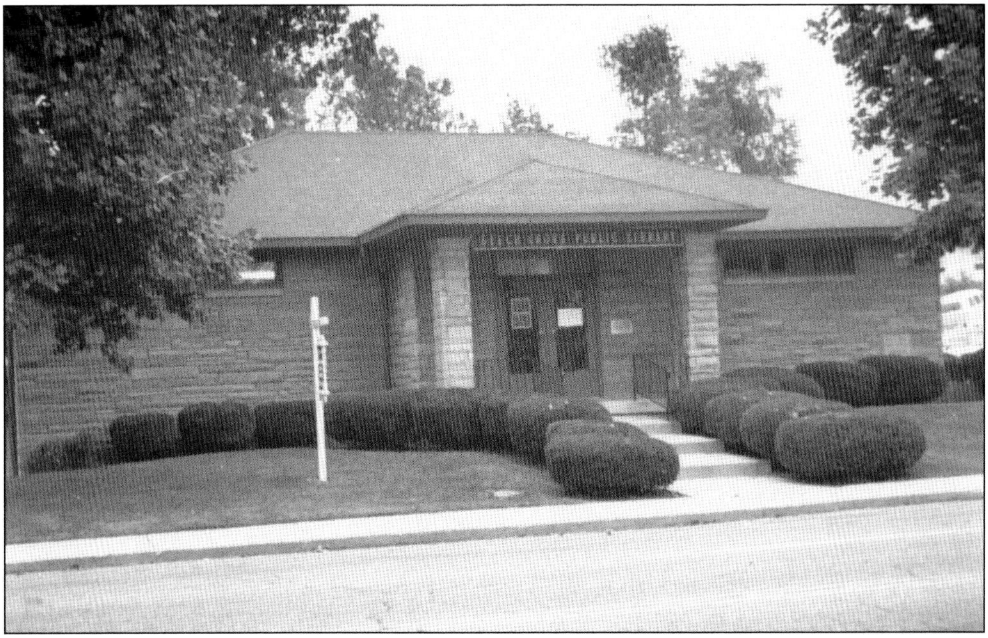

During the 1950s, librarian Helen Hurst continually reported rapidly growing patronage and crowded space. This was no secret to those who frequently visited the facility, and along with civic and government leaders, plans were developed for facility expansion. The two-level addition opened in 1966, but the lower level remained uncompleted until 1972, when a dedicated children's room was finished. The photographs show the main entry to the library (above) and expansion construction (below). The Hein home, built in 1915 by early resident Dr. Adams, was sold to the library for expansion. Over the years, the library's collection has grown significantly from a handful of books, to 9,000 volumes in 1954, to the modern collection at the facility today. Additional improvements have occurred throughout the years, including the addition of a history research room containing the collection of the Beech Grove Historical Society, a café, and a gift shop.

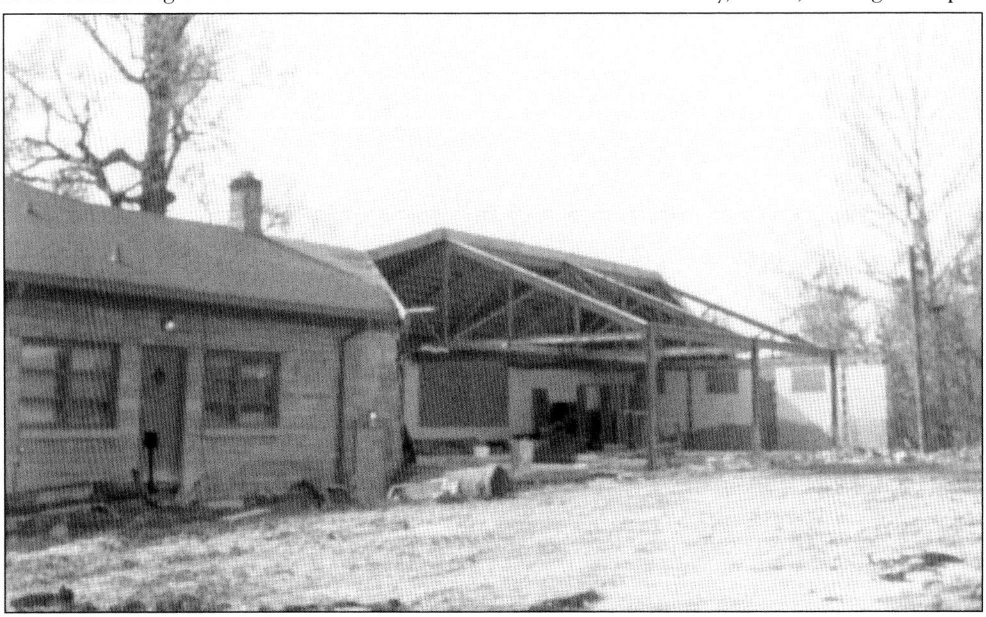

The library was a busy place from the very beginning. This photograph, portraying the excited buzz of patrons, was taken at the opening of the first storefront location in 1951. The checkout desk was hopping, trying to quench everyone's thirst for the latest book. While people still go to the library for a good read, services have expanded to include meeting rooms, educational classes, and computer access and training.

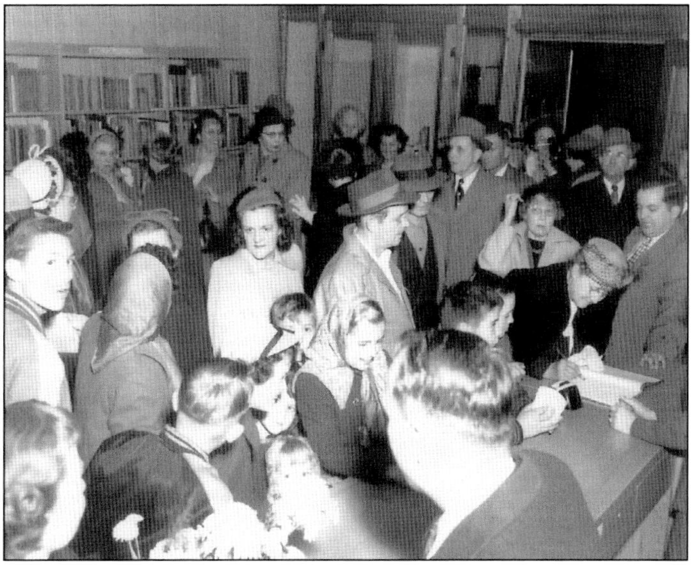

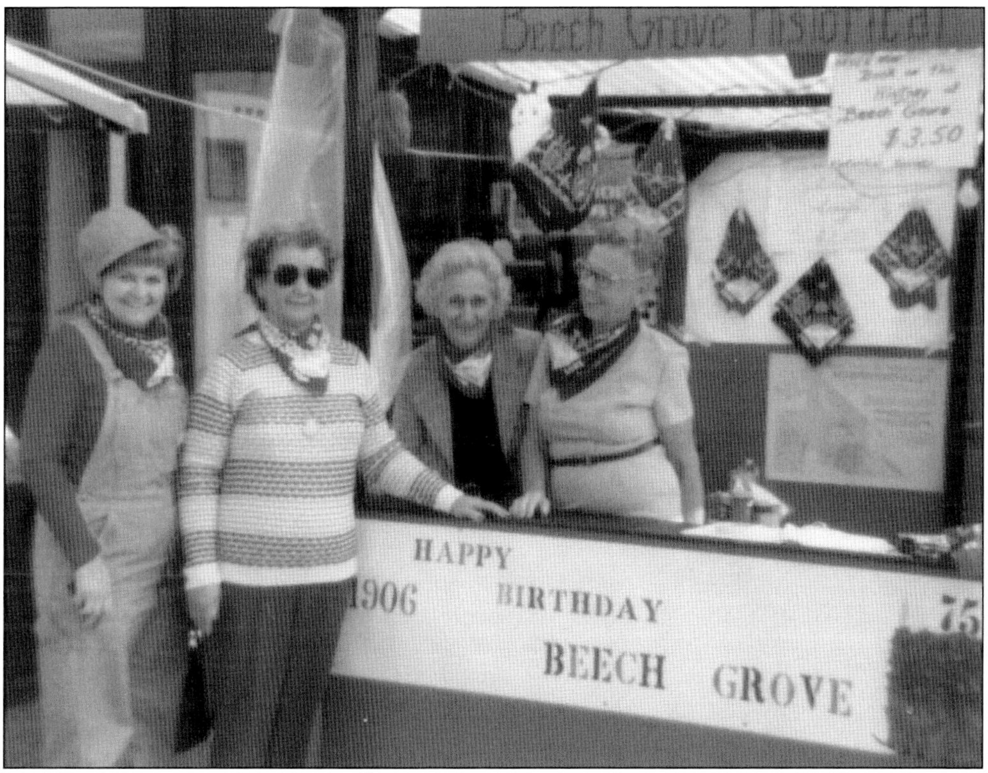

The Beech Grove Historical Society, currently on hiatus, formed in 1978 during a series of community history classes at Beech Grove Middle School. From research and preparation of a formal history for Beech Grove's Diamond Jubilee, including production of a slide presentation named "Beech Roots," the society was built on the efforts of three teachers and 15 students. A reorganization in 1979 brought the society an adult focus.

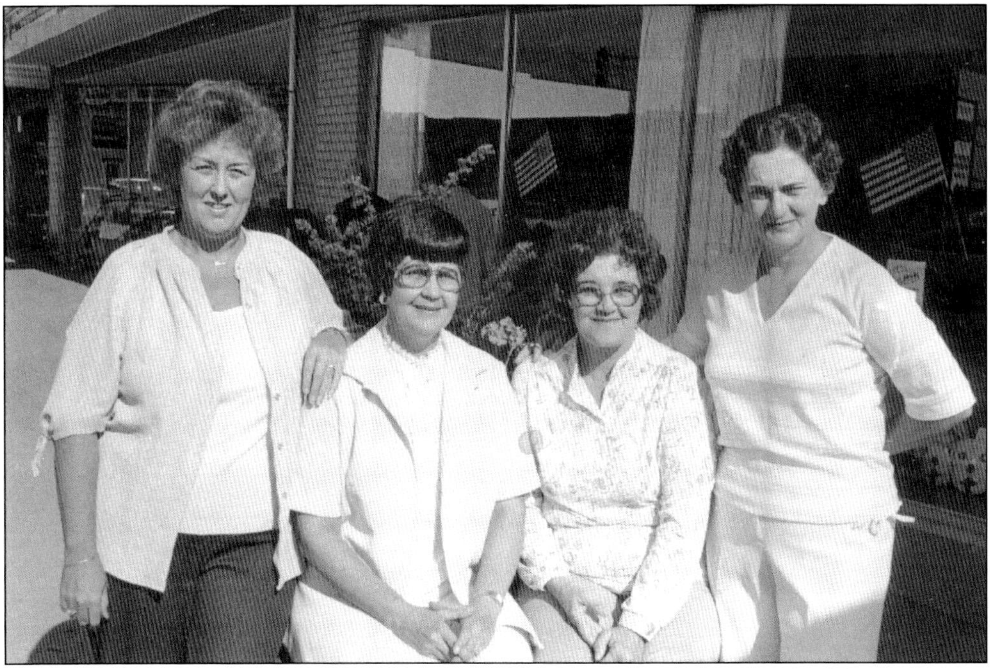

The community initiated efforts to address the concerns, situations, and needs of the city's aging population. Arising from the research efforts of an Indiana University student intern, Mayor Geshwiler appointed a committee to look at enriching the lives of the city's seniors. The Central Indiana Council on Aging awarded Beech Grove a grant for transportation and outreach. With the city's match, the Beech Grove Senior Center became reality in a small room in city hall. In 1976, a permanent building was purchased, and in subsequent years facilities, services, and outreach have expanded. A growing senior center staff is seen above in 1981, and below the center's Beech Grove People Mover goes tooling down the streets of Beech Grove in 1983. The city also purchased an old high school bus in 1978, which was reconditioned and upgraded by employees at the Amtrak Shops as a community service, demonstrating the continuing relationship between the Shops and the city.

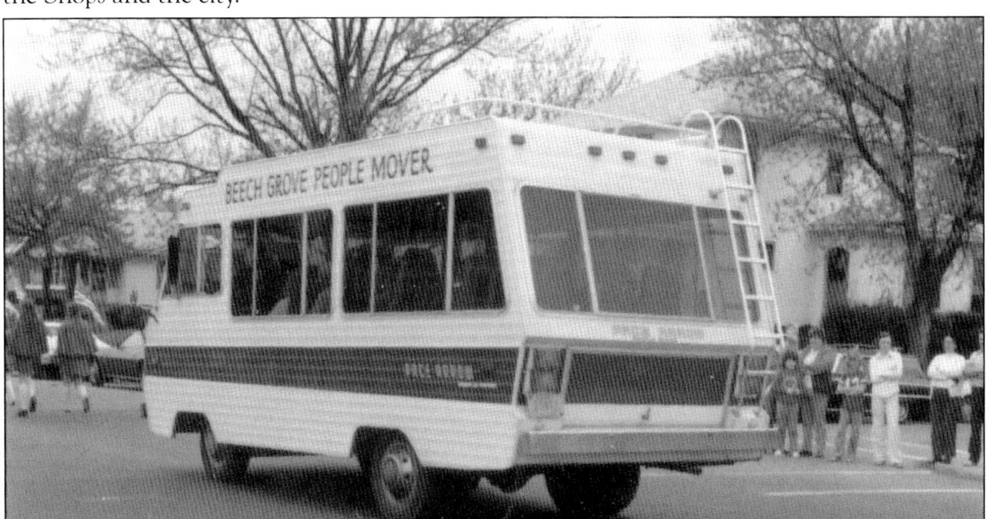

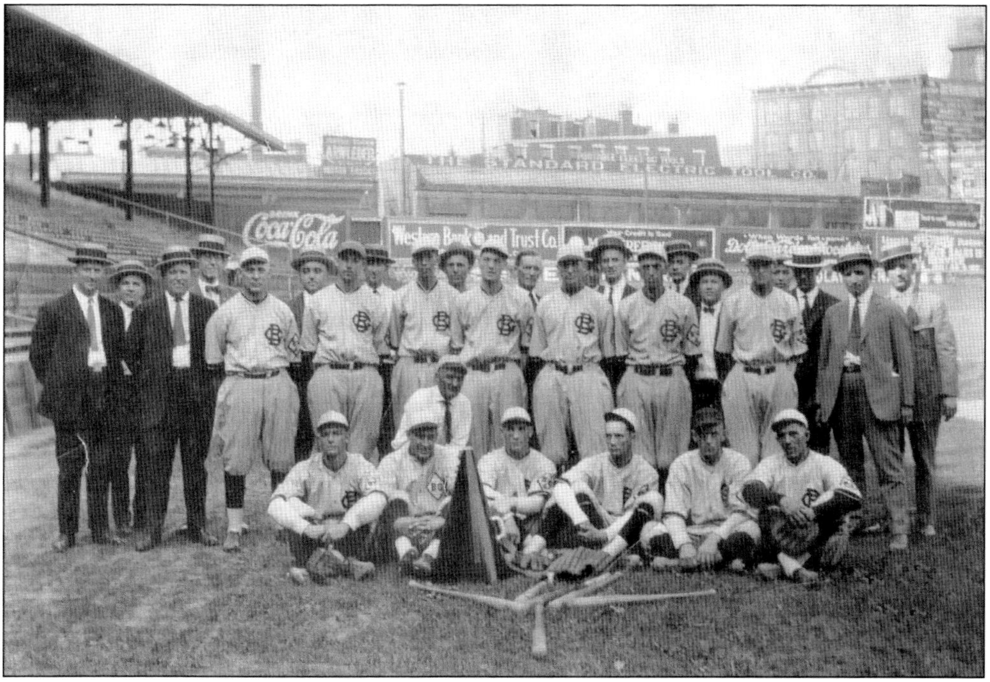

The image above is definitely fitting of the line, "Take me out to the ballgame!" Adding to the quality of life in Beech Grove was the excitement of semiprofessional baseball. While this 1920s photograph of Beech Grove's team was not taken in Beech Grove, the city did have an impressive baseball facility. In 1929, Beech Grove's New York Central Shops baseball team won the league championship, seen below. The popularity and success of Big Four AA baseball is apparent in this display of trophies. Along with basketball court action at the high school and racing and other sports in Indianapolis, Beech Grove sport fans seldom had idle time.

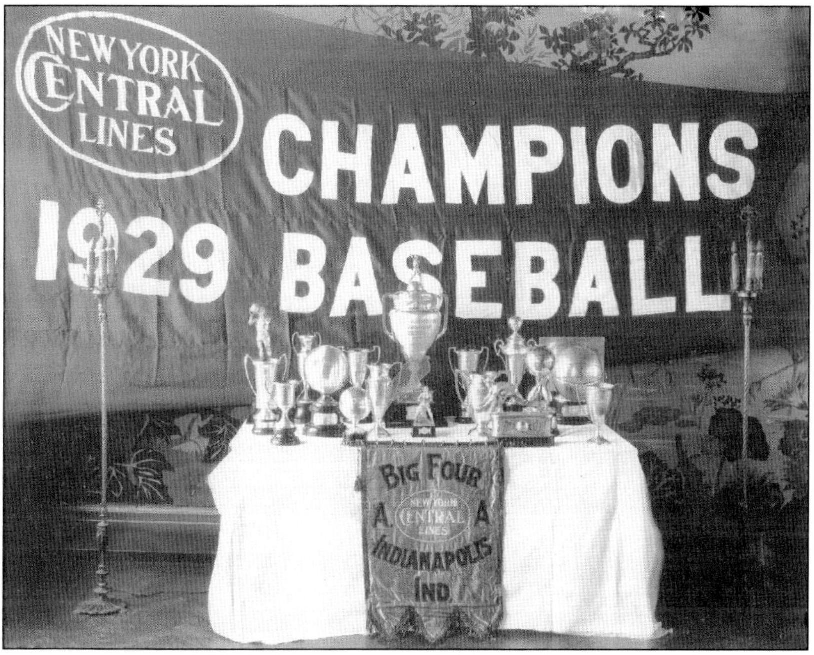

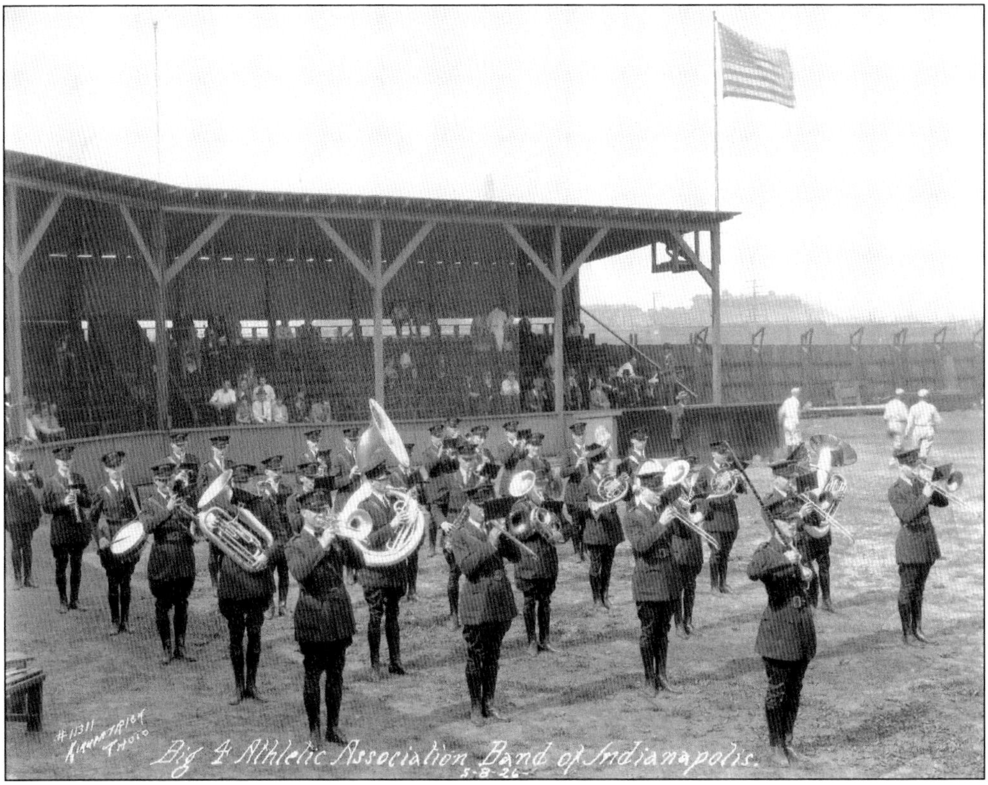

Included in both of these 1920s action and posed images, the Big Four Association Band is seen at the long-gone Beech Grove baseball stadium, which was located between First and Fifth Avenues in the heart of town. The town relied on the railroad band to play at celebrations since Beech Grove, as both a town and a city, never had an organized community band. The community was basically left without a musical performance unit from the time that the Big Four Band folded until the high school band was formed in the 1950s. The Big Four Association Band played throughout Indiana at various parades and events.

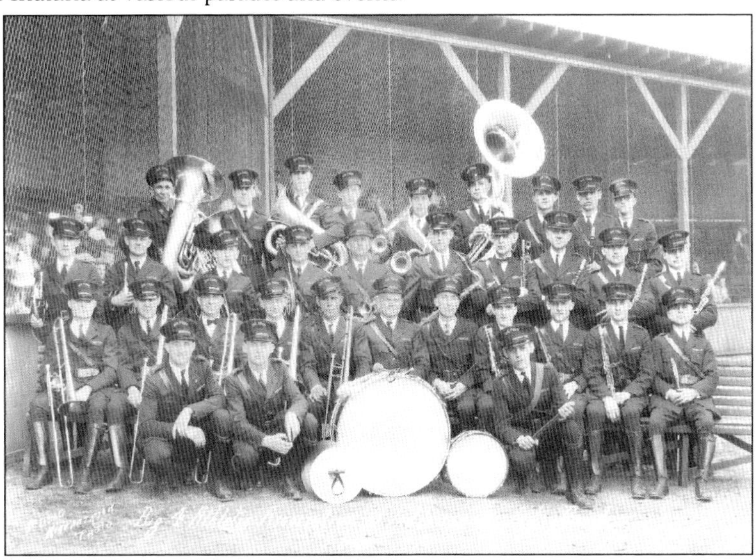

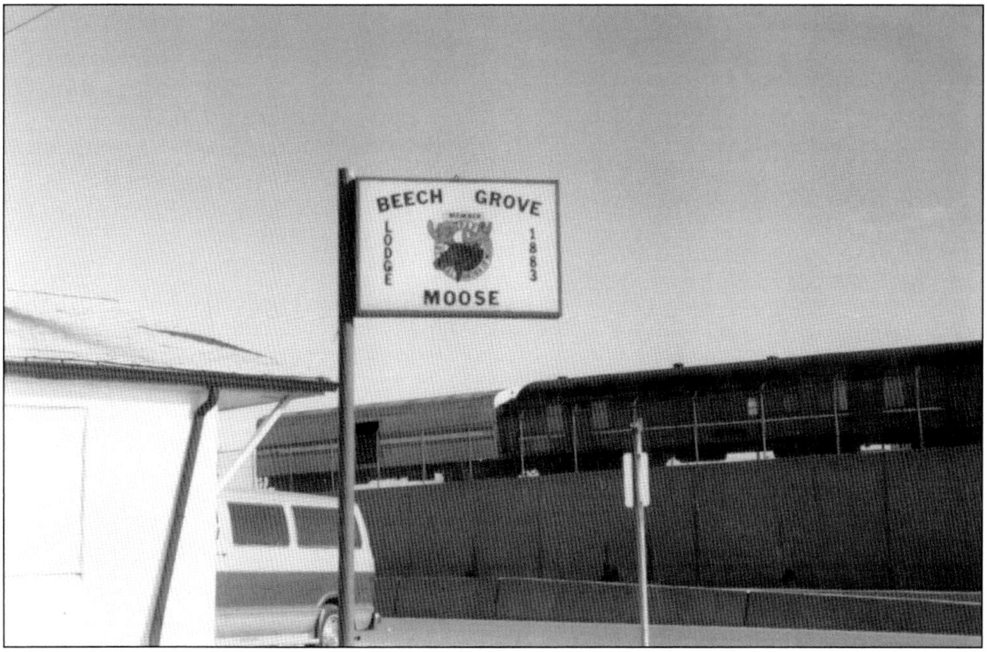

From early meetings at city hall that began on April 27, 1962, the membership of the Beech Grove Moose Lodge grew and built a "home" at 92 South First Avenue in 1970, pictured above. Suffering a devastating fire in 1980, the lodge rebuilt and continues a strong community presence. It is directly across Emerson Avenue from the railroad Shops where many of the members are employed. The Beech Grove Jaycee Civic Center's residential location is pictured in the 1981 photograph below. Through the years, Beech Grove residents have supported several civic organizations, including the Lions Club, Promoter's Club, Art League, Veterans of Foreign Wars, American Legion, Masonic Lodge, and others.

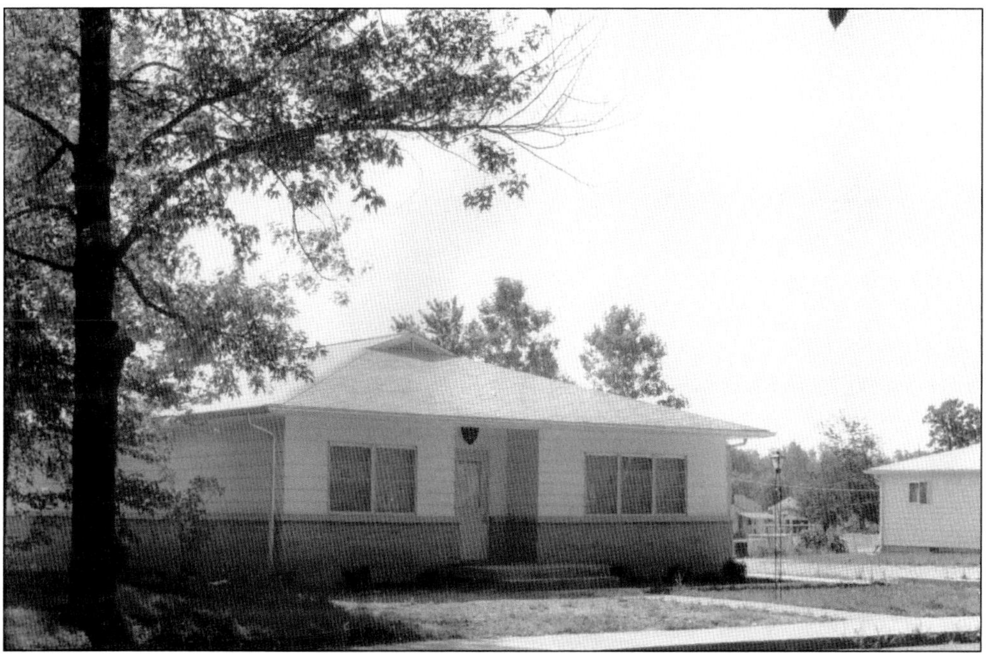

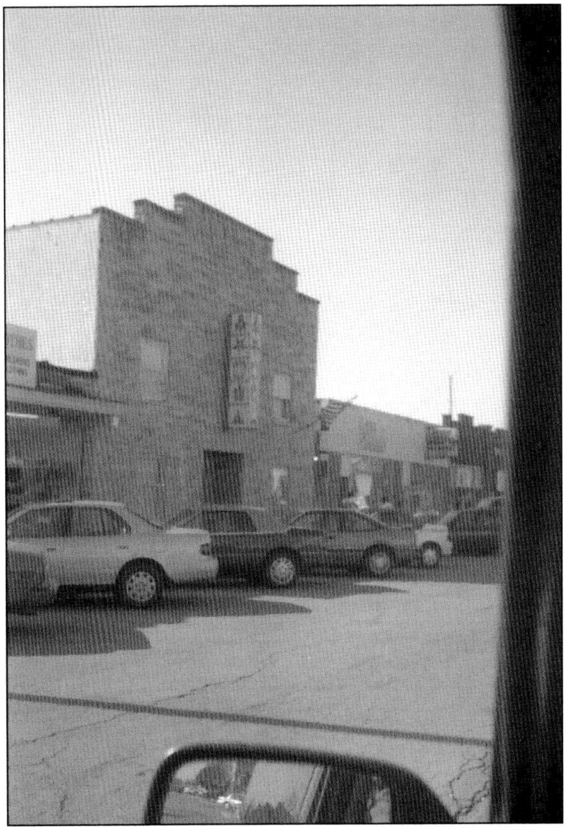

Beech Grove's Masonic Lodge, the first major civic organization in town, was chartered in 1913. The present site (left) was built in 1941 in the midst of increasing membership and became one of the larger brotherhoods in Indiana. Gerald Prather, contractor for the 617 Main Street building, was the first lodge Mason to attain the Master Mason degree at the temple. Pres. Harry Truman (below, center of the front row) visited on October 15, 1948, after his election whistle-stop speeches in Kokomo and at the War Memorial in Indianapolis. The father of Seaman Donald Bauermeister mentioned to Truman that his son would be conferred the third degree of Freemasonry in Beech Grove that night and invited the president to attend. Much to the father's surprise, Truman arrived to participate in the ceremonies. This was the first time a U.S. president had visited an Indiana Masonic lodge.

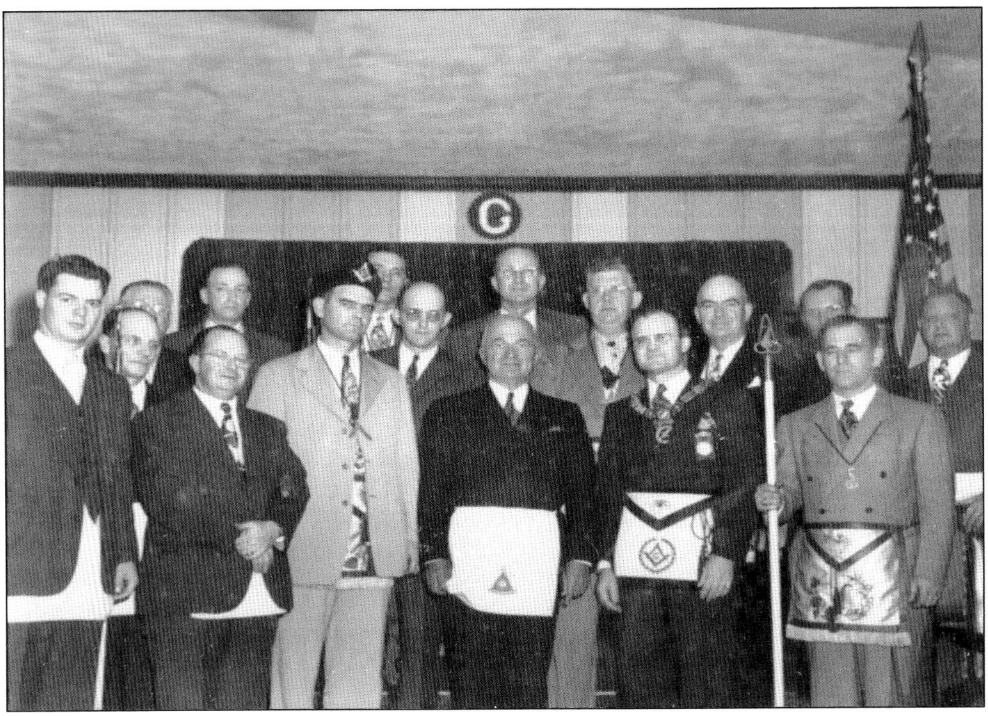

Five

Beyond the Train Station

While the lure of employment at the Shops has been instrumental in the growth and identity of Beech Grove, the true face of the city is found in the local businesses and residents of the community. Encompassing 4.3 square miles of Marion County, at an elevation that would meet the top of the Soldiers and Sailors Monument in Indianapolis, Beech Grove remains an independent and proud community of about 6,000 households. The residents enjoy clean, safe streets, bountiful employment, and the nearby amenities of one of the country's largest cities—all while living in a small-town oasis. The landscapes are lush and mature, residents are friendly, and Main Street is picturesque and welcoming.

Beyond the railroad industry, across Emerson Avenue, Beech Grove remains a testament to progressive, planned living. Not particularly wealthy, problems resulting from growth were solved by an involved community that worked together for the common good. If ever there were an American city that defined middle-class America, Beech Grove would surely contend.

Amazingly self-contained, the city provides all the necessities of life within the partiality of four Marion County townships: Perry, Franklin, Center, and Warren. A resident could be born, attend school, begin a family, recreate, receive health care attention, age, die, and be buried—all without ever leaving the city limits.

Yet the heart of any city remains its business district. While later years brought the addition of large chain stores, most of which dot Emerson Avenue and the area around the I-465 exit ramps, the city retains its charm through the local businesses that still call Beech Grove home. Nightlife meant a movie at one of three theaters, or maybe a few games of bowling, a stroll along Beech Creek, or a nightcap at the Grove. The pace here is slower, speeding is not tolerated, and the streets from Indianapolis change names and address numbering at the Beech Creek city limits, signaling to visitors that they are someplace different.

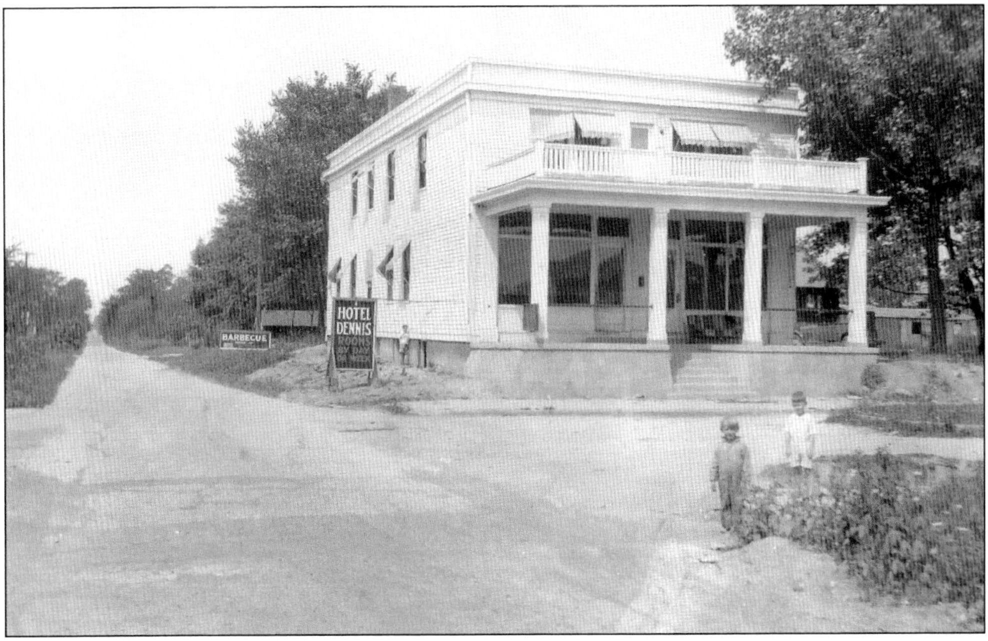

In this 1930 view of Albany Street, looking west from Fourth Avenue, the Hotel Dennis stands alone to welcome travelers and workers in need of a room, rented by the day or week. The sign to the rear of the building advertises a barbeque dinner. The area surrounding the boardinghouse depicts very little development. Current hoteliers in the area include Red Roof Inn, La Quinta, and other national chains.

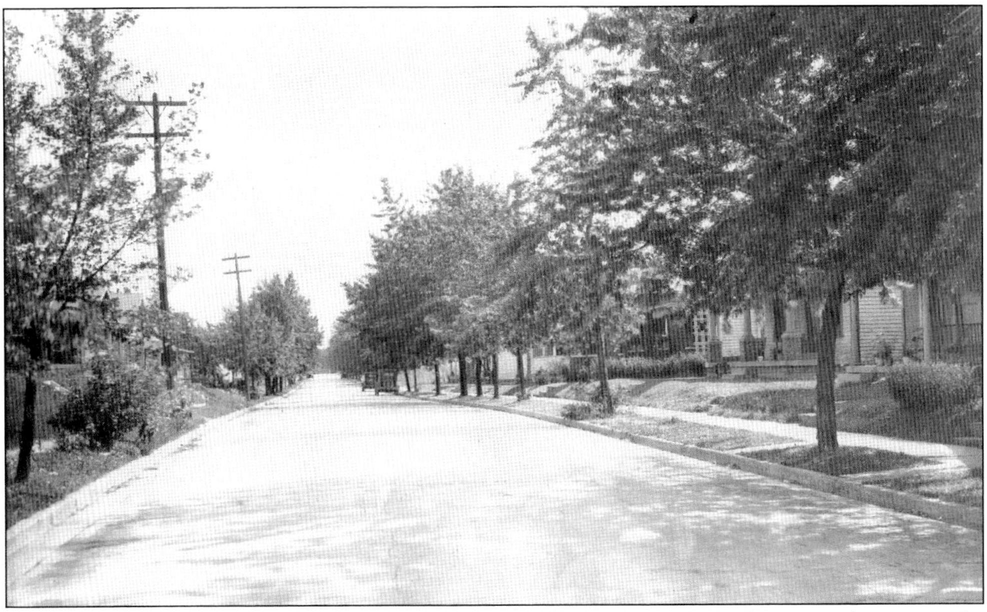

In this 1930 view of Fourth Avenue, looking south from Main Street, the quiet character of a typical Beech Grove neighborhood is evident. A little more than a decade earlier, this street was dirt and development was mostly in the planning stages. While housing was not elaborate, sidewalks were laid—an amenity usually reserved for pricier planned developments—and trees were saved whenever possible, giving the landscape a mature quality.

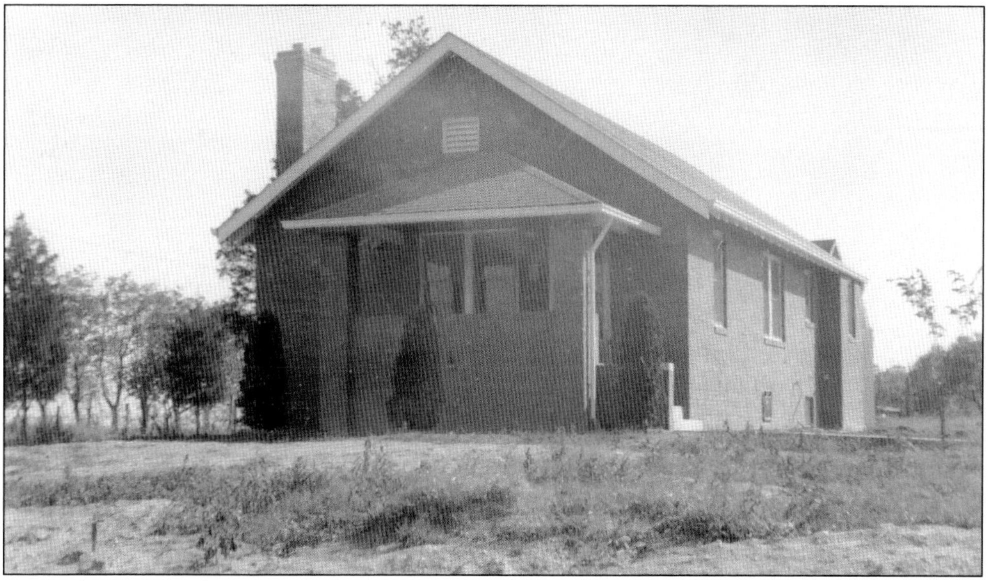

Leo and Lena Besselman were the first couple in Beech Grove to take advantage of newly created, government-backed Federal Housing Administration loans. These loans made the American dream of home ownership much more achievable, and the simplified financing was another motivator for young families to seek a mortgage. Beech Grove had the jobs that provided adequate income to make house payments.

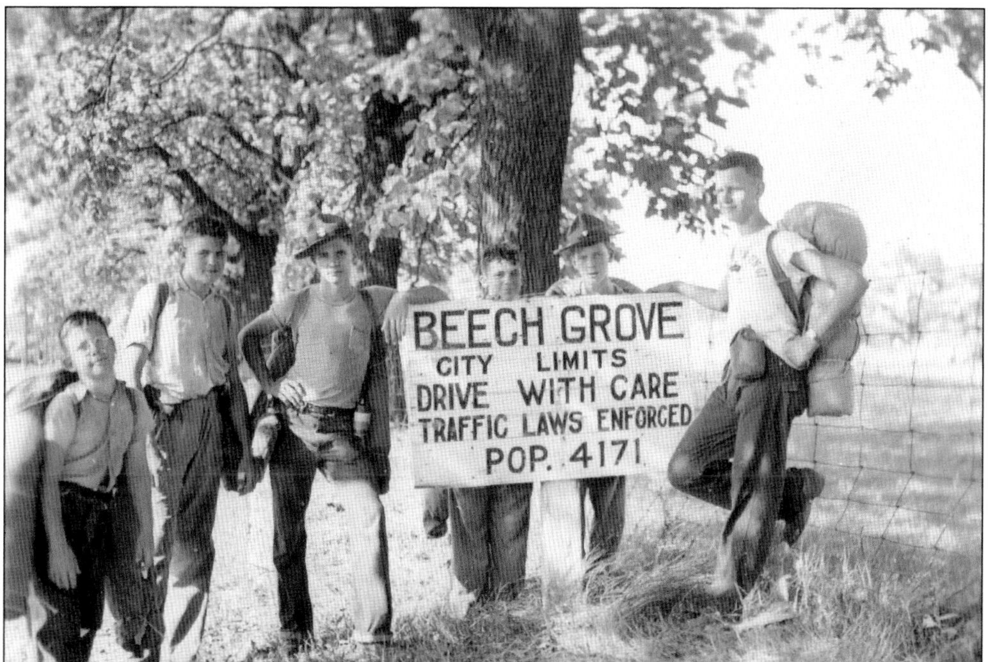

Boy Scouts fictitiously guard entry into Beech Grove. This 1942 photograph shows, from left to right, Jim Greenfield, Bill Chappel, Dick Greenfield, and Bill Do taking a short break on a sunny day. While this sign is hand-stenciled and simply states, "Drive with care. Traffic laws enforced," it is a message that rings true to this day. Locals know better than to speed.

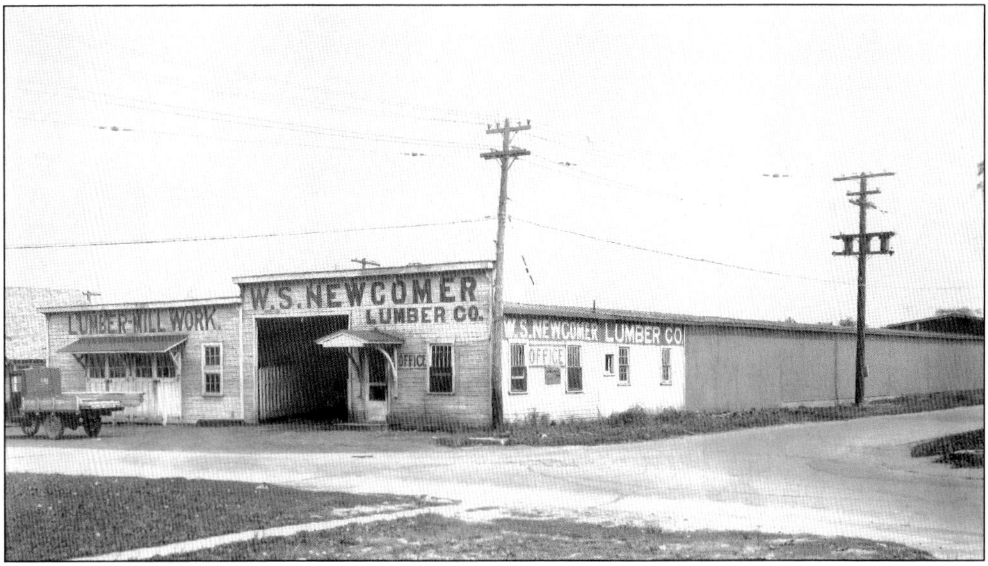

Newcomer Lumber and Millworks has been a fixture in the Beech Grove community for decades. The business is seen in 1930 (above) and 1964 (below) at the same, albeit remodeled, location. The Enco Service Station, with expensive 30¢-per-gallon gas, neighbored Newcomer through the 1960s. The lumberyard's initial success was due to business from the Shops and, in subsequent years, the accompanying residential growth. Integrated into the community, Newcomer's longevity can be attributed to business savvy in being cognizant of the changing customer base and needs, partnered with tradition. If a person needs lumber in Beech Grove, the answer is Newcomer.

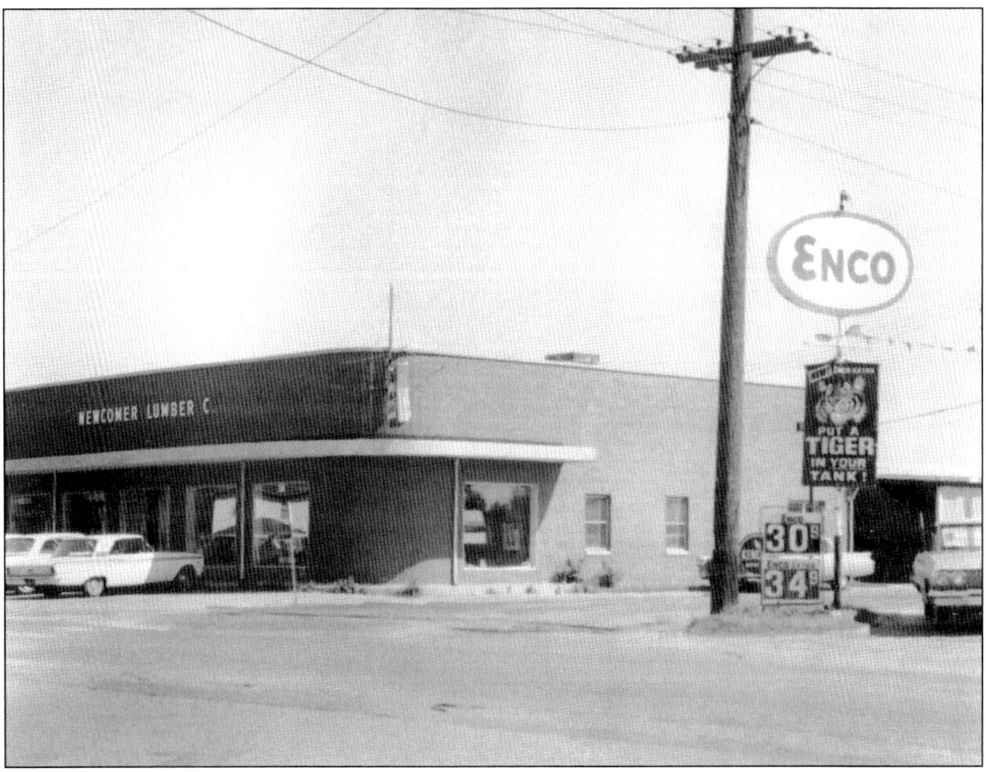

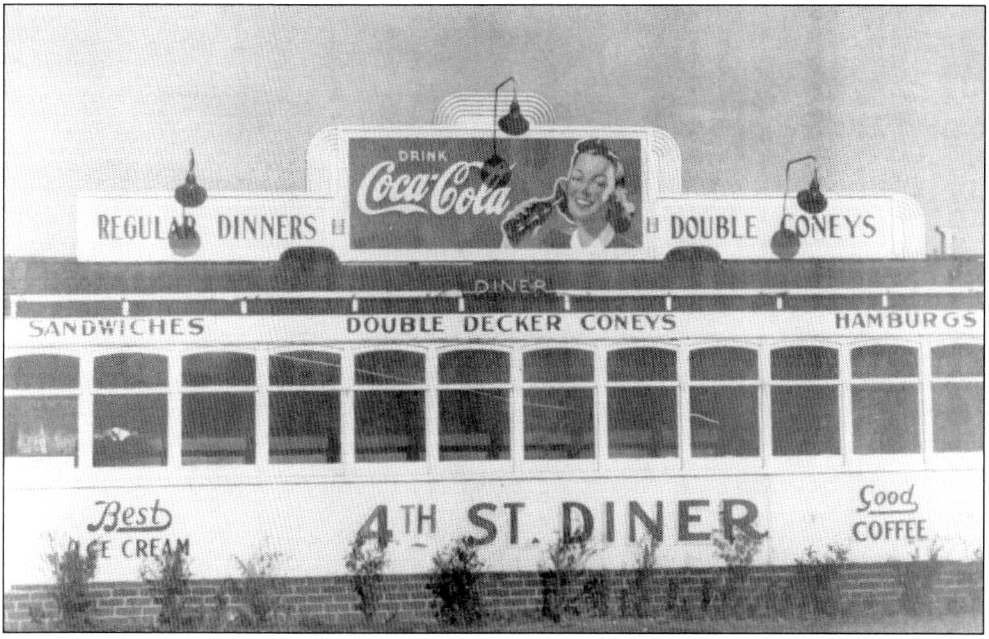

Inexpensive food was served with a smile at the Fourth Street Diner. The signs promise the "best" ice cream, "good" coffee, Coca-Cola, and the diner's famous double-decker coney hot dogs, but regular, homemade dinners were also on the menu. Before McDonald's, Burger King, Taco Bell, and other fast-food giants nestled close to city limits, small local eateries fed the hungry city.

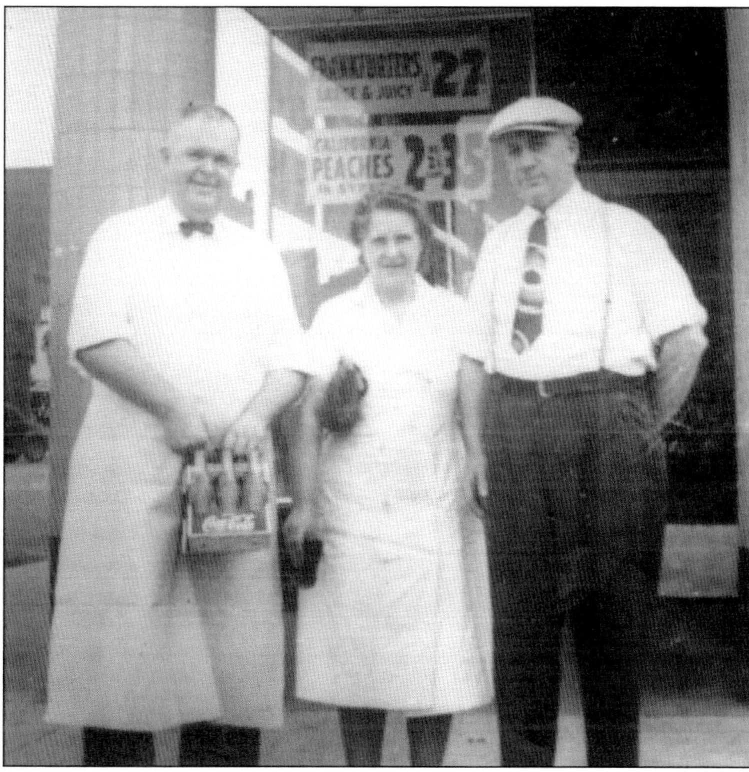

Dressed, groomed, and ready for work, Ray Warrick (right) visits with Marie and Otto Tulley. Ray had a snack bar at Sixth Avenue and Main Street, while Otto managed the downtown Standard Food Market. For the most part, local merchants knew each other and their customers by name well into the 1950s.

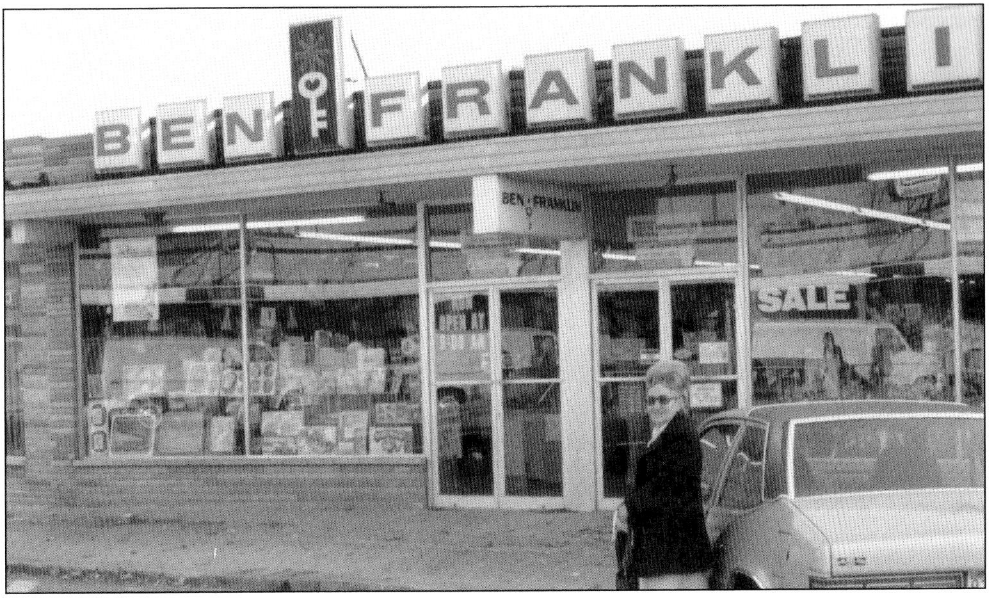

What small town would be complete without a five-and-dime store? Beech Grove had a branch of the nationally known Ben Franklin dime store chain. The store was alive and well as seen in this 1964 photograph. Manager Mike Brown stocked the shelves deep and also special-ordered merchandise for his regular customers. He never wanted to forfeit business to larger Indianapolis retailers.

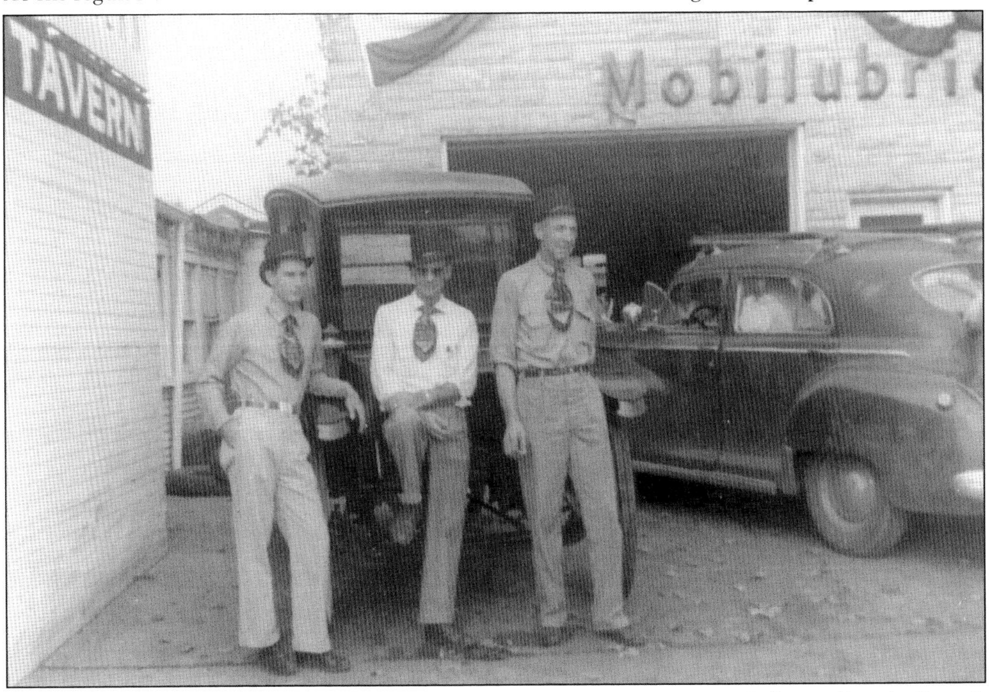

Dressed like gangsters for fun, these gentlemen are resting against a truck during Beech Grove's 50th anniversary celebration. The Mobile station in the background stood at Fourth Avenue and Main Street and competed with several downtown independent operators. The passage of time saw Shell and Speedway stations make their way to the city's outskirts, and the independent service stations slowly vanished.

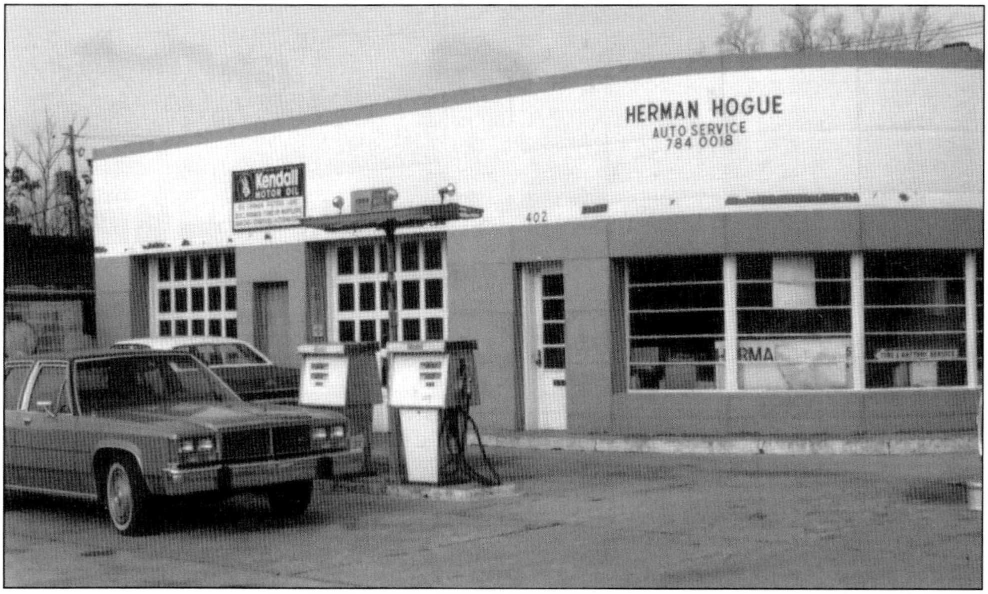

Herman Hogue Auto Service was both a successful gas and service station and a community landmark. The station (above) always appeared busy, and often Herman Hogue (right) personally pumped gas for his customers. In addition to a unique curved building and a location at the main entry to downtown, the service station had another one-of-a-kind feature in Hogue himself. He was friendly, knew no strangers, was well liked, and is fondly remembered by local residents. His business did not have the quickest, flashiest service, or the least expensive gas in town, and his auto bays were not spotlessly clean, but the charm and character of the station, and the reason people returned, rested with its namesake.

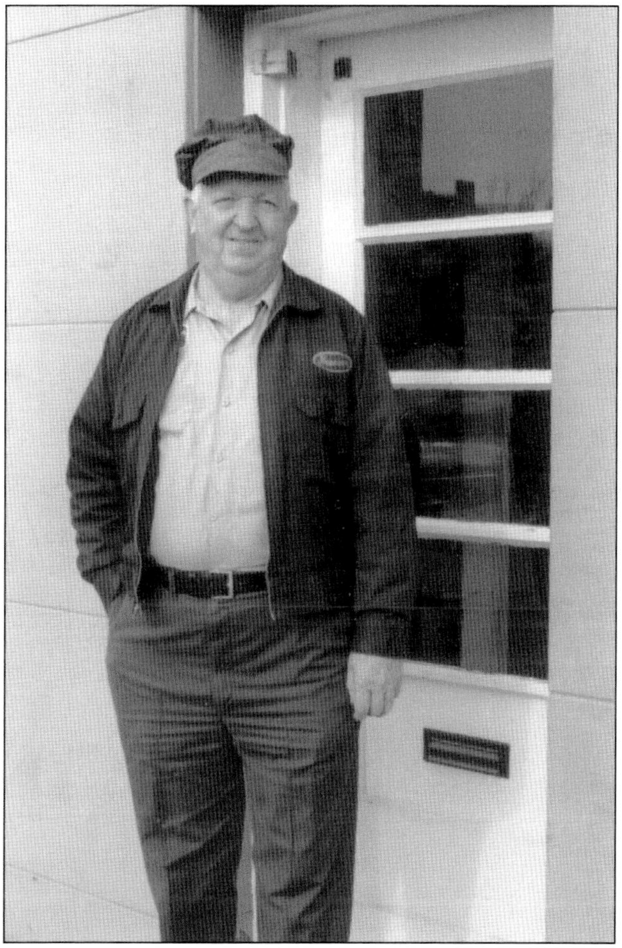

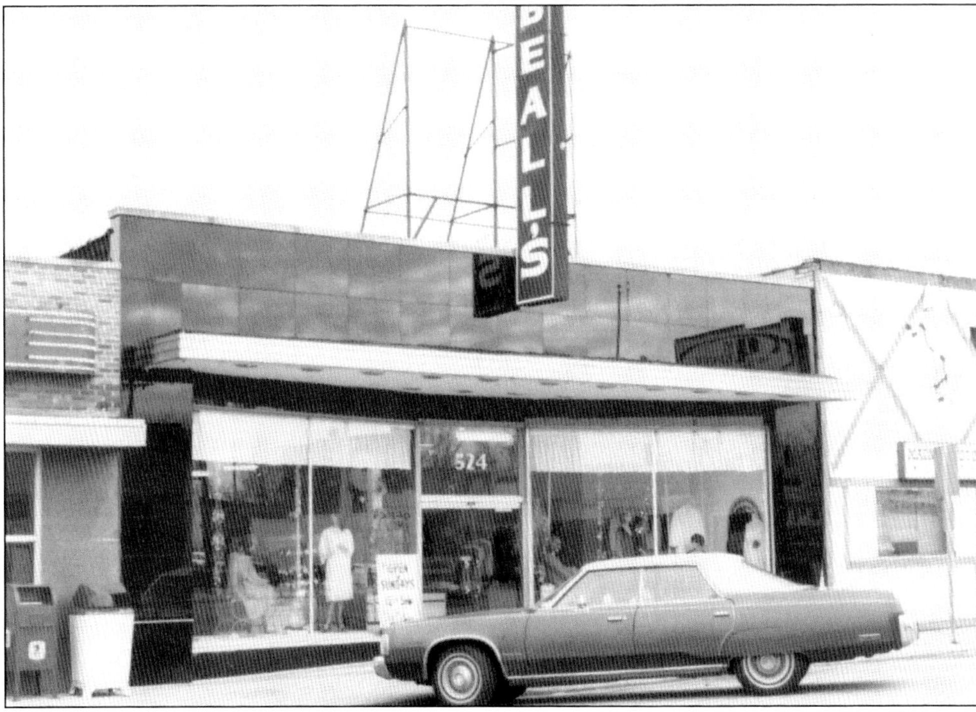

Shopping in Beech Grove was a welcome treat for natives. Being close to Indianapolis, the Main Street stores received additional business from big city customers. Beall's clothing store (above) was a popular spot for family apparel, while Sally's (below) provided fine women's outfits and elaborate dresses. Popular Main Street merchants through the years included Star Christian Supplies, Beech Grove Meat Market, Eckstein Shoes and Repairing, Key Auto Parts, and a host of others. Main Street was also the home to various service businesses, including Little and Sons Funeral Home, several service stations, and Merchant's National Bank, located at Seventh Avenue and Main Street.

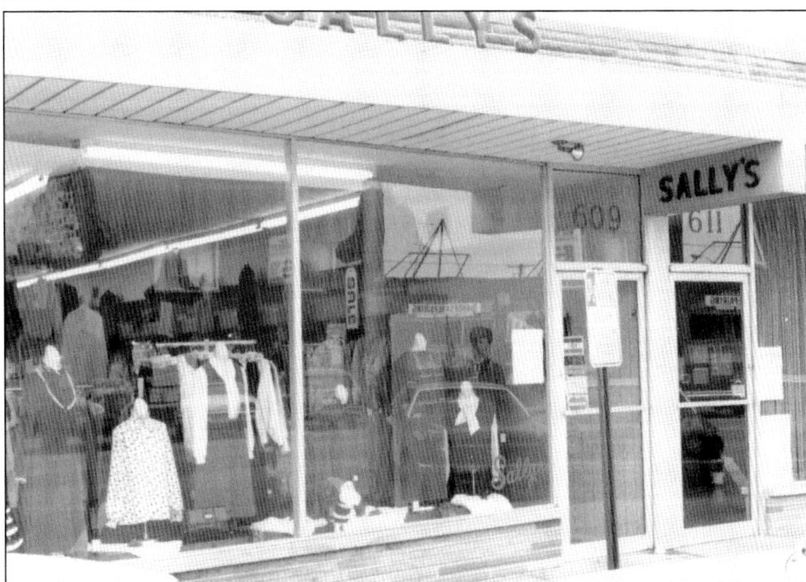

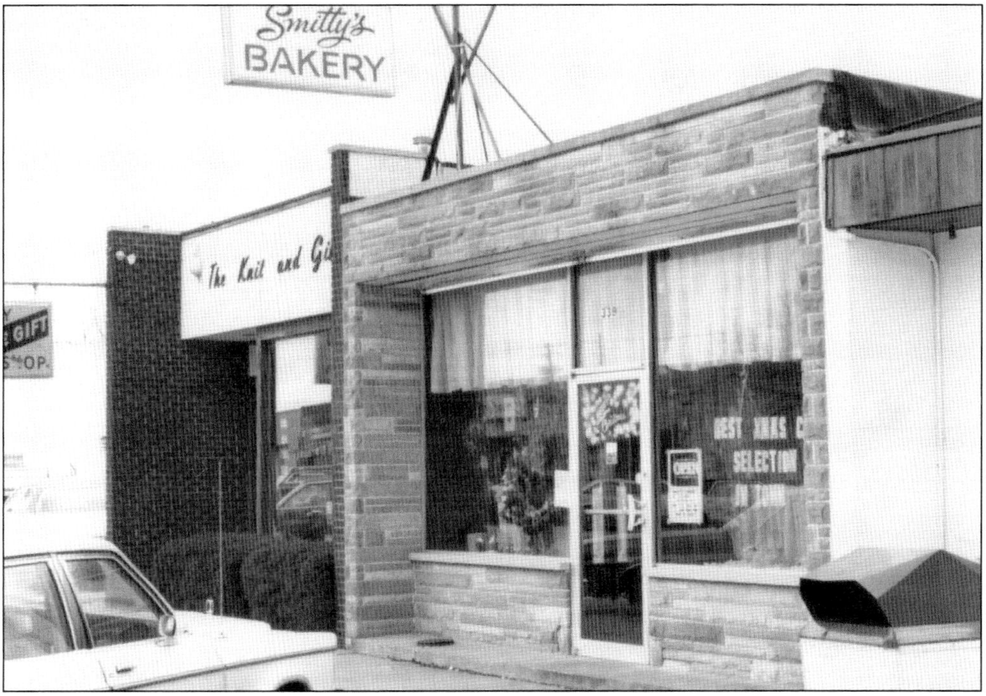

Smitty's Bakery, located at 339 Main Street, was another Beech Grove institution. Jack Smith began the business on a shoestring budget, armed with a strong work ethic and secret recipes. People drove from miles around to savor a pastry or bite into a chocolate chip cookie. Smith's son Mike eventually took over the business from his father, expanded operations, and then eventually shuttered the doors.

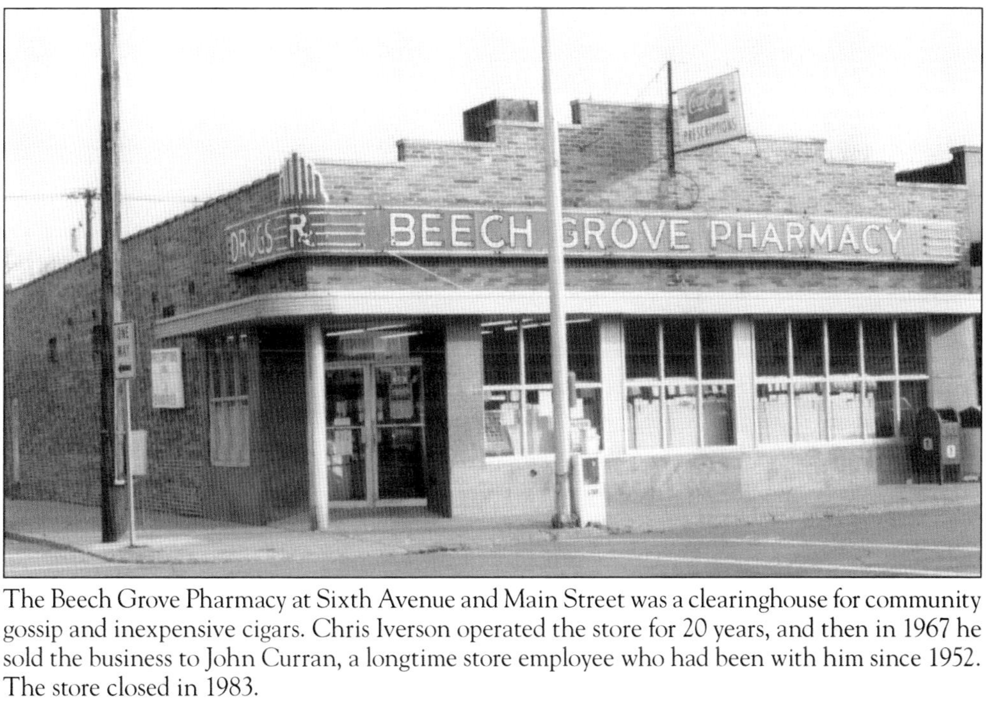

The Beech Grove Pharmacy at Sixth Avenue and Main Street was a clearinghouse for community gossip and inexpensive cigars. Chris Iverson operated the store for 20 years, and then in 1967 he sold the business to John Curran, a longtime store employee who had been with him since 1952. The store closed in 1983.

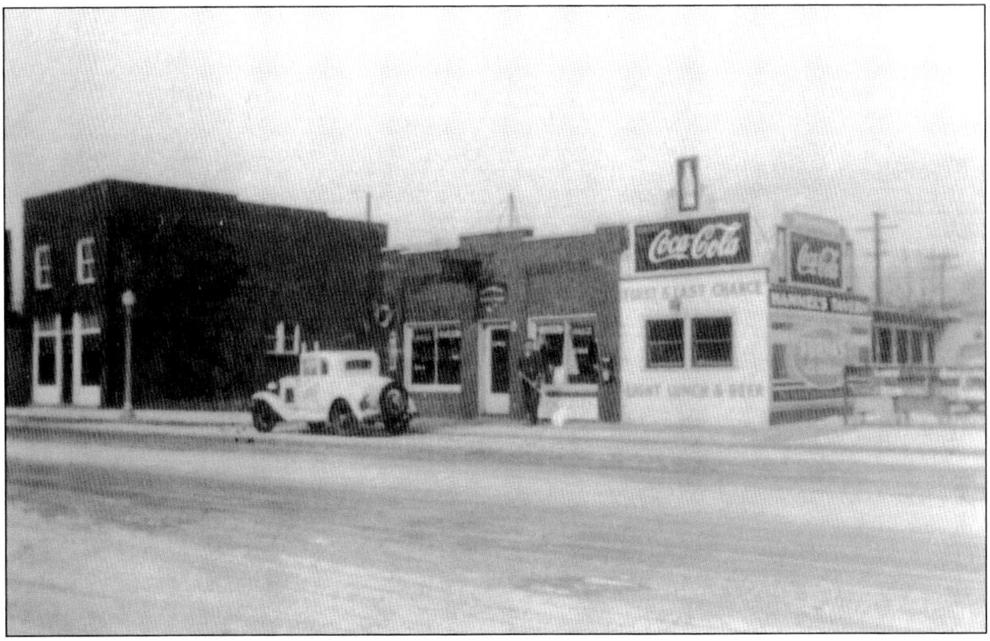

Pictured above is Hammel's Tavern around 1930, located next to Brennan's Barber Shop at Fourth Avenue and Main Street. It was a Beech Grove tradition. Over the years, the tavern was also home to a confectionery but settled on spirits for livelihood. In a 1956 photograph seen below, Hammel's is decorated in celebration of Beech Grove's 50th anniversary. Aside from the decorative flags, the tavern remained virtually unchanged through the years. Under family ownership, the bar was a true part of the community, actively supporting civic events and initiatives. Through the years, Hammel's Tavern served many area patrons their first legal alcoholic drink.

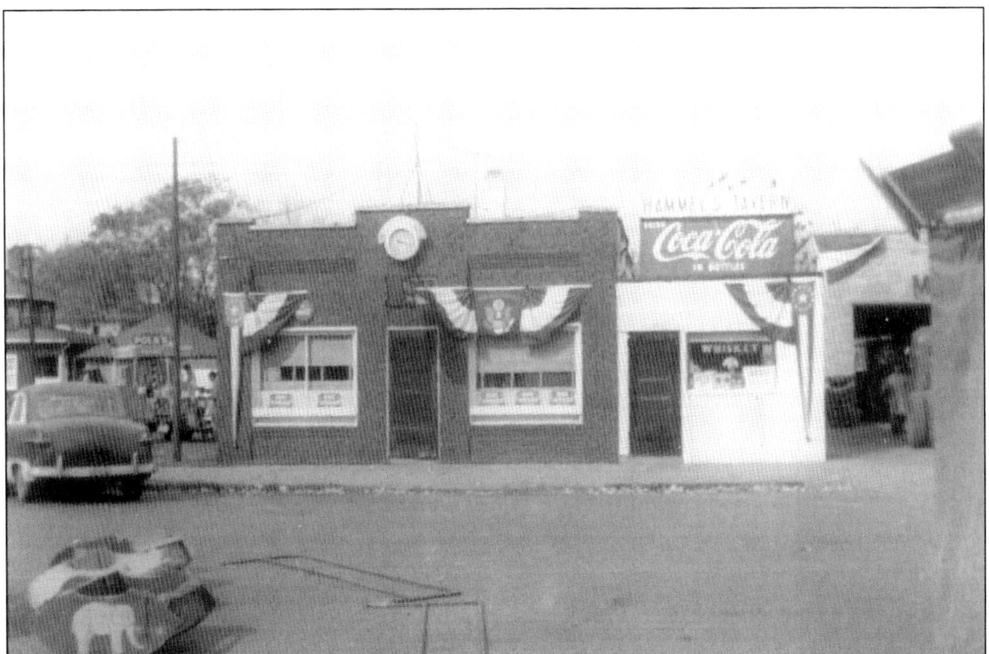

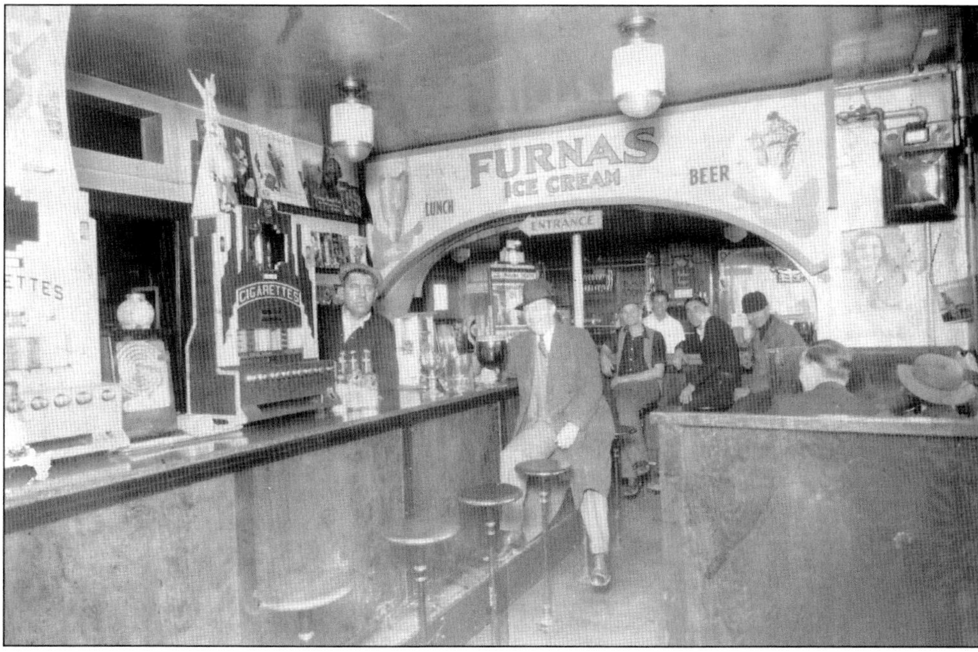

Photographed here is the interior of Hammel's Tavern as it appeared in the late 1930s. Known as a confectionery, patrons could get a pack of smokes and a shot of whiskey with their Furnas ice cream. Bartender Bob Spargur is ready for action behind the bar, while proprietor Omer Hammel sits and chats.

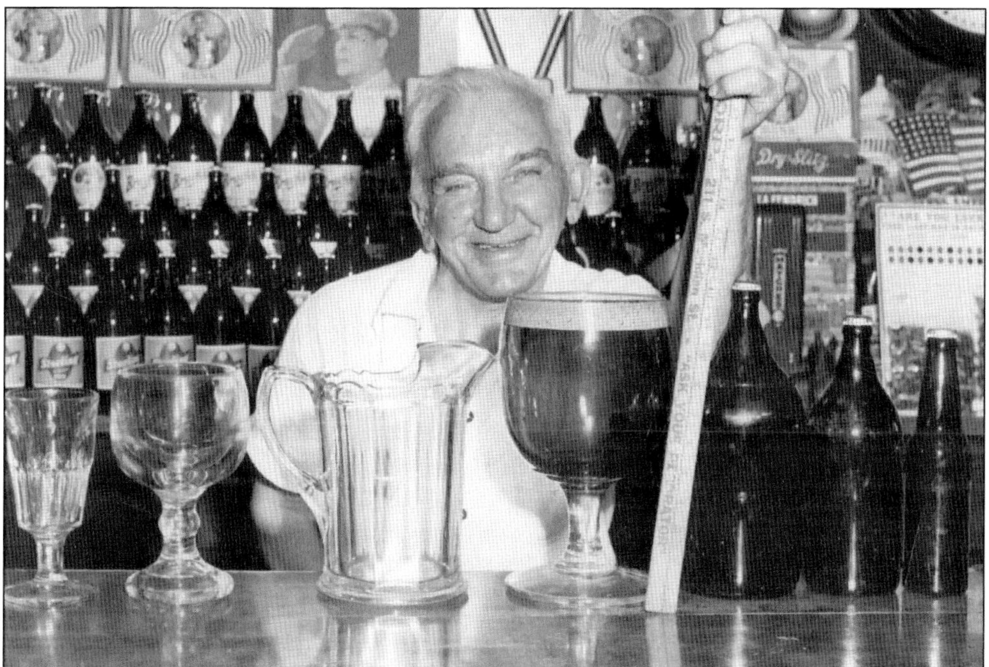

Guess who is at the beer tap? During World War II, Hammel's was known for serving the biggest glasses of beer in town. Seen here are traditional beer glasses from nearby competitors. Even a beer pitcher is no match for Hammel's goliath goblet of brew, always served with a smile.

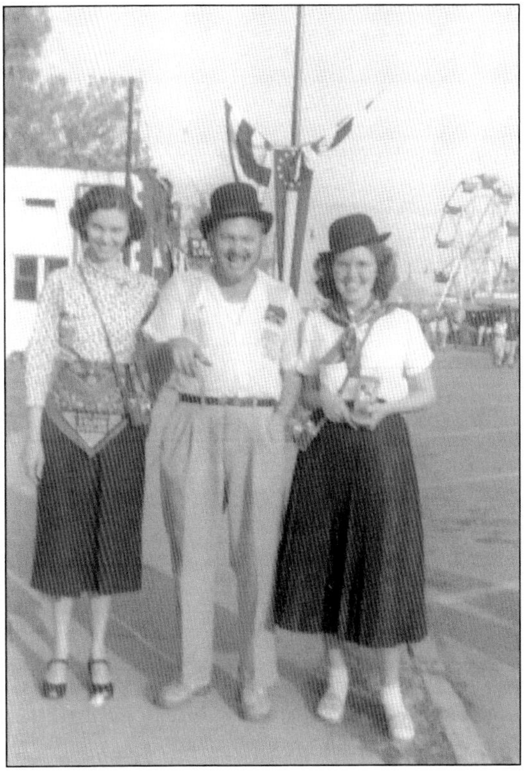

Beech Grove knows how to throw a party! The city's 50th anniversary celebration, complete with midway rides, food vendors, music, and merriment, provided residents in attendance with many fond memories. From left to right, volunteers Dolly Shockley, Walt Zignaver, and Virginia Hammel are ready to work serving the anticipated crowds.

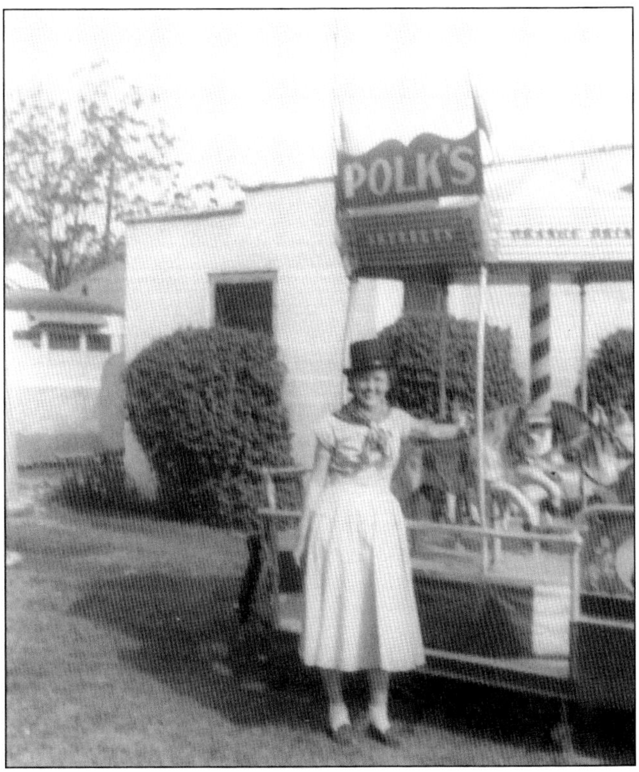

Virginia Hammel is standing in front of Polk's merry-go-round concession at Beech Grove's 50th anniversary celebration, demonstrating the Hammel family's continual commitment to the community. This ride was one of many brought to the event by various independent contractors. The historic event was the largest in Beech Grove's history and attracted people from across the region.

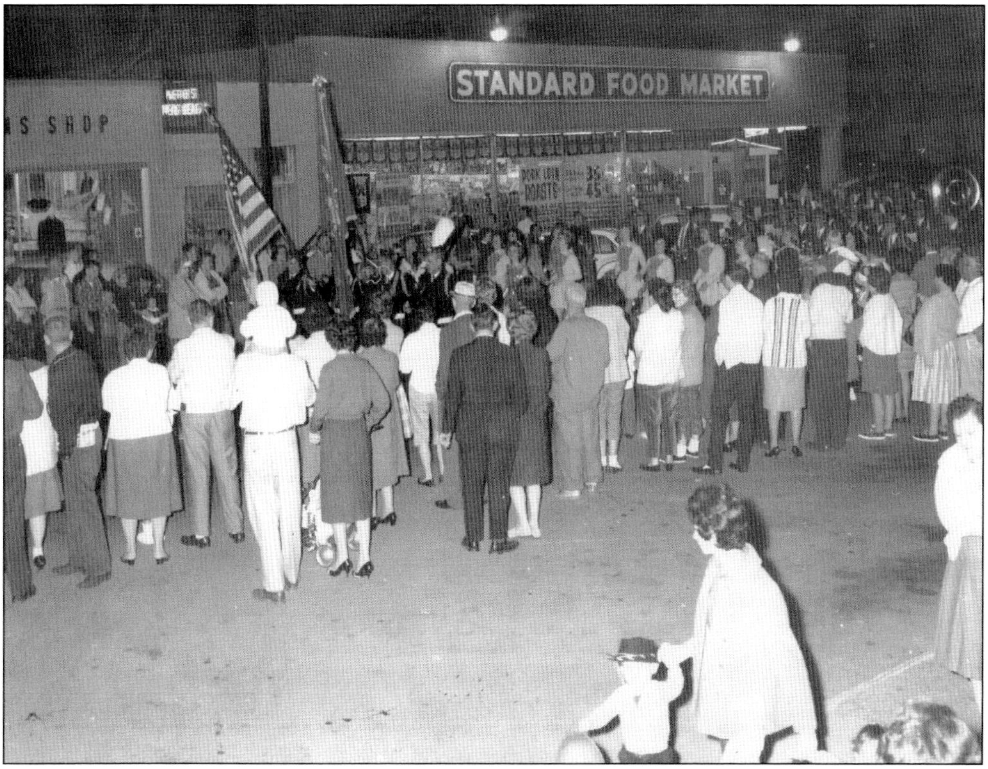

Festivities lasted well into the night. Usually downtown was quiet after the workday, but on this very special occasion, the band played as darkness fell upon the crowd gathered in front of Main Street's Standard Food Market and other businesses. The event drew entertainment, and accompanying crowds, to the excited city.

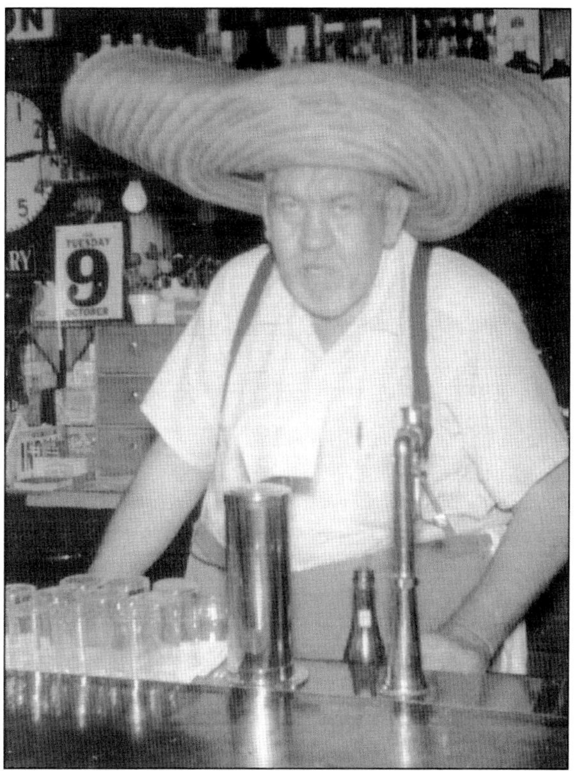

It was October 9, 1956, and Beech Grove's 50th anniversary celebration at Hammel's Tavern was definitely the place to be. Hammel's famous bartender looks to be enjoying himself in suspenders and a sombrero. While the event was primarily a family affair, the man behind the bar confirms the event offered something for everyone.

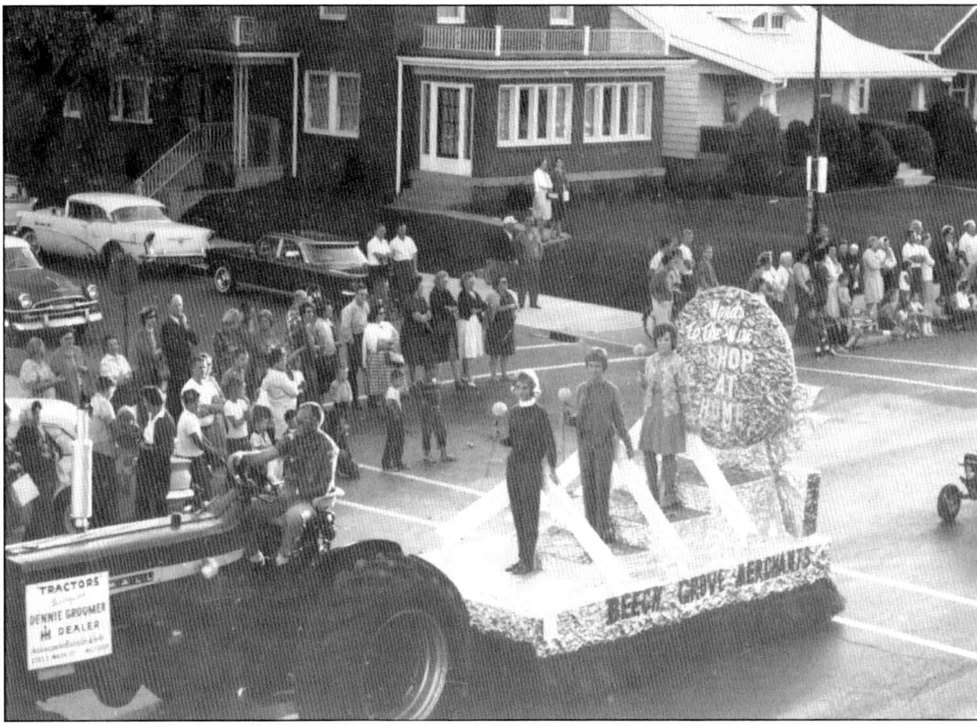

The Beech Grove Promoter's Club has sponsored an annual fall festival along Main Street since 1959. This mid-1960s photograph shows the Beech Grove Merchant's float, promoting the message, "Shop at Home." If the float did not get the attention of the crowd, the three attractive ladies holding lollipops surely did. The Promoter's Club also sponsors the city's annual Fourth of July celebration in Sarah Bolton Park. The much-anticipated annual event brings several thousand spectators to Beech Grove for picnicking and fun during the day and an elaborate fireworks display after dark. Year after year, this annual celebration remains Beech Grove's most attended one-day event.

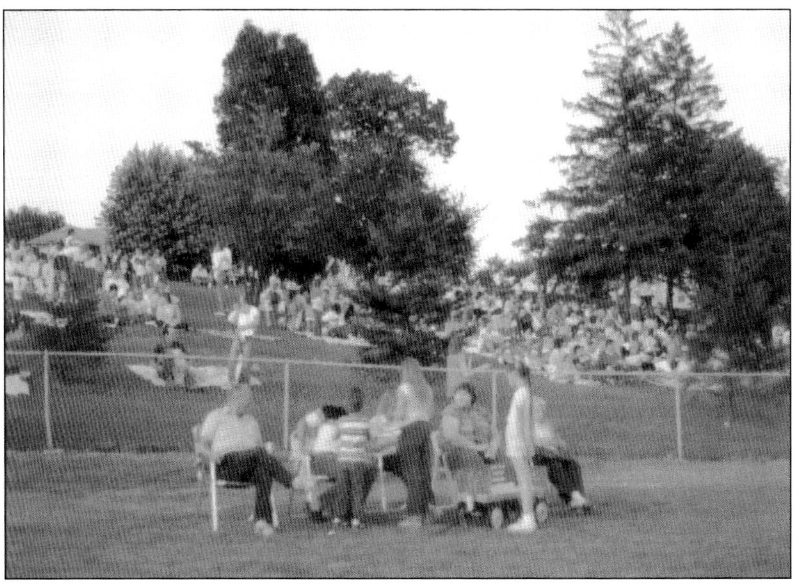

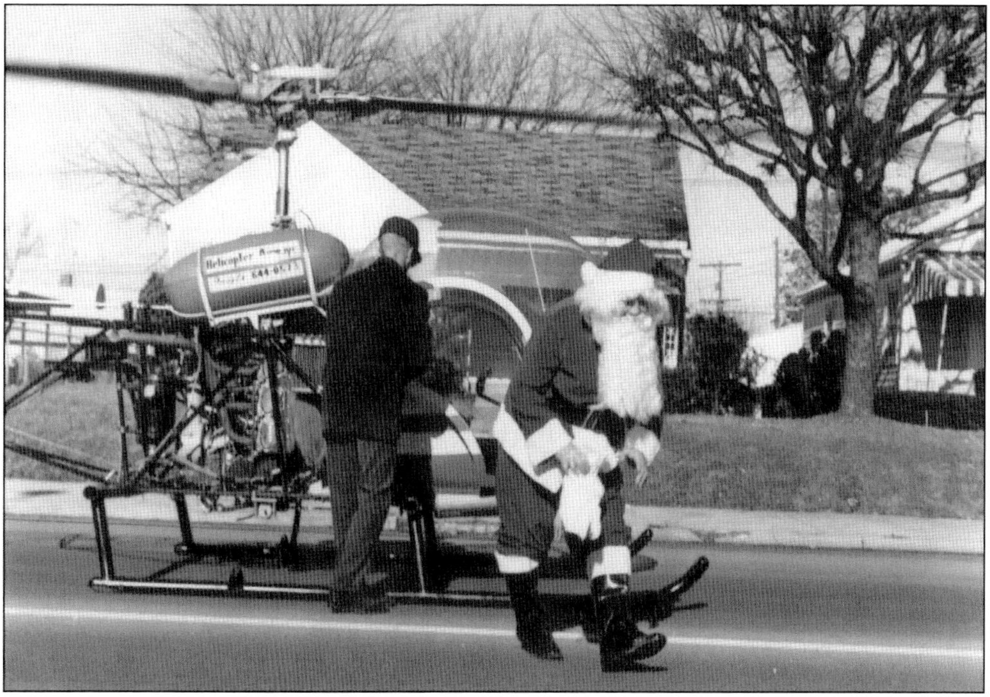

Santa arriving and departing by helicopter was another family treat provided by the Promoter's Club to welcome the Yuletide season. The arrival of Santa called attention to the many shopping opportunities existing within the city. Merchant's provided special sales and giveaways to make the jolly old soul's annual visit exciting for all children, especially the young at heart.

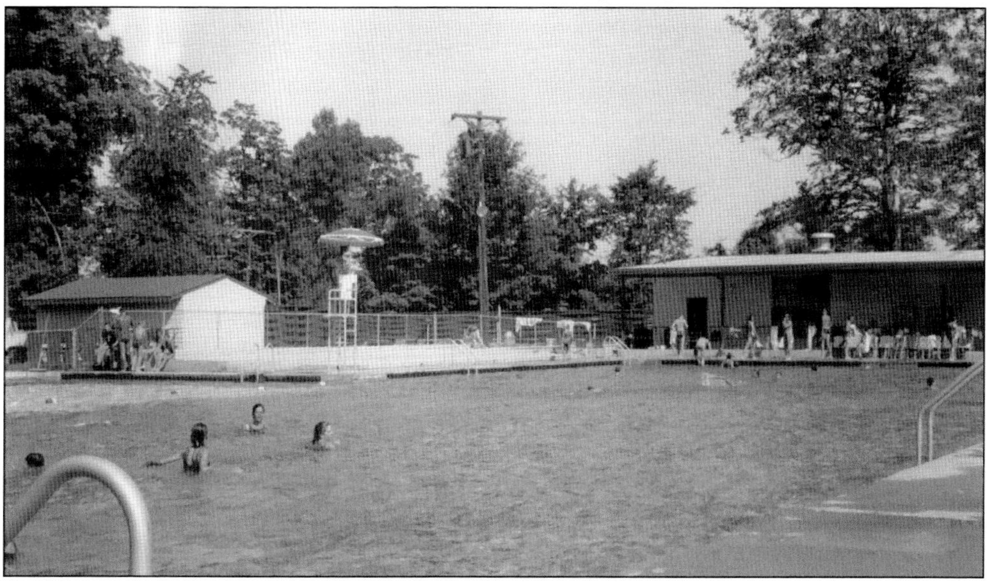

The Olympia Club, a private family recreational swim club, opened in Beech Grove in 1956. Beech Grove never had a public swimming pool, so the new facility offered an alternative to a dip in Lick Creek. Aside from the pool, the club had space to hold dances and other events. Like most similar clubs of the era, the Olympia closed in the 1970s due to changing social and economic conditions.

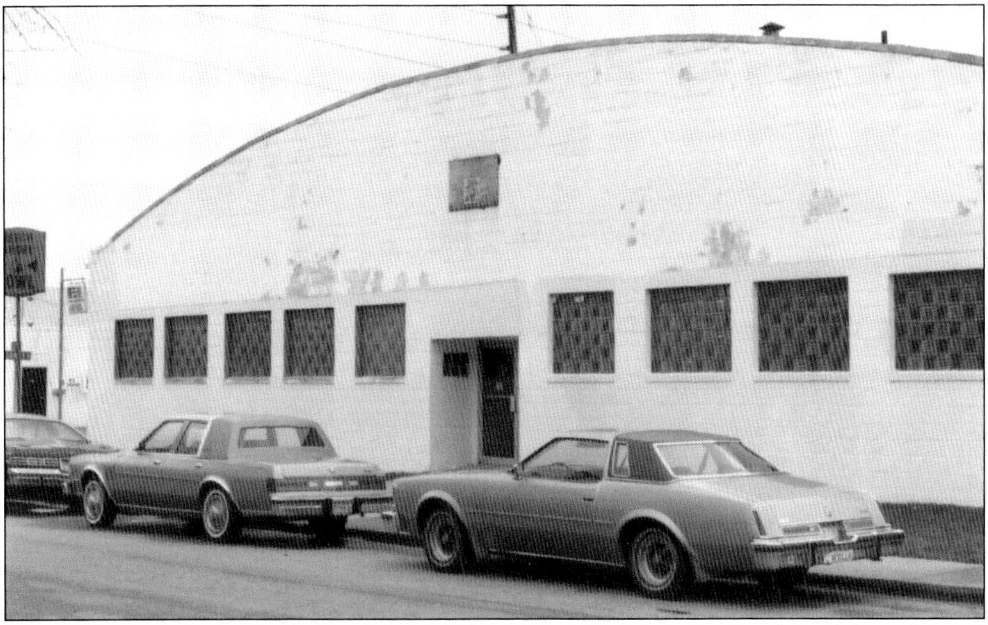

In spite of development to the south, where the massive 80-lane Expo Bowl nestled just beyond the city's limits, Beech Grove Bowl continues to entertain bowlers to this day. Located at 95 North Second Avenue, the facility is plainly visible from highly traveled Emerson Avenue. In addition to the bowling centers, Beech Grove was home to three movie theaters, the last to disappear being the Grove Theater.

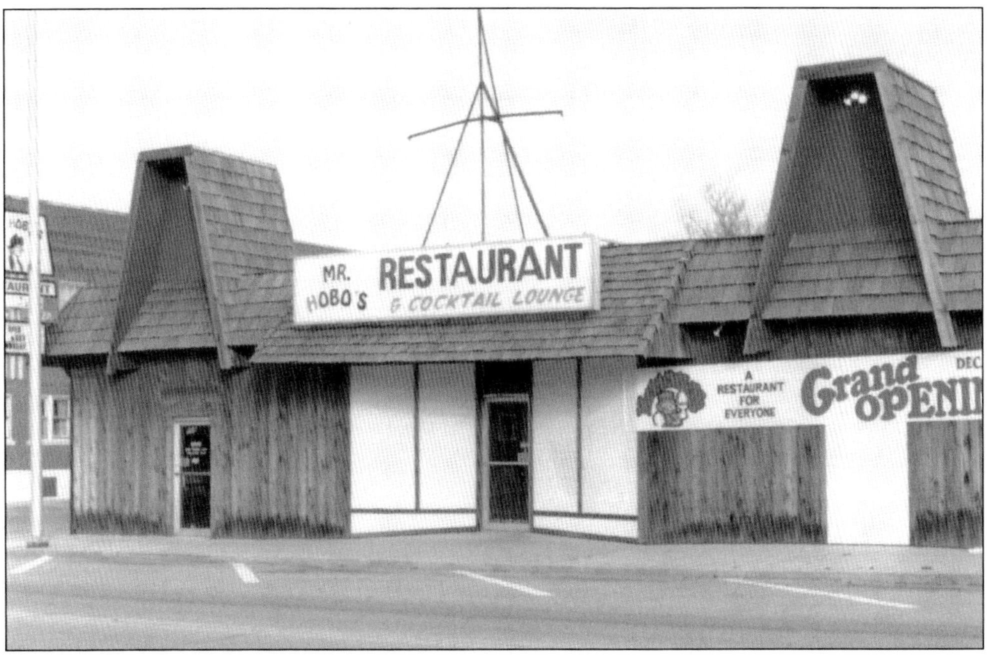

Mr. Hobo's Restaurant is seen shortly after opening. The restaurant is now gone, but other independent restaurants continue to thrive in the city, including Glory Days, Napoli Villa Italian Restaurant, The Diner, and Ball Park Pizza, which is ironically located on Seventh Avenue near land once occupied by the city's baseball stadium.

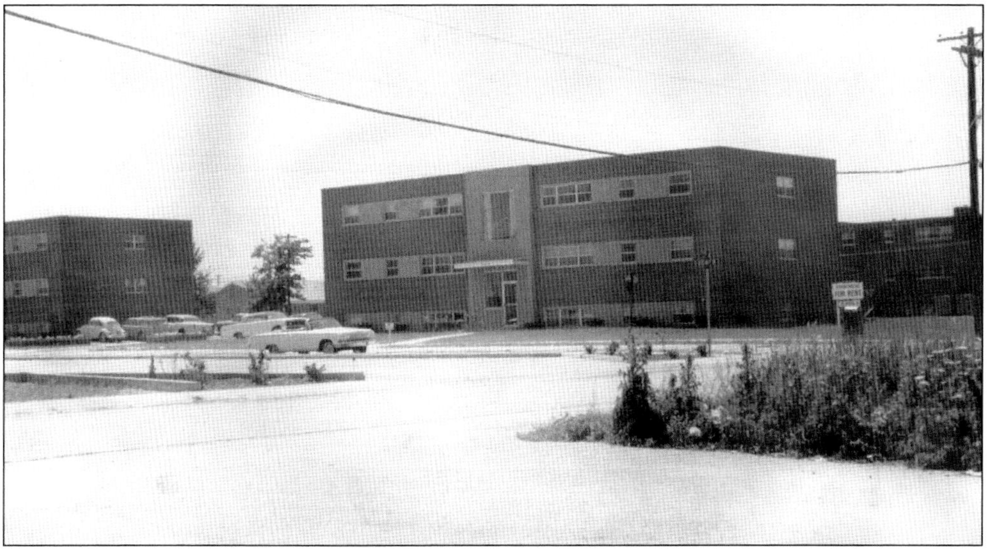

Times change and so do the residential needs of a city. This is a picture of the Par Main Apartments in 1964. Along with the Diplomat Apartments at Troy and Twenty-fifth Avenue, both complexes stand as the first such housing options in Beech Grove. The city of 15,000 residents has relatively few apartments or other rental units and a high percentage of owner-occupied residences.

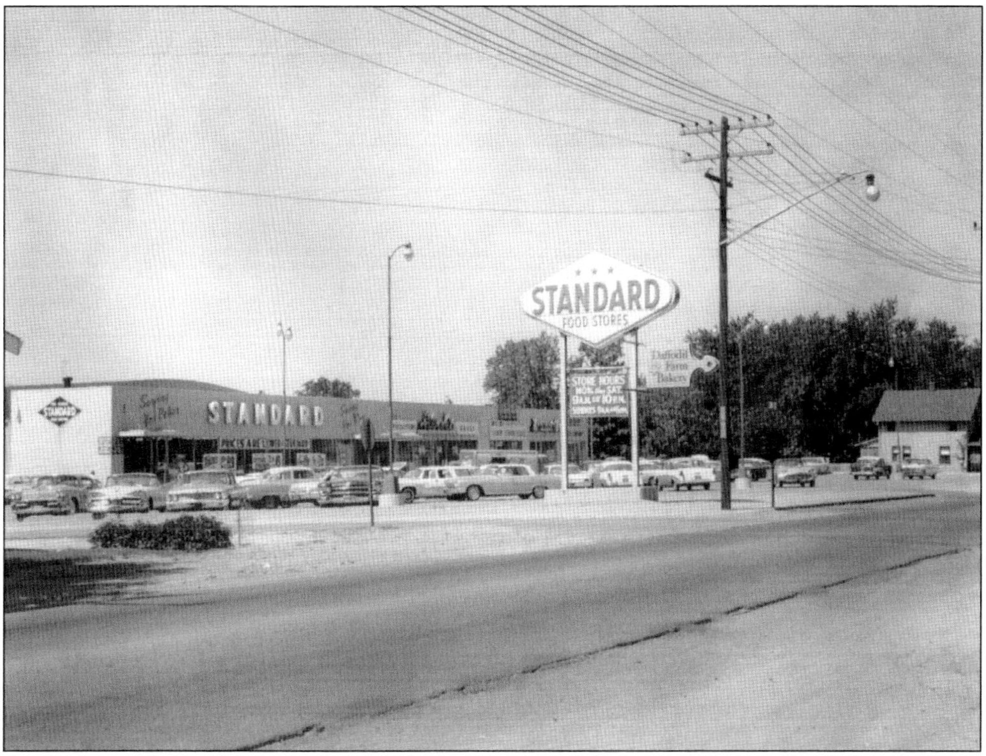

A new, modern shopping center was built at Eighteenth Avenue and Albany Street. The old Standard Food Market relocated to the center from Main Street, signaling shifting consumer preferences. While parking could be a hassle downtown, the new shopping center offered ample parking spaces, becoming an instant hit with residents.

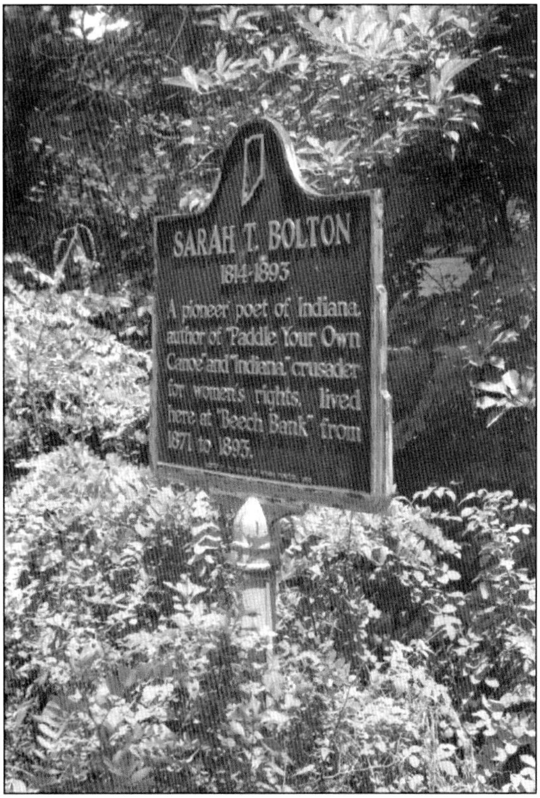

This historical marker indicates the location of "Beech Bank," Sarah Bolton's Beech Grove home. A portion of her estate became the largest park in the city. The land is nestled along the banks of Lick Creek, providing an inviting respite from city life. Bolton's grandson Lloyd B. Mann Jr. visited the city and spoke at Beech Grove High School on January 9, 1981.

This miniature train was displayed at the Beech Grove Shops during Family Day in 1997. The Shops play a prominent role in the history of Beech Grove and remain integral to the city's continued prosperity. While not much news travels from the Amtrak facility, the operation quietly watches over Beech Grove. Likewise, the city is ever vigilant to the welfare of its longtime partner in progress and prosperity.

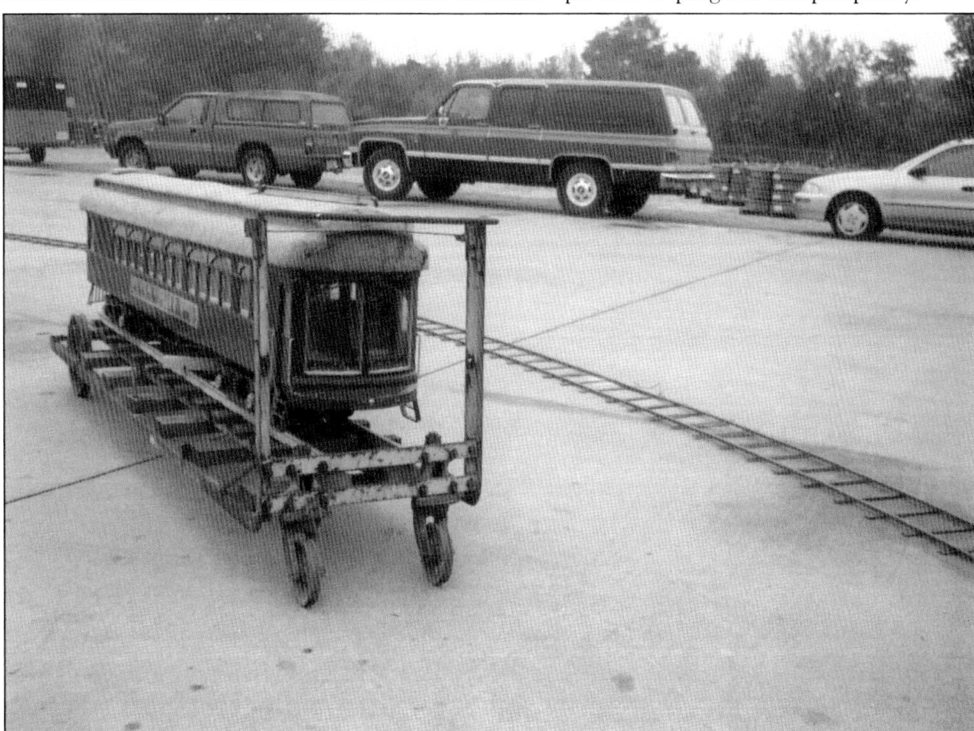

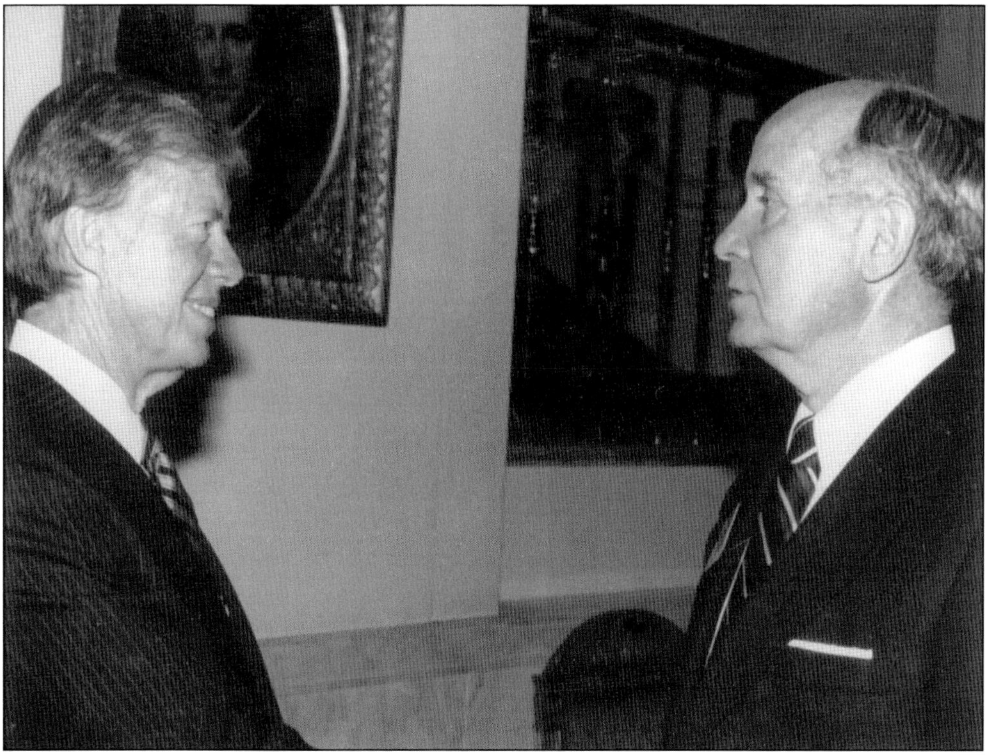

Pres. Jimmy Carter shakes the hand of Mayor Elton Geshwiler. From the days when, as a young boy, he aided his father's campaign for the Beech Grove Town Board, until the time when Elton became the city's (and Indiana's) longest-serving mayor, Geshwiler successfully managed bipartisanship. Geshwiler gave his entire life to serving the city he loved, including 32 years as mayor. Without his guidance, Beech Grove would not be today's safe, progressive city. In Geshwiler's 1999 *Indianapolis Star* obituary, Mayor Warner Wiley stated, "Everything in the city of Beech Grove has Elton's name on it." While this certainly is an exaggeration, Beech Grove would be a very different community today without the work, influence, love, and sacrifices of the Geshwiler family. Likewise, the Shops, overlooking the modern gateway to Beech Grove (below), remain a constant reminder of how both histories intertwine.

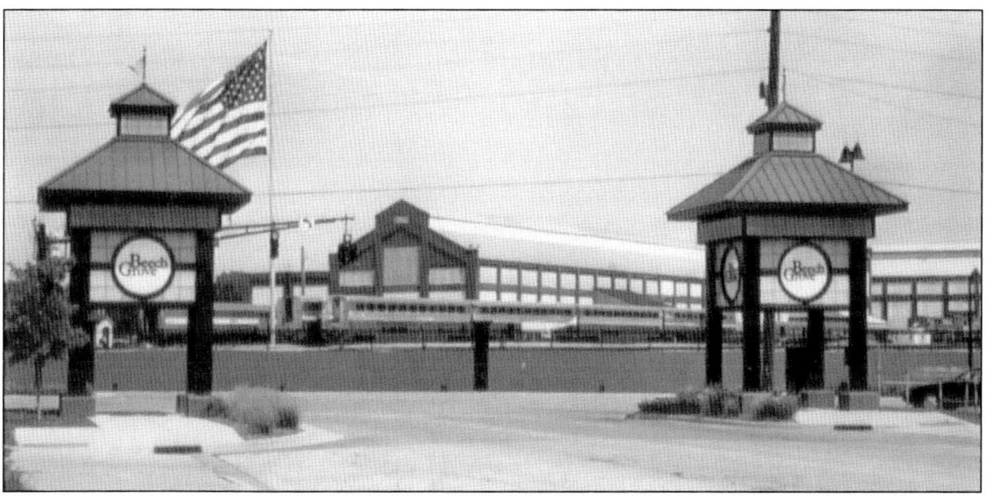

Discover Thousands of Local History Books Featuring Millions of Vintage Images

Arcadia Publishing, the leading local history publisher in the United States, is committed to making history accessible and meaningful through publishing books that celebrate and preserve the heritage of America's people and places.

Find more books like this at
www.arcadiapublishing.com

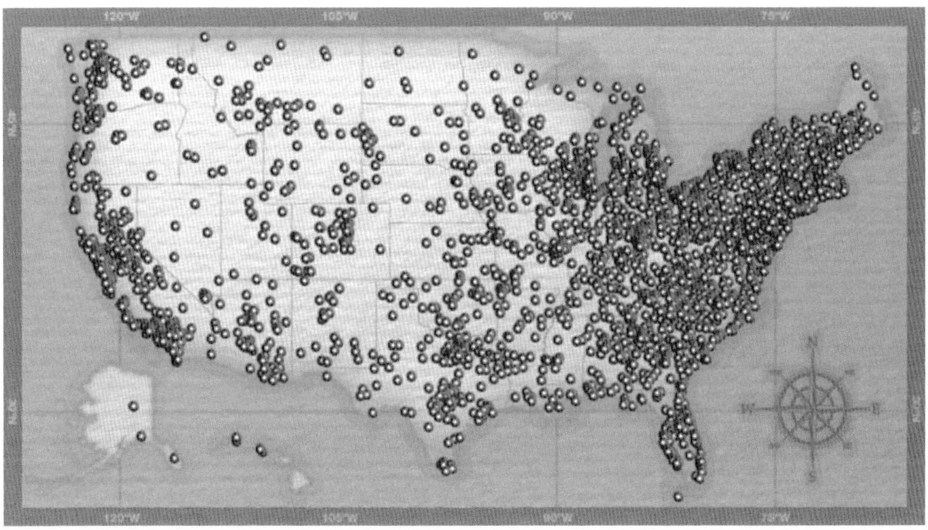

Search for your hometown history, your old stomping grounds, and even your favorite sports team.

Consistent with our mission to preserve history on a local level, this book was printed in South Carolina on American-made paper and manufactured entirely in the United States. Products carrying the accredited Forest Stewardship Council (FSC) label are printed on 100 percent FSC-certified paper.

MADE IN THE USA